STEVEN PINKER

The Sense of Style

The Thinking Person's Guide to Writing in the 21st Century

PENGUIN BOOKS

To Susan Pinker and Robert Pinker
who have a way with words

PENGUIN BOOKS

UK | USA | Canada | Ireland | Australia
India | New Zealand | South Africa

Penguin Books is part of the Penguin Random House group of companies
whose addresses can be found at global.penguinrandomhouse.com.

First published in the United States of America by Viking Penguin,
a member of Penguin Group (USA) LLC 2014
First published in Great Britain by Allen Lane 2014
Published in Penguin Books 2015

001

Text copyright © Steven Pinker, 2014

Illustration credits
Page 52: MacNelly editorial, © Jeff MacNelly—distributed by King Features; 57:
CartoonStock; 61: James Stevenson / The New Yorker Collection /www.cartoonbank.com;
79: *Shoe* © 1993 Jeff MacNelly—distributed by King Features; 202: *Bizarro* used with
permission of Dan Piraro, King Features Syndicate and the Cartoonist Group. All rights
reserved; 256 and 260: Ryan North; 284: © 2007 Harry Bliss. Used with permission of
Pippin Properties, Inc.; 294: Copyright 2008 by Debbie Ridpath Ohi. Reprinted by
permission of Curtis Brown, Ltd.; 297: William Haefeli / The New Yorker Collection /
www.cartoonbank.com; 298: *Zippy the Pinhead* © 1997 Griffith—distributed by King
Features Syndicate, world rights reserved; 301: xkcd.com
Credits for certain illustrations appear adjacent to the respective works.

The moral right of the author has been asserted

Printed in Great Britain by Clays Ltd, St Ives plc

A CIP catalogue record for this book is available from the British Library

ISBN: 978-0-241-95771-4

www.greenpenguin.co.uk

MIX
Paper from
responsible sources
FSC
www.fsc.org   FSC® C018179

Penguin Random House is committed to a
sustainable future for our business, our readers
and our planet. This book is made from Forest
Stewardship Council® certified paper.

PENGUIN BOOKS

THE SENSE OF STYLE

'The world is full of writing about writing. *The Sense of Style* is different – and better – for two reasons. One, it avoids the silly it-were-better-in-my-day stuff; and two, it is informed by the research of academic linguists, as well as by Pinker's own field of psychology. It is also entertaining . . . Pinker is unafraid to overthrow received wisdom . . . an absorbing book, and a helpful one . . . a much-needed corrective to the fatuous "everything's going to hell in a handcart" approach that characterizes most of the public debate about language' Tom Chivers, *The Times Literary Supplement*

'Ignore the glut of grammar books out there, pick this one' James McConnachie, *Sunday Times, Books of the Year*

'Charming and erudite . . . wit and insight . . . such a gem' *Time*

'Gentle humour accompanies Mr Pinker's good sense throughout the book, an antidote to bestselling, operatically irate usage guides that disparage those who disagree as idiots or barbarians. Mr Pinker explains eloquently not just what to do, but also why' *Economist*

'Pinker is a witty and personable guide . . . A thoughtful guide, tough-minded and up to date, for people who think they can write well but are willing to believe that they could write better' Henry Hitchings, *Guardian*

'A canny and punchy polemic' Stevie Davies, *Independent*

'Clear, scholarly and refreshingly free of prescriptions . . . will benefit anyone who aims to write well and with flair' *New Statesman*

'Pinker's linguistical learning . . . is considerable. His knowledge of grammar is extensive and runs deep. He also takes a scarcely hidden delight in exploding tradition' *Wall Street Journal*

'Only Steven Pinker could have written this marvellous book, and thank heaven he has. "Good writing can flip the way the world is perceived," he writes, and *The Sense of Style* will flip the way you think about good writing. Pinker's curiosity and delight illuminate every page, and when he says style can make the world a better place,

ABOUT THE AUTHOR

An award-winning cognitive scientist and public intellectual, Steven Pinker is also Chair of the Usage Panel of the American Heritage Dictionary and the lauded author of bestsellers such as *The Language Instinct*, *Words and Rules*, *The Better Angels of Our Nature* and *The Stuff of Thought: Language as a Window into Human Nature*. He is Johnstone Family Professor in the Department of Psychology at Harvard University and lives in Boston and Truro, Massachusetts.

Contents

Prologue

I love style manuals. Ever since I was assigned Strunk and White's *The Elements of Style* in an introductory psychology course, the writing guide has been among my favorite literary genres. It's not just that I welcome advice on the lifelong challenge of perfecting the craft of writing. It's also that credible guidance on writing must itself be well written, and the best of the manuals are paragons of their own advice. William Strunk's course notes on writing, which his student E. B. White turned into their famous little book, was studded with gems of self-exemplification such as "Write with nouns and verbs," "Put the emphatic words of a sentence at the end," and best of all, his prime directive, "Omit needless words." Many eminent stylists have applied their gifts to explaining the art, including Kingsley Amis, Jacques Barzun, Ambrose Bierce, Bill Bryson, Robert Graves, Tracy Kidder, Stephen King, Elmore Leonard, F. L. Lucas, George Orwell, William Safire, and of course White himself, the beloved author of *Charlotte's Web* and *Stuart Little*. Here is the great essayist reminiscing about his teacher:

> In the days when I was sitting in his class, he omitted so many needless words, and omitted them so forcibly and with such eagerness

and obvious relish, that he often seemed in the position of having shortchanged himself—a man left with nothing more to say yet with time to fill, a radio prophet who had outdistanced the clock. Will Strunk got out of this predicament by a simple trick: he uttered every sentence three times. When he delivered his oration on brevity to the class, he leaned forward over his desk, grasped his coat lapels in his hands, and, in a husky, conspiratorial voice, said, "Rule Seventeen. Omit needless words! Omit needless words! Omit needless words!"[1]

I like to read style manuals for another reason, the one that sends botanists to the garden and chemists to the kitchen: it's a practical application of our science. I am a psycholinguist and a cognitive scientist, and what is style, after all, but the effective use of words to engage the human mind? It's all the more captivating to someone who seeks to explain these fields to a wide readership. I think about how language works so that I can best explain how language works.

But my professional acquaintance with language has led me to read the traditional manuals with a growing sense of unease. Strunk and White, for all their intuitive feel for style, had a tenuous grasp of grammar.[2] They misdefined terms such as *phrase, participle,* and *relative clause,* and in steering their readers away from passive verbs and toward active transitive ones they botched their examples of both. *There were a great number of dead leaves lying on the ground,* for instance, is not in the passive voice, nor does *The cock's crow came with dawn* contain a transitive verb. Lacking the tools to analyze language, they often struggled when turning their intuitions into advice, vainly appealing to the writer's "ear." And they did not seem to realize that some of the advice contradicted itself: "Many a tame sentence . . . can be made lively and emphatic by substituting a transitive in the active voice" uses the passive voice to warn against the passive voice. George Orwell, in his vaunted "Politics and the English Language," fell into the same trap when, without irony, he derided prose in which "the passive voice is wherever possible used in preference to the active."[3]

Self-contradiction aside, we now know that telling writers to avoid the passive is bad advice. Linguistic research has shown that the passive construction has a number of indispensable functions because of the way it engages a reader's attention and memory. A skilled writer should know what those functions are and push back against copy editors who, under the influence of grammatically naïve style guides, blue-pencil every passive construction they spot into an active one.

Style manuals that are innocent of linguistics also are crippled in dealing with the aspect of writing that evokes the most emotion: correct and incorrect usage. Many style manuals treat traditional rules of usage the way fundamentalists treat the Ten Commandments: as unerring laws chiseled in sapphire for mortals to obey or risk eternal damnation. But skeptics and freethinkers who probe the history of these rules have found that they belong to an oral tradition of folklore and myth. For many reasons, manuals that are credulous about the inerrancy of the traditional rules don't serve writers well. Although some of the rules can make prose better, many of them make it worse, and writers are better off flouting them. The rules often mash together issues of grammatical correctness, logical coherence, formal style, and standard dialect, but a skilled writer needs to keep them straight. And the orthodox stylebooks are ill equipped to deal with an inescapable fact about language: it changes over time. Language is not a protocol legislated by an authority but rather a wiki that pools the contributions of millions of writers and speakers, who ceaselessly bend the language to their needs and who inexorably age, die, and get replaced by their children, who adapt the language in their turn.

Yet the authors of the classic manuals wrote as if the language they grew up with were immortal, and failed to cultivate an ear for ongoing change. Strunk and White, writing in the early and middle decades of the twentieth century, condemned then-new verbs like *personalize, finalize, host, chair,* and *debut,* and warned writers never to use *fix* for "repair" or *claim* for "declare." Worse, they justified their peeves with cockamamie rationalizations. The verb *contact,* they argued, is "vague and self-important. Do not *contact* people; get in touch with them, look them up, phone them, find them, or meet them." But of course the vagueness of *to contact* is exactly why it caught on: sometimes a writer doesn't need to know how one person will get in touch with another, as long as he does so. Or consider this head-scratcher, concocted to explain why a writer should never use a number word with *people*, only with *persons:* "If of 'six people' five went away, how many people would be left? Answer: one people." By the same logic, writers should avoid using numbers with irregular plurals such as *men, children,* and *teeth* ("If of 'six children' five went away . . .").

In the last edition published in his lifetime, White did acknowledge some changes to the language, instigated by "youths" who "speak to other youths in a tongue of their own devising: they renovate the language with a wild vigor, as they would a basement apartment." White's condescension to these "youths" (now in their retirement years) led him to predict the passing of *nerd, psyched, ripoff, dude, geek,* and *funky,* all of which have become entrenched in the language.

The graybeard sensibilities of the style mavens come not just from an underappreciation of the fact of language change but from a lack of reflection on their own psychology. As people age, they confuse changes in themselves with changes in the world, and changes in the world with moral decline—the illusion of the good old days.[4] And so every generation believes that the kids today are degrading the language and taking civilization down with it:[5]

The common language is disappearing. It is slowly being crushed to death under the weight of verbal conglomerate, a pseudospeech at once both pretentious and feeble, that is created daily by millions of blunders and inaccuracies in grammar, syntax, idiom, metaphor, logic, and common sense. . . . In the history of modern English there is no period in which such victory over thought-in-speech has been so widespread.—1978

Recent graduates, including those with university degrees, seem to have no mastery of the language at all. They cannot construct a simple declarative sentence, either orally or in writing. They cannot spell common, everyday words. Punctuation is apparently no longer taught. Grammar is a complete mystery to almost all recent graduates.—1961

From every college in the country goes up the cry, "Our freshmen can't spell, can't punctuate." Every high school is in disrepair because its pupils are so ignorant of the merest rudiments.—1917

The vocabularies of the majority of high-school pupils are amazingly small. I always try to use simple English, and yet I have talked to classes when quite a minority of the pupils did not comprehend more than half of what I said.—1889

Unless the present progress of change [is] arrested . . . there can be no doubt that, in another century, the dialect of the Americans will become utterly unintelligible to an Englishman.—1833

Our language (I mean the English) is degenerating very fast. . . . I begin to fear that it will be impossible to check it.—1785

Complaints about the decline of language go at least as far back as the invention of the printing press. Soon after William Caxton set up the first one in England in 1478, he lamented, "And certaynly our langage now vsed veryeth ferre from what whiche was vsed and spoken when I was borne." Indeed, moral panic about the decline of writing may be as old as writing itself:

The cartoon is not much of an exaggeration. According to the English scholar Richard Lloyd-Jones, some of the clay tablets deciphered from ancient Sumerian include complaints about the deteriorating writing skills of the young.[6]

My discomfort with the classic style manuals has convinced me that we need a writing guide for the twenty-first century. It's not that I have the desire, to say nothing of the ability, to supplant *The Elements of Style*. Writers can profit by reading more than one style guide, and much of Strunk and White (as it is commonly called) is as timeless as it is charming. But much of it is not. Strunk was born in 1869, and today's writers cannot base their craft exclusively on the advice of a man who developed his sense of style before the invention of the telephone (let alone the Internet), before the advent of modern linguistics and cognitive science, before the wave of informalization that swept the world in the second half of the twentieth century.

A manual for the new millennium cannot just perpetuate the diktats of earlier manuals. Today's writers are infused by the spirit of scientific skepticism and the ethos of questioning authority. They should not be satisfied with "That's the way it's done" or "Because I said so," and they deserve not to be patronized at any age. They rightly expect *reasons* for any advice that is foisted upon them.

Today we can provide the reasons. We have an understanding of grammatical phenomena which goes well beyond the traditional taxonomies based on crude analogies with Latin. We have a body of research on the mental dynamics of reading: the waxing and waning of memory load as readers comprehend a passage, the incrementing of their knowledge as they come to grasp its meaning, the blind alleys that can lead them astray. We have a body of history and criticism which can distinguish the rules that enhance clarity, grace, and emotional resonance from those that are based on myths and misunderstandings. By replacing dogma about usage with reason and evidence, I hope not just to avoid giving ham-fisted advice but to make the advice that I do give easier to remember than a list of dos and don'ts. Providing reasons should also allow writers and editors to apply the guidelines judiciously, mindful of what they are designed to accomplish, rather than robotically.

"The sense of style" has a double meaning. The word *sense*, as in "the sense of sight" and "a sense of humor," can refer to a faculty of mind, in this case the faculties of comprehension that resonate to a well-crafted sentence. It can also refer to "good sense" as opposed to "nonsense," in this case the ability to discriminate between the principles that improve the quality of prose and the superstitions, fetishes, shibboleths, and initiation ordeals that have been passed down in the traditions of usage.

The Sense of Style is not a reference manual in which you can find the answer to every question about hyphenation and capitalization. Nor is it a remedial guide for badly educated students who have yet to master the mechanics of a sentence. Like the classic guides, it is designed for people who know how to write and want to write better. This includes students who hope to improve the quality of their papers, aspiring critics and journalists who want to start a blog or column or series of reviews, and professionals who seek a cure for their academese, bureaucratese, corporatese, legalese, medicalese, or officialese. The book is also written for readers who seek no help in writing but are interested in letters and literature and curious about the ways in which the sciences of mind can illuminate how language works at its best.

My focus is on nonfiction, particularly genres that put a premium on clarity and coherence. But unlike the authors of the classic guides, I don't equate these virtues with plain words, austere expression, and formal style.[7] You can write with clarity and with flair, too. And though the emphasis is on nonfiction, the explanations should be useful to fiction writers as well, because many principles of style apply whether the world being written about is real or imaginary. I like to think they might also be helpful to poets, orators, and other creative wordsmiths, who need to know the canons of pedestrian prose to flout them for rhetorical effect.

People often ask me whether anyone today even cares about style. The English language, they say, faces a new threat in the rise of the

Internet, with its texting and tweeting, its email and chatrooms. Surely the craft of written expression has declined since the days before smartphones and the Web. You remember those days, don't you? Back in the 1980s, when teenagers spoke in fluent paragraphs, bureaucrats wrote in plain English, and every academic paper was a masterpiece in the art of the essay? (Or was it the 1970s?) The problem with the Internet-is-making-us-illiterate theory, of course, is that bad prose has burdened readers in every era. Professor Strunk tried to do something about it in 1918, when young Elwyn White was a student in his English class at Cornell.

What today's doomsayers fail to notice is that the very trends they deplore consist in oral media—radio, telephones, and television—giving way to written ones. Not so long ago it was radio and television that were said to be ruining the language. More than ever before, the currency of our social and cultural lives is the written word. And no, not all of it is the semiliterate ranting of Internet trolls. A little surfing will show that many Internet users value language that is clear, grammatical, and competently spelled and punctuated, not just in printed books and legacy media but in e-zines, blogs, Wikipedia entries, consumer reviews, and even a fair proportion of email. Surveys have shown that college students are writing more than their counterparts in earlier generations did, and that they make no more errors per page of writing.[8] And contrary to an urban legend, they do not sprinkle their papers with smileys and instant-messaging abbreviations like IMHO and L8TR, any more than previous generations forgot how to use prepositions and articles out of the habit of omitting them from their telegrams. Members of the Internet generation, like all language users, fit their phrasing to the setting and audience, and have a good sense of what is appropriate in formal writing.

Style still matters, for at least three reasons. First, it ensures that writers will get their messages across, sparing readers from squandering their precious moments on earth deciphering opaque prose. When the effort fails, the result can be calamitous—as Strunk and White put it, "death on the highway caused by a badly worded road sign, heartbreak among lovers caused by a misplaced phrase in a well-intentioned letter, anguish of a traveler expecting to be met at a railroad station and not being met because of a slipshod telegram." Governments and corporations have found that small improvements in clarity can prevent vast amounts of error, frustration, and waste,[9] and many countries have recently made clear language the law of the land.[10]

Second, style earns trust. If readers can see that a writer cares about consistency and accuracy in her prose, they will be reassured that the writer cares about those virtues in conduct they cannot see as easily. Here is how one technology executive explains why he rejects job applications filled with errors of grammar and punctuation: "If it takes someone more than 20 years to notice how to properly use *it's*, then that's not a learning curve I'm comfortable with."[11] And if that isn't enough to get you to brush up your prose, consider the discovery of the dating site OkCupid that sloppy grammar and spelling in a profile are "huge turn-offs." As one client said, "If you're trying to date a woman, I don't expect flowery Jane Austen prose. But aren't you trying to put your best foot forward?"[12]

Style, not least, adds beauty to the world. To a literate reader, a crisp sentence, an arresting metaphor, a witty aside, an elegant turn of phrase are among life's greatest pleasures. And as we shall see in the first chapter, this thoroughly impractical virtue of good writing is where the practical effort of mastering good writing must begin.

Chapter 1

GOOD WRITING

REVERSE-ENGINEERING GOOD PROSE AS
THE KEY TO DEVELOPING A WRITERLY EAR

Education is an admirable thing," wrote Oscar Wilde, "but it is well to remember from time to time that nothing that is worth knowing can be taught."[1] In dark moments while writing this book, I sometimes feared that Wilde might be right. When I polled some accomplished writers about which style manuals they had consulted during their apprenticeships, the most common answer I got was "none." Writing, they said, just came naturally to them.

I'd be the last to doubt that good writers are blessed with an innate dose of fluency with syntax and memory for words. But no one is born with skills in English composition per se. Those skills may not have come from stylebooks, but they must have come from somewhere.

That somewhere is the writing of other writers. Good writers are avid readers. They have absorbed a vast inventory of words, idioms, constructions, tropes, and rhetorical tricks, and with them a sensitivity to how they mesh and how they clash. This is the elusive "ear" of a skilled writer—the tacit sense of style which every honest stylebook, echoing Wilde, confesses cannot be explicitly taught. Biographers of great authors always try to track down the books their subjects read when they were young, because they know these sources hold the key to their development as writers.

I would not have written this book if I did not believe, contra Wilde, that many principles of style really can be taught. But the starting point for becoming a good writer is to be a good reader. Writers acquire their technique by spotting, savoring, and reverse-engineering examples of good prose. The goal of this chapter is to provide a glimpse of how that is done. I have picked four passages of twenty-first-century prose, diverse in style and content, and will think aloud as I try to understand what makes them work. My intent is not to honor these passages as if I were bestowing a prize, nor to hold them up as models for you to emulate. It's to illustrate, via a peek into my stream of consciousness, the habit of lingering over good writing wherever you find it and reflecting on what makes it good.

Savoring good prose is not just a more effective way to develop a writerly ear than obeying a set of commandments; it's a more inviting one. Much advice on style is stern and censorious. A recent bestseller advocated "zero tolerance" for errors and brandished the words *horror, satanic, ghastly,* and *plummeting standards* on its first page. The classic manuals, written by starchy Englishmen and rock-ribbed Yankees, try to take all the fun out of writing, grimly adjuring the writer to avoid offbeat words, figures of speech, and playful alliteration. A famous piece of advice from this school crosses the line from the grim to the infanticidal: "Whenever you feel an impulse to perpetrate a piece of exceptionally fine writing, obey it—wholeheartedly—and delete it before sending your manuscript to press. *Murder your darlings.*"[2]

An aspiring writer could be forgiven for thinking that learning to write is like negotiating an obstacle course in boot camp, with a sergeant barking at you for every errant footfall. Why not think of it instead as a form of pleasurable mastery, like cooking or photography? Perfecting the craft is a lifelong calling, and mistakes are part of the game. Though the quest for improvement may be informed by lessons and honed by practice, it must first be kindled by a delight in the best work of the masters and a desire to approach their excellence.

———

We are going to die, and that makes us the lucky ones. Most people are never going to die because they are never going to be born. The potential people who could have been here in my place but who will in fact never see the light of day outnumber the sand grains of Arabia. Certainly those unborn ghosts include greater poets than Keats, scientists greater than Newton. We know this because the set of possible people allowed by our DNA so massively exceeds the set of actual people. In the teeth of these stupefying odds it is you and I, in our ordinariness, that are here.

In the opening lines of Richard Dawkins's *Unweaving the Rainbow,* the uncompromising atheist and tireless advocate of science explains why his worldview does not, as the romantic and the religious fear, extinguish a sense of wonder or an appreciation of life.[3]

We are going to die, and that makes us the lucky ones. Good writing starts strong. Not with a cliché ("Since the dawn of time"), not with a banality ("Recently, scholars have been increasingly concerned with the question of . . ."), but with a contentful observation that provokes curiosity. The reader of *Unweaving the Rainbow* opens the book and is walloped with a reminder of the most dreadful fact we know, and on its heels a paradoxical elaboration. We're lucky because we'll die? Who wouldn't want to find out how this mystery will be solved? The starkness of the paradox is reinforced by the diction and meter: short, simple words, a stressed monosyllable followed by six iambic feet.*

Most people are never going to die. The resolution to the paradox—that a bad thing, dying, implies a good thing, having lived—is explained with parallel constructions: *never going to die . . . never going to be born.* The next sentence restates the contrast, also in parallel language, but avoids

———

* Technical terms are defined in the Glossary.

the tedium of repeating words yet again by juxtaposing familiar idioms that have the same rhythm: *been here in my place . . . see the light of day.*

the sand grains of Arabia. A touch of the poetic, better suited to the grandeur that Dawkins seeks to invoke than a colorless adjective like *massive* or *enormous.* The expression is snatched from the brink of cliché by its variant wording (*sand grains* rather than *sands*) and by its vaguely exotic feel. The phrase *sands of Arabia*, though common in the early nineteenth century, has plunged in popularity ever since, and there is no longer even a place that is commonly called Arabia; we refer to it as Saudi Arabia or the Arabian Peninsula.[4]

unborn ghosts. A vivid image to convey the abstract notion of a mathematically possible combination of genes, and a wily repurposing of a supernatural concept to advance a naturalistic argument.

greater poets than Keats, scientists greater than Newton. Parallel wording is a powerful trope, but after dying and being born, being here in my place and seeing the light of day, enough is enough. To avoid monotony Dawkins inverts the structure of one of the lines in this couplet. The phrase subtly alludes to another meditation on unrealized genius, "Some mute inglorious Milton here may rest," from Thomas Gray's "Elegy Written in a Country Churchyard."

In the teeth of these stupefying odds. The idiom brings to mind the menacing gape of a predator, reinforcing our gratitude for being alive: to come into existence we narrowly escaped a mortal threat, namely the high odds against it. How high? Every writer faces the challenge of finding a superlative in the English word-hoard that has not been inflated by hyperbole and overuse. *In the teeth of these incredible odds? In the teeth of these awesome odds?* Meh. Dawkins has found a superlative—to render into a stupor, to make stupid—that still has the power to impress.

Good writing can flip the way the world is perceived, like the silhouette in psychology textbooks which oscillates between a goblet and two faces. In six sentences Dawkins has flipped the way we think of death, and has stated a rationalist's case for an appreciation of life in words so stirring that many humanists I know have asked that it be read at their funerals.

What is it that makes a person the very person that she is, herself alone and not another, an integrity of identity that persists over time, undergoing changes and yet still continuing to be—until she does not continue any longer, at least not unproblematically?

I stare at the picture of a small child at a summer's picnic, clutching her big sister's hand with one tiny hand while in the other she has a precarious hold on a big slice of watermelon that she appears to be struggling to have intersect with the small *o* of her mouth. That child is me. But why is she me? I have no memory at all of that summer's day, no privileged knowledge of whether that child succeeded in getting the watermelon into her mouth. It's true that a smooth series of contiguous physical events can be traced from her body to mine, so that we would want to say that her body *is* mine; and perhaps bodily identity is all that our personal identity consists in. But bodily persistence over time, too, presents philosophical dilemmas. The series of contiguous physical events has rendered the child's body so different from the one I glance down on at this moment; the very atoms that composed her body no longer compose mine. And if our bodies are dissimilar, our points of view are even more so. Mine would be as inaccessible to her—just let *her* try to figure out [Spinoza's] *Ethics*—as hers is now to me. Her thought processes, prelinguistic, would largely elude me.

Yet she is me, that tiny determined thing in the frilly white pinafore. She has continued to exist, survived her childhood illnesses, the near-drowning in a rip current on Rockaway Beach at the age of twelve, other dramas. There are presumably adventures that she— that is that I—can't undergo and still continue to be herself. Would I then be someone else or would I just no longer be? Were I to lose all sense of myself—were schizophrenia or demonic possession, a coma or progressive dementia to remove me from myself—would it be I who would be undergoing those trials, or would I have quit the premises? Would there then be someone else, or would there be no one?

Is death one of those adventures from which I can't emerge as myself? The sister whose hand I am clutching in the picture is dead. I wonder every day whether she still exists. A person whom one has loved seems altogether too significant a thing to simply vanish altogether from the world. A person whom one loves *is* a world, just as one knows oneself to be a world. How can worlds like these simply cease altogether? But if my sister does exist, then *what* is she, and what makes that thing that she now is identical with the beautiful girl laughing at her little sister on that forgotten day?

In this passage from *Betraying Spinoza,* the philosopher and novelist Rebecca Newberger Goldstein (to whom I am married) explains the philosophical puzzle of personal identity, one of the problems that engaged the Dutch-Jewish thinker who is the subject of her book.[5] Like her fellow humanist Dawkins, Goldstein analyzes the vertiginous enigma of existence and death, but their styles could not be more different—a reminder of the diverse ways that the resources of language can be deployed to illuminate a topic. Dawkins's could fairly be called masculine, with its confrontational opening, its cold abstractions, its aggressive imagery, its glorification of alpha males. Goldstein's is personal, evocative, reflective, yet intellectually just as rigorous.

at least not unproblematically. The categories of grammar reflect the building blocks of thought—time, space, causality, matter—and a philosophical wordsmith can play with them to awaken her readers to metaphysical conundrums. Here we have an adverb, *unproblematically,* modifying the verb *continue,* an ellipsis for *continue to be.* Ordinarily *to be* is not the kind of verb that can be modified by an adverb. To be or not to be—it's hard to see shades of gray there. The unexpected adverb puts an array of metaphysical, theological, and personal questions on the table before us.

a big slice of watermelon that she appears to be struggling to have intersect with the small o *of her mouth.* Good writing is understood with the mind's eye.[6] The unusual description of the familiar act of eating in terms of its geometry—a piece of fruit intersecting with an *o*—

forces the reader to pause and conjure a mental image of the act rather than skating over a verbal summary. We find the little girl in the photograph endearing not because the author has stooped to telling us so with words like *cute* or *adorable* but because we can see her childlike mannerisms for ourselves—as the author herself is doing when pondering the little alien who somehow is her. We see the clumsiness of a small hand manipulating an adult-sized object; the determination to master a challenge we take for granted; the out-of-sync mouth anticipating the sweet, juicy reward. The geometric language also prepares us for the prelinguistic thinking that Goldstein introduces in the next paragraph: we regress to an age at which "to eat" and even "to put in your mouth" are abstractions, several levels removed from the physical challenge of making an object intersect with a body part.

That child is me. But why is she me? . . . [My point of view] would be as inaccessible to her . . . as hers is now to me. . . . There are presumably adventures that she—that is that I—can't undergo and still continue to be herself. Would I then be someone else? Goldstein repeatedly juxtaposes nouns and pronouns in the first and third person: *that child . . . me; she . . . I . . . herself; I . . . someone else.* The syntactic confusion about which grammatical person belongs in which phrase reflects our intellectual confusion about the very meaning of the concept "person." She also plays with *to be,* the quintessentially existential verb, to engage our existential puzzlement: *Would I then be someone else or would I just no longer be? . . . Would there then be someone else, or would there be no one?*

frilly white pinafore. The use of an old-fashioned word for an old-fashioned garment helps date the snapshot for us, without the cliché *faded photograph.*

The sister whose hand I am clutching in the picture is dead. After eighteen sentences that mix wistful nostalgia with abstract philosophizing, the reverie is punctured by a stark revelation. However painful it must have been to predicate the harsh word *dead* of a beloved sister, no euphemism—*has passed away, is no longer with us*—could have ended that sentence. The topic of the discussion is how we struggle to reconcile the indubitable fact of death with our incomprehension of the possibility that a person can no longer exist. Our linguistic ancestors parlayed that incomprehension into euphemisms like *passed on* in which death consists of a journey to a remote location. Had Goldstein settled for these weasel words, she would have undermined her analysis before it began.

I wonder every day whether she still exists. A person whom one has loved seems altogether too significant a thing to simply vanish altogether from the world. A person whom one loves is *a world, just as one knows oneself to be a world. How can worlds like these simply cease altogether?* This passage fills my eyes every time I read it, and not just because it is about a sister-in-law I will never meet. With a spare restatement of what philosophers call the hard problem of consciousness (*A person . . . is a world, just as one knows oneself to be a world*), Goldstein creates an effect that is richly emotional. The puzzlement in having to make sense of this abstract philosophical conundrum mingles with the poignancy of having to come to terms with the loss of someone we love. It is not just the selfish realization that we have been robbed of their third-person company, but the unselfish realization that they have been robbed of their first-person experience.

The passage also reminds us of the overlap in techniques for writing fiction and nonfiction. The interweaving of the personal and the philosophical in this excerpt is being used as an expository device, to help us understand the issues that Spinoza wrote about. But it is also a theme that runs through Goldstein's fiction, namely that the obsessions of academic philosophy—personal identity, consciousness, truth, will, meaning, morality—are of a piece with the obsessions of human beings as they try to make sense of their lives.

———

Maurice Sendak, Author of Splendid Nightmares, Dies at 83

Maurice Sendak, widely considered the most important children's book artist of the 20th century, who wrenched the picture book out of the safe, sanitized world of the nursery and plunged it into the dark, terrifying, and hauntingly beautiful recesses of the human psyche, died on Tuesday in Danbury, Conn. . . .

Roundly praised, intermittently censored, and occasionally eaten, Mr. Sendak's books were essential ingredients of childhood for the generation born after 1960 or thereabouts, and in turn for their children.

PAULINE PHILLIPS, FLINTY ADVISER TO MILLIONS AS DEAR ABBY, DIES AT 94

Dear Abby: My wife sleeps in the raw. Then she showers, brushes her teeth and fixes our breakfast—still in the buff. We're newlyweds and there are just the two of us, so I suppose there's really nothing wrong with it. What do you think?—Ed
Dear Ed: It's O.K. with me. But tell her to put on an apron when she's frying bacon.

Pauline Phillips, a California housewife who nearly 60 years ago, seeking something more meaningful than mah-jongg, transformed herself into the syndicated columnist Dear Abby—and in so doing became a trusted, tart-tongued adviser to tens of millions—died on Wednesday in Minneapolis. . . .

With her comic and flinty yet fundamentally sympathetic voice, Mrs. Phillips helped wrestle the advice column from its weepy Victorian past into a hard-nosed 20th-century present. . . .

Dear Abby: Our son married a girl when he was in the service. They were married in February and she had an 8 1/2-pound baby girl in August. She said the baby was premature. Can an 8 1/2-pound baby be this premature?—Wanting to Know
Dear Wanting: The baby was on time. The wedding was late. Forget it.

Mrs. Phillips began her life as the columnist Abigail Van Buren in 1956. She quickly became known for her astringent, often genteelly risqué, replies to queries that included the marital, the medical, and sometimes both at once.

HELEN GURLEY BROWN, WHO GAVE "SINGLE GIRL" A LIFE IN FULL, DIES AT 90

Helen Gurley Brown, who as the author of *Sex and the Single Girl* shocked early-1960s America with the news that unmarried women not only had sex but thoroughly enjoyed it—and who as the editor of *Cosmopolitan* magazine spent the next three decades telling those women precisely how to enjoy it even more—died on Monday in Manhattan. She was 90, though parts of her were considerably younger. . . .

As *Cosmopolitan*'s editor from 1965 until 1997, Ms. Brown was widely credited with being the first to introduce frank discussions of sex into magazines for women. The look of women's magazines today—a sea of voluptuous models and titillating cover lines— is due in no small part to her influence.

My third selection, also related to death, showcases yet another tone and style, and stands as further proof that good writing does not fit into a single formula. With deadpan wit, an affection for eccentricity, and a deft use of the English lexicon, the linguist and journalist Margalit Fox has perfected the art of the obituary.[7]

plunged [the picture book] into the dark, terrifying, and hauntingly beautiful recesses of the human psyche; a trusted, tart-tongued adviser to tens of millions; a sea of voluptuous models and titillating cover lines. When you have to capture a life in just eight hundred words, you have to choose those words carefully. Fox has found some mots justes and packed them into readable phrases which put the lie to the lazy excuse that you can't sum up a complex subject—in this case a life's accomplishments—in just a few words.

Roundly praised, intermittently censored, and occasionally eaten. This is a zeugma: the intentional juxtaposition of different senses of a single word. In this list, the word *books* is being used in the sense of both their narrative content (which can be *praised* or *censored*) and their physical form (which can be *eaten*). Along with putting a smile on the reader's face, the zeugma subtly teases the bluenoses who objected to the nudity in Sendak's drawings by juxtaposing their censorship with the innocence of the books' readership.

and in turn for their children. A simple phrase that tells a story—a generation of children grew up with such fond memories of Sendak's books that they read them to their own children—and that serves as an understated tribute to the great artist.

Dear Abby: My wife sleeps in the raw. Beginning the obit with a bang, this sample column instantly brings a pang of nostalgia to the millions of readers who grew up reading Dear Abby, and graphically introduces her life's work to those who did not. We see for ourselves, rather than having to be told about, the offbeat problems, the waggish replies, the (for her time) liberal sensibility.

Dear Abby: Our son married a girl when he was in the service. The deliberate use of surprising transitions—colons, dashes, block quotations—is one of the hallmarks of lively prose.[8] A lesser writer might have introduced this with the plodding "Here is another example of a column by Mrs. Phillips," but Fox interrupts her narration without warning to redirect our gaze to Phillips in her prime. A writer, like a cinematographer, manipulates the viewer's perspective on an ongoing story, with the verbal equivalent of camera angles and quick cuts.

the marital, the medical, and sometimes both at once. Killjoy style manuals tell writers to avoid alliteration, but good prose is enlivened with moments of poetry, like this line with its pleasing meter and its impish pairing of *marital* and *medical*.

She was 90, though parts of her were considerably younger. A sly twist on the formulaic reporting and ponderous tone of conventional obituaries. We soon learn that Brown was a champion of women's sexual self-definition, so we understand the innuendo about cosmetic surgery as good-natured rather than catty—as a joke that Brown herself would have enjoyed.

hauntingly, flinty, tart-tongued, weepy, hard-nosed, astringent, genteelly, risqué, voluptuous, titillating. In selecting these uncommon adjectives and adverbs, Fox defies two of the commonest advisories in the stylebooks: Write with nouns and verbs, not adjectives and adverbs, and Never use an uncommon, fancy word when a common, plain one will do.

But the rules are badly stated. It's certainly true that a lot of turgid prose is stuffed with polysyllabic Latinisms (*cessation* for *end, eventuate in* for *cause*) and flabby adjectives (*is contributive to* instead of *contributes to, is determinative of* instead of *determines*). And showing off with fancy words you barely understand can make you look pompous and occasionally ridiculous. But a skilled writer can enliven and sometimes electrify her prose with the judicious insertion of a surprising word. According to studies of writing quality, a varied vocabulary and the use of unusual words are two of the features that distinguish sprightly prose from mush.[9]

The best words not only pinpoint an idea better than any alternative but echo it in their sound and articulation, a phenomenon called phonesthetics, the feeling of sound.[10] It's no coincidence that *haunting* means "haunting" and *tart* means "tart," rather than the other way around; just listen to your voice and sense your muscles as you articulate them. *Voluptuous* has a voluptuous give-and-take between the lips and the tongue, and *titillating* also gives the tongue a workout while titillating the ear with a coincidental but unignorable overlap with a naughty word. These associations make *a sea of voluptuous models and titillating cover lines* more lively than *a sea of sexy models and provocative cover lines.* And *a sea of pulchritudinous models* would have served as a lesson on how not to choose words: the ugly *pulchritude* sounds like the opposite of what it means, and it is one of those words that no one ever uses unless they are trying to show off.

But sometimes even show-off words can work. In her obituary of the journalist Mike McGrady, who masterminded a 1979 literary hoax in which a deliberately awful bodice ripper became an international bestseller, Fox wrote, "*Naked Came the Stranger* was written by 25

Newsday journalists in an era when newsrooms were arguably more relaxed and inarguably more bibulous."[11] The playful *bibulous,* "tending to drink too much," is related to *beverage* and *imbibe* and calls to mind babbling, bobbling, bubbling, and burbling. Readers who want to become writers should read with a dictionary at hand (several are available as smartphone apps), and writers should not hesitate to send their readers there *if* the word is dead-on in meaning, evocative in sound, and not so obscure that the reader will never see it again. (You can probably do without *maieutic, propaedeutic,* and *subdoxastic.*) I write with a thesaurus, mindful of the advice I once read in a bicycle repair manual on how to squeeze a dent out of a rim with Vise-Grip pliers: "Do *not* get carried away with the destructive potential of this tool."

———

From the early years of the twentieth century to well past its middle age, nearly every black family in the American South, which meant nearly every black family in America, had a decision to make. There were sharecroppers losing at settlement. Typists wanting to work in an office. Yard boys scared that a single gesture near the planter's wife could leave them hanging from an oak tree. They were all stuck in a caste system as hard and unyielding as the red Georgia clay, and they each had a decision before them. In this, they were not unlike anyone who ever longed to cross the Atlantic or the Rio Grande.

It was during the First World War that a silent pilgrimage took its first steps within the borders of this country. The fever rose without warning or notice or much in the way of understanding by those outside its reach. It would not end until the 1970s and would set into motion changes in the North and South that no one, not even the people doing the leaving, could have imagined at the start of it or dreamed would take a lifetime to play out.

Historians would come to call it the Great Migration. It would become perhaps the biggest underreported story of the twentieth century. . . .

The actions of the people in this book were both universal and distinctly American. Their migration was a response to an economic and social structure not of their making. They did what humans have done for centuries when life became untenable— what the pilgrims did under the tyranny of British rule, what the Scotch-Irish did in Oklahoma when the land turned to dust, what the Irish did when there was nothing to eat, what the European Jews did during the spread of Nazism, what the landless in Russia, Italy, China, and elsewhere did when something better across the ocean called to them. What binds these stories together was the back-against-the-wall, reluctant yet hopeful search for something better, any place but where they were. They did what human beings looking for freedom, throughout history, have often done.

They left.

In *The Warmth of Other Suns,* the journalist Isabel Wilkerson ensured that the story of the Great Migration would be underreported no longer.[12] Calling it "great" is no exaggeration. The movement of millions of African Americans from the Deep South to Northern cities set off the civil rights movement, redrew the urban landscape, rewrote the agenda of American politics and education, and transformed American culture and, with it, world culture.

Wilkerson not only rectifies the world's ignorance about the Great Migration, but with twelve hundred interviews and crystalline prose she makes us understand it in its full human reality. We live in an era of social science, and have become accustomed to understanding the social world in terms of "forces," "pressures," "processes," and "developments." It is easy to forget that those "forces" are statistical summaries of the deeds of millions of men and women who act on their beliefs in pursuit of their desires. The habit of submerging the individual into abstractions can lead not only to bad science (it's not as if the "social forces" obeyed Newton's laws) but to dehumanization. We are apt to think, "I (and my kind) choose to do things for reasons; he (and his kind) are part of a social process." This was a moral of Orwell's essay

"Politics and the English Language," which warned against dehumanizing abstraction: "Millions of peasants are robbed of their farms and sent trudging along the roads with no more than they can carry: this is called *transfer of population* or *rectification of frontiers*." With an allergy to abstraction and a phobia of cliché, Wilkerson trains a magnifying glass on the historical blob called "the Great Migration" and reveals the humanity of the people who compose it.

From the early years of the twentieth century to well past its middle age. Not even the chronology is described in conventional language: the century is an aging person, a contemporary of the story's protagonists.

Typists wanting to work in an office. Not "denial of economic opportunities." By invoking a moderately skilled occupation from an earlier era, Wilkerson invites us to imagine the desperation of a woman who has acquired a proficiency that could lift her from the cotton fields to a professional office but who is denied the chance because of the color of her skin.

Yard boys scared that a single gesture near the planter's wife could leave them hanging from an oak tree. Not "oppression," not "the threat of violence," not even "lynching," but a horrific physical image. We even see what kind of tree it is.

as hard and unyielding as the red Georgia clay. Once again prose is brought to life with a snatch of poetry, as in this simile with its sensual image, its whiff of allusion (I think of Martin Luther King's "red hills of Georgia"), and its lyrical anapest meter.

anyone who ever longed to cross the Atlantic or the Rio Grande. Not "immigrants from Europe or Mexico." Once again the people are not sociological categories. The author forces us to visualize bodies in motion and to remember the motives that pulled them along.

what the pilgrims did . . . what the Scotch-Irish did . . . what the European Jews did . . . what the landless in Russia, Italy, China, and elsewhere did. Wilkerson begins the paragraph by stating that the actions of her protagonists are universal, but she does not rest with that generalization. She nominates the Great Migration for inclusion in a list of storied emigrations (expressed in pleasingly parallel syntax), whose descendants doubtless include many of her readers. Those readers are implicitly invited to apply their respect for their ancestors' courage and sacrifice to the forgotten pilgrims of the Great Migration.

when the land turned to dust, not "the Dust Bowl"; *when there was nothing to eat,* not "the Potato Famine"; *the landless,* not "the peasants."* Wilkerson will not allow us to snooze through a recitation of familiar verbiage. Fresh wording and concrete images force us to keep updating the virtual reality display in our minds.

They left. Among the many dumb rules of paragraphing foisted on students in composition courses is the one that says that a paragraph may not consist of a single sentence. Wilkerson ends a richly descriptive introductory chapter with a paragraph composed of exactly two syllables. The abrupt ending and the expanse of blankness at the bottom of the page mirror the finality of the decision to move and the uncertainty of the life that lay ahead. Good writing finishes strong.

The authors of the four passages share a number of practices: an insistence on fresh wording and concrete imagery over familiar verbiage and abstract summary; an attention to the readers' vantage point and the target of their gaze; the judicious placement of an uncommon word or idiom against a backdrop of simple nouns and verbs; the use of parallel syntax; the occasional planned surprise; the presentation of a telling detail that obviates an explicit pronouncement; the use of meter and sound that resonate with the meaning and mood.

The authors also share an attitude: they do not hide the passion and relish that drive them to tell us about their subjects. They write as if they have something important to say. But no, that doesn't capture it. They write as if they have something important to *show.* And that, we shall see, is a key ingredient in the sense of style.

Chapter 2

A WINDOW ONTO THE WORLD

CLASSIC STYLE AS AN ANTIDOTE FOR ACADEMESE,
BUREAUCRATESE, CORPORATESE, LEGALESE,
OFFICIALESE, AND OTHER KINDS OF STUFFY PROSE

Writing is an unnatural act.[1] As Charles Darwin observed, "Man has an instinctive tendency to speak, as we see in the babble of our young children, whereas no child has an instinctive tendency to bake, brew, or write." The spoken word is older than our species, and the instinct for language allows children to engage in articulate conversation years before they enter a schoolhouse. But the written word is a recent invention that has left no trace in our genome and must be laboriously acquired throughout childhood and beyond.

Speech and writing differ in their mechanics, of course, and that is one reason children must struggle with writing: it takes practice to reproduce the sounds of language with a pencil or a keyboard. But they differ in another way, which makes the acquisition of writing a lifelong challenge even after the mechanics have been mastered. Speaking and writing involve very different kinds of human relationship, and only the one associated with speech comes naturally to us. Spoken conversation is instinctive because social interaction is instinctive: we speak to those with whom we are on speaking terms. When we engage our conversational partners, we have an inkling of what they know and what they might be interested in learning, and as we chat with them, we monitor their eyes, their face, and their posture. If they need clarification, or cannot swallow an assertion, or have something to add, they can break into the conversation or follow up in turn.

We enjoy none of this give-and-take when we cast our bread upon the waters by sending a written missive out into the world. The recipients are invisible and inscrutable, and we have to get through to them without knowing much about them or seeing their reactions. At the time that we write, the reader exists only in our imaginations. Writing is above all an act of pretense. We have to visualize ourselves in some kind of conversation, or correspondence, or oration, or soliloquy, and put words into the mouth of the little avatar who represents us in this simulated world.

The key to good style, far more than obeying any list of commandments, is to have a clear conception of the make-believe world in which you're pretending to communicate. There are many possibilities. A person thumb-typing a text message can get away with acting as if he is taking part in a real conversation.* A college student who writes a term paper is pretending that he knows more about his subject than the reader and that his goal is to supply the reader with information she needs, whereas in reality his reader typically knows more about the subject than he does and has no need for the information, the actual goal of the exercise being to give the student practice for the real thing. An activist composing a manifesto, or a minister drafting a sermon, must write as if they are standing in front of a crowd and whipping up their emotions.

Which simulation should a writer immerse himself in when composing a piece for a more generic readership, such as an essay, an article, a review, an editorial, a newsletter, or a blog post? The literary scholars Francis-Noël Thomas and Mark Turner have singled out one model of prose as an aspiration for such writers today. They call it classic style, and explain it in a wonderful little book called *Clear and Simple as the Truth*.

The guiding metaphor of classic style is seeing the world. The writer

---

* To avoid the awkwardness of strings of *he or she*, I have borrowed a convention from linguistics and will consistently refer to a generic writer of one sex and a generic reader of the other. The male gender won the coin toss, and will represent the writer in this chapter; the roles will alternate in subsequent ones.

can see something that the reader has not yet noticed, and he orients the reader's gaze so that she can see it for herself. The purpose of writing is presentation, and its motive is disinterested truth. It succeeds when it aligns language with the truth, the proof of success being clarity and simplicity. The truth can be known, and is not the same as the language that reveals it; prose is a window onto the world. The writer knows the truth before putting it into words; he is not using the occasion of writing to sort out what he thinks. Nor does the writer of classic prose have to argue for the truth; he just needs to present it. That is because the reader is competent and can recognize the truth when she sees it, as long as she is given an unobstructed view. The writer and the reader are equals, and the process of directing the reader's gaze takes the form of a conversation.

A writer of classic prose must simulate two experiences: showing the reader something in the world, and engaging her in conversation. The nature of each experience shapes the way that classic prose is written. The metaphor of showing implies that there is something to see. The things in the world the writer is pointing to, then, are *concrete*: people (or other animate beings) who move around in the world and interact with objects.[2] The metaphor of conversation implies that the reader is *cooperative*. The writer can count on her to read between the lines, catch his drift, and connect the dots, without his having to spell out every step in his train of thought.[3]

Classic prose, Thomas and Turner explain, is just one kind of style, whose invention they credit to seventeenth-century French writers such as Descartes and La Rochefoucauld. The differences between classic style and other styles can be appreciated by comparing their stances on the communication scenario: how the writer imagines himself to be related to the reader, and what the writer is trying to accomplish.

Classic style is not a contemplative or romantic style, in which a writer tries to share his idiosyncratic, emotional, and mostly ineffable reactions to something. Nor is it a prophetic, oracular, or oratorical style, where the writer has the gift of being able to see things that no one else can, and uses the music of language to unite an audience.

Less obviously, classic style differs from practical style, like the language of memos, manuals, term papers, and research reports. (Traditional stylebooks such as Strunk and White are mainly guides to practical style.) In practical style, the writer and reader have defined roles (supervisor and employee, teacher and student, technician and customer), and the writer's goal is to satisfy the reader's need. Writing in practical style may conform to a fixed template (a five-paragraph essay, a report in a scientific journal), and it is brief because the reader needs the information in a timely manner. Writing in classic style, in contrast, takes whatever form and whatever length the writer needs to present an interesting truth. The classic writer's brevity "comes from the elegance of his mind, never from pressures of time or employment."[4]

Classic style also differs subtly from plain style, where everything is in full view and the reader needs no help in seeing anything. In classic style the writer has worked hard to find something worth showing and the perfect vantage point from which to see it. The reader may have to work hard to discern it, but her efforts will be rewarded. Classic style, Thomas and Turner explain, is aristocratic, not egalitarian: "Truth is available to all who are willing to work to achieve it, but truth is certainly not commonly possessed by all and is no one's birthright."[5] *The early bird gets the worm*, for example, is plain. *The early bird gets the worm, but the second mouse gets the cheese* is classic.

Classic style overlaps with plain and practical styles. And all three differ from self-conscious, relativistic, ironic, or postmodern styles, in which "the writer's chief, if unstated, concern is to escape being convicted of philosophical naiveté about his own enterprise." As Thomas and Turner note, "When we open a cookbook, we completely put aside—and expect the author to put aside—the kind of question that leads to the heart of certain philosophic and religious traditions. Is it possible to talk about cooking? Do eggs really exist? Is food something about which knowledge is possible? Can anyone else ever tell us anything true about cooking? . . . Classic style similarly puts aside as inappropriate philosophical questions about its enterprise. If it took those questions up, it could never get around to treating its subject, and its purpose is exclusively to treat its subject."[6]

The different prose styles are not sharply demarcated, and many kinds of writing blend the different styles or alternate between them. (Academic writing, for example, tends to mix practical and self-conscious styles.) Classic style is an ideal. Not all prose should be classic, and not all writers can carry off the pretense. But knowing the hallmarks of classic style will make anyone a better writer, and it is the strongest cure I know for the disease that enfeebles academic, bureaucratic, corporate, legal, and official prose.

At first glance classic style sounds naïve and philistine, suited only to a world of concrete goings-on. Not so. Classic style is not the same as the common but unhelpful advice to "avoid abstraction." Sometimes we do have to write about abstract ideas. What classic style does is explain them as if they were objects and forces that would be recognizable to anyone standing in a position to see them. Let's see how classic style is used by the physicist Brian Greene to explain one of the most exotic ideas the human mind has ever entertained, the theory of multiple universes.[7]

Greene begins with the observation by astronomers in the 1920s that galaxies were moving away from each other:

If space is now expanding, then at ever earlier times the universe must have been ever smaller. At some moment in the distant past, everything we now see—the ingredients responsible for every planet, every star, every galaxy, even space itself—must have been compressed to an infinitesimal speck that then swelled outward, evolving into the universe as we know it.

The big-bang theory was born. . . . Yet scientists were aware that the big-bang theory suffered from a significant shortcoming. Of all things, it leaves out the bang. Einstein's equations do a wonderful job of describing how the universe evolved from a split second after the bang, but the equations break down (similar to the error message returned by a calculator when you try to divide 1 by 0) when applied to the extreme environment of the universe's earliest moment. The big bang thus provides no insight into what might have powered the bang itself.

Greene does not tut-tut over the fact that this reasoning depends on complex mathematics. Instead he shows us, with images and everyday examples, what the math reveals. We accept the theory of the big bang by watching a movie of expanding space running backwards. We appreciate the abstruse concept of equations breaking down through an example, division by zero, which we can understand for ourselves in either of two ways. We can think it through: What could dividing a number into zero parts actually mean? Or we can punch the numbers into our calculators and see the error message ourselves.

Greene then tells us that astronomers recently made a surprising discovery, which he illustrates with an analogy:

> Just as the pull of earth's gravity slows the ascent of a ball tossed upward, the gravitational pull of each galaxy on every other must be slowing the expansion of space. . . . [But] far from slowing down, the expansion of space went into overdrive about 7 billion years ago and has been speeding up ever since. That's like gently tossing a ball upward, having it slow down initially, but then rocket upward ever more quickly.

But soon they found an explanation, which he illustrates with a looser simile:

> We're all used to gravity being a force that does only one thing: pull objects toward each other. But in Einstein's . . . theory of relativity, gravity can also . . . push things apart. . . . If space contains . . . an invisible energy, sort of like an invisible mist that's uniformly spread through space, then the gravity exerted by the energy mist would be repulsive.

The dark energy hypothesis, however, led to yet another mystery:

When the astronomers deduced how much dark energy would have to permeate every nook and cranny of space to account for the observed cosmic speedup, they found a number that no one has been able to explain . . . :

.000000000000000000000000000000000000000000000000
000000000000000000000000000000000000000000000000
00000000000000000000000000000000138.

By displaying this number in all its multi-zeroed glory, Greene impresses upon us the fact that it is very small yet oddly precise. He then points out that it is hard to explain that value because it seems to be fine-tuned to allow life on earth to come into being:

In universes with larger amounts of dark energy, whenever matter tries to clump into galaxies, the repulsive push of the dark energy is so strong that the clump gets blown apart, thwarting galactic formation. In universes whose dark-energy value is much smaller, the repulsive push changes to an attractive pull, causing those universes to collapse back on themselves so quickly that again galaxies wouldn't form. And without galaxies, there are no stars, no planets, and so in those universes there's no chance for our form of life to exist.

To the rescue comes an idea which (Greene showed us earlier) explained the bang in the big bang. According to the theory of inflationary cosmology, empty space can spawn other big bangs, creating a vast number of other universes: a multiverse. This makes the precise value of dark energy in our universe less surprising:

We find ourselves in this universe and not another for much the same reason we find ourselves on earth and not on Neptune— we find ourselves where conditions are ripe for our form of life.

Of course! As long as there are many planets, one of them is likely to be at a hospitable distance from the sun, and no one thinks it's sensible to ask why we find ourselves on that planet rather than on Neptune. So it would be if there are many universes.

But scientists still faced a problem, which Greene illustrates with an analogy:

> Just as it takes a well-stocked shoe store to guarantee you'll find your size, only a well-stocked multiverse can guarantee that our universe, with its peculiar amount of dark energy, will be represented. On its own, inflationary cosmology falls short of the mark. While its never-ending series of big bangs would yield an immense collection of universes, many would have similar features, like a shoe store with stacks and stacks of sizes 5 and 13, but nothing in the size you seek.

The piece that completes the puzzle is string theory, according to which "the tally of possible universes stands at the almost incomprehensible 10^{500}, a number so large it defies analogy."

> By combining inflationary cosmology and string theory, . . . the stock room of universes overflows: in the hands of inflation, string theory's enormously diverse collection of possible universes become actual universes, brought to life by one big bang after another. Our universe is then virtually guaranteed to be among them. And because of the special features necessary for our form of life, that's the universe we inhabit.

In just three thousand words, Greene has caused us to understand a mind-boggling idea, with no apology that the physics and math behind the theory might be hard for him to explain or for readers to understand. He narrates a series of events with the confidence that anyone looking at them will know what they imply, because the examples he has chosen are *exact*. Division by zero is a perfect example of "equations breaking down"; gravity tugs at a tossed ball in exactly the way it slows cosmic expansion; the improbability of finding a precisely specified item in a small pool of possibilities applies to both the sizes of shoes in a store and the values of physical constants in a multiverse. The examples are not so much metaphors or analogies as they are *actual instances* of the phenomena he is explaining, and they are instances that readers can see with their own eyes. This is classic style.

It may not be a coincidence that Greene, like many scientists since Galileo, is a lucid expositor of difficult ideas, because the ideal of classic prose is congenial to the worldview of the scientist. Contrary to the common misunderstanding in which Einstein proved that everything is relative and Heisenberg proved that observers always affect what they observe, most scientists believe that there are objective truths about the world and that they can be discovered by a disinterested observer.

By the same token, the guiding image of classic prose could not be further from the worldview of relativist academic ideologies such as postmodernism, poststructuralism, and literary Marxism. And not coincidentally, it was scholars with these worldviews who consistently won the annual Bad Writing Contest, a publicity stunt held by the philosopher Denis Dutton during the late 1990s.[8] First place in 1997 went to the eminent critic Fredric Jameson for the opening sentence of his book on film criticism:

> The visual is essentially pornographic, which is to say that it has its end in rapt, mindless fascination; thinking about its attributes becomes an adjunct to that, if it is unwilling to betray its object; while the most austere films necessarily draw their energy from the attempt to repress their own excess (rather than from the more thankless effort to discipline the viewer).

The assertion that "the visual is essentially pornographic" is not, to put it mildly, a fact about the world that anyone can see. The phrase "which is to say" promises an explanation, but it is just as baffling: can't something have "its end in rapt, mindless fascination" without being pornographic? The puzzled reader is put on notice that *her* ability to understand the world counts for nothing; her role is to behold the enigmatic pronouncements of the great scholar. Classic writing, with its assumption of equality between writer and reader, makes the reader feel like a genius. Bad writing makes the reader feel like a dunce.

The winning entry for 1998, by another eminent critic, Judith Butler, is also a defiant repudiation of classic style:

> The move from a structuralist account in which capital is understood to structure social relations in relatively homologous ways to a view of hegemony in which power relations are subject to repetition, convergence, and rearticulation brought the question of temporality into the thinking of structure, and marked a shift from a form of Althusserian theory that takes structural totalities as theoretical objects to one in which the insights into the contingent possibility of structure inaugurate a renewed conception of hegemony as bound up with the contingent sites and strategies of the rearticulation of power.

A reader of this intimidating passage can marvel at Butler's ability to juggle abstract propositions about still more abstract propositions, with no real-world referent in sight. We have a move from an account of an understanding to a view with a rearticulation of a question, which reminds me of the Hollywood party in *Annie Hall* where a movie producer is overheard saying, "Right now it's only a notion, but I think I can get money to make it into a concept, and later turn it into an idea." What the reader cannot do is understand it—to see with her own eyes what Butler is seeing. Insofar as the passage has a meaning at all, it seems to be that some scholars have come to realize that power can change over time.

The abstruseness of the contest winners' writing is deceptive. Most academics can effortlessly dispense this kind of sludge, and many students, like Zonker Harris in this *Doonesbury* cartoon, acquire the skill without having to be taught:

Doonesbury © 1972 G. B. Trudeau. Reprinted with permission of Universal Uclick. All rights reserved.

Just as deceptive is the plain language of Greene's explanation of the multiverse. It takes cognitive toil and literary dexterity to pare an argument to its essentials, narrate it in an orderly sequence, and illustrate it with analogies that are both familiar and accurate. As Dolly Parton said, "You wouldn't *believe* how much it costs to look this cheap."

The confident presentation of an idea in classic style should not be confused with an arrogant insistence that it is correct. Elsewhere in his essay, Greene does not hide the fact that many of his fellow physicists think that string theory and the multiverse are extravagant and unproven. He only wants readers to understand them. Thomas and Turner explain that the reader of classic prose "may conclude that a text is masterful, classic, and completely wrong."[9]

And for all its directness, classic style remains a pretense, an imposture, a stance. Even scientists, with their commitment to seeing the world as it is, are a *bit* postmodern. They recognize that it's hard to know the truth, that the world doesn't just reveal itself to us, that we understand the world through our theories and constructs, which are not pictures but abstract propositions, and that our ways of understanding the world must constantly be scrutinized for hidden biases. It's just that good writers don't flaunt this anxiety in every passage they write; they artfully conceal it for clarity's sake.

Remembering that classic style is a pretense also makes sense of the seemingly outlandish requirement that a writer know the truth before putting it into words and not use the writing process to organize and clarify his thoughts. Of course no writer works that way, but that is irrelevant. The goal of classic style is to make it *seem* as if the writer's thoughts were fully formed before he clothed them in words. As with the celebrity chef in the immaculate television kitchen who pulls a perfect soufflé out of the oven in the show's final minute, the messy work has been done beforehand and behind the scenes.

The rest of this chapter is organized as follows. The first subsection introduces the concept of "metadiscourse," followed by one of its principal manifestations, the use of signposting. The second subsection reviews three issues: the problem of focusing on a description of professional activity rather than an exposition of subject matter, the overuse of apologetic language, and the disadvantages of excessive hedging. Following this, the third subsection explains the issue of prespecified verbal formulas. The fourth subsection covers issues having to do with excessive abstraction, including overuse of nominalizations and passives. Finally, I will review the main points of the preceding discussion.

Did you get all that?

I didn't think so. That tedious paragraph was filled with metadiscourse—verbiage about verbiage, such as *subsection, review,* and *discussion.* Inexperienced writers often think they're doing the reader a favor by guiding her through the rest of the text with a detailed preview. In reality, previews that read like a scrunched-up table of contents are there to help the writer, not the reader. At this point in the presentation, the terms mean nothing to the reader, and the list is too long and arbitrary to stay in memory for long.

The previous paragraph reviewed the concept of metadiscourse. This paragraph introduces one of its primary manifestations, the phenomenon of signposting.

Clumsy writers do a lot of that, too. They unthinkingly follow the advice to say what you're going to say, say it, and then say what you've said. The advice comes from classical rhetoric, and it makes sense for long orations: if a listener's mind momentarily wanders, the passage she has missed is gone forever. It's not as necessary in writing, where a reader can backtrack and look up what she's missed. And it can be intrusive in classic style, which simulates a conversation. You would never announce to a companion, "I'm going to say three things to you. The first thing I'm going to say is that a woodpecker has just landed on that tree." You'd just say it.

The problem with thoughtless signposting is that the reader has to put more work into understanding the signposts than she saves in seeing what they point to, like complicated directions for a shortcut which take longer to figure out than the time the shortcut would save. It's better if the route is clearly enough laid out that every turn is obvious when you get to it. Good writing takes advantage of a reader's expectations of where to go next. It accompanies the reader on a journey, or arranges the material in a logical sequence (general to specific, big to small, early to late), or tells a story with a narrative arc.

It's not that authors should avoid signposting altogether. Even casual chitchat has some signposting. *Let me tell you a story. To make a long story short. In other words. As I was saying. Mark my words. Did you hear the one about the minister, the priest, and the rabbi?* Like all writing decisions, the amount of signposting requires judgment and compromise: too much, and the reader bogs down in reading the signposts; too little, and she has no idea where she is being led.

The art of classic prose is to signpost sparingly, as we do in conversation, and with a minimum of metadiscourse. One way to introduce a topic without metadiscourse is to open with a question:

This chapter discusses the factors that cause names to rise and fall in popularity.	What makes a name rise and fall in popularity?

Another is to use the guiding metaphor behind classic style, vision. The content in a passage of writing is treated like a happening in the world that can be seen with one's eyeballs:

The preceding paragraph demonstrated that parents sometimes give a boy's name to a girl, but never vice versa.	As we have seen, parents sometimes give a boy's name to a girl, but never vice versa.

And since seeing implies seers, we no longer have to refer to paragraphs "demonstrating" some things and sections "summarizing" other things, as if blocks of printing had a mind of their own. The active parties are the writer and the reader, who are taking in the spectacle together, and the writer can refer to them with the good old pronoun *we*. That supplies him with still other metaphors that can replace metadiscourse, such as moving together or cooperating on a project:

The previous section analyzed the source of word sounds. This section raises the question of word meanings.	Now that we have explored the source of word sounds, we arrive at the puzzle of word meanings.
The first topic to be discussed is proper names.	Let's begin with proper names.

As for the advice to say what you said, the key is the expression "in other words." There's no sense in copying a sentence from every paragraph and pasting them together at the end. That just forces the reader to figure out the point of those sentences all over again, and it is tantamount to a confession that the author isn't presenting ideas (which can always be clothed in different language) but just shuffling words around the page. A summary should repeat enough of the key words to allow the reader to connect it back to the earlier passages that spelled out the points in detail. But those words should be fitted into new sentences that work together as a coherent passage of prose in its own right. The summary should be self-contained, almost as if the material being summarized had never existed.

Metadiscourse is not the only form of self-consciousness that bogs down professional prose. Another is a confusion of the writer's subject matter with his line of work. Writers live in two universes. One is the world of the thing they study: the poetry of Elizabeth Bishop, the development of language in children, the Taiping Rebellion in China. The other is the world of their profession: getting articles published, going to conferences, keeping up with the trends and gossip. Most of a researcher's waking hours are spent in the second world, and it's easy for him to confuse the two. The result is the typical opening of an academic paper:

> In recent years, an increasing number of psychologists and linguists have turned their attention to the problem of child language acquisition. In this article, recent research on this process will be reviewed.

No offense, but very few people are interested in how professors spend their time. Classic style ignores the hired help and looks directly at what they are being paid to study:

> All children acquire the ability to speak a language without explicit lessons. How do they accomplish this feat?

To be fair, sometimes the topic of conversation really *is* the activity of researchers, such as an overview intended to introduce graduate students or other insiders to the scholarly literature in their chosen profession. But researchers are apt to lose sight of whom they are writing for, and narcissistically describe the obsessions of their guild rather than what the audience really wants to know. Professional narcissism is by no means confined to academia. Journalists assigned to an issue often cover the coverage, creating the notorious media echo chamber. Museum signs explain how the shard in the showcase fits into a classification of pottery styles rather than who made it or what it was used for. Music and movie guides are dominated by data on how much money a work grossed the weekend it was released, or how many weeks it spent in the theaters or on the charts. Governments and corporations organize their Web sites around their bureaucratic structure rather than the kinds of information a user seeks.

Self-conscious writers are also apt to whinge about how what they're about to do is so terribly difficult and complicated and controversial:

What are intractable conflicts? "Intractability" is a controversial concept, which means different things to different people.

Resilience to stress is a complex multidimensional construct. Although there is no one universally accepted definition of resilience, it is generally understood as the ability to bounce back from hardship and trauma.

The problem of language acquisition is extremely complex. It is difficult to give precise definitions of the concept of "language" and the concept of "acquisition" and the concept of "children." There is much uncertainty about the interpretation of experimental data and a great deal of controversy surrounding the theories. More research needs to be done.

The last of these quotations is a pastiche, but the other two are real, and all are typical of the inward-looking style that makes academic writing so tedious. In classic style, the writer credits the reader with enough intelligence to realize that many concepts aren't easy to define and that many controversies aren't easy to resolve. She is there to see what the writer will do about it.

Another bad habit of self-conscious writing is the prissy use of quotation marks—sometimes called shudder quotes or scare quotes—to distance the writer from a common idiom:

By combining forces, you could make the "whole more than the sum of its parts."

But this is not the "take home message."

They may be able to "think outside the box" even when everybody else has a fixed approach, but they do not always note when "enough is enough."

It began as a movement led by a few "young turks" against an "old guard" who dominated the profession.

She is a "quick study" and has been able to educate herself in virtually any area that interests her.

The authors seem to be saying, "I couldn't think of a more dignified way of putting this, but please don't think I'm a flibbertigibbet who talks this way; I really am a serious scholar." The problem goes beyond prissiness. In the last example, taken from a letter of recommendation, are we supposed to think that the student is a quick study, or that she is a "quick study"—someone who is alleged or rumored by others to be a quick study, but really isn't? The use of shudder quotes is taken to an extreme in the agonizingly self-conscious, defiantly un-classic style of postmodernism, which rejects the possibility that any word can ever refer to anything, or even that there is an objectively existing world for words to refer to. Hence the 2004 headline in the satirical newspaper *The Onion* on the passing of postmodernism's leading light: JACQUES DERRIDA "DIES."

Quotation marks have a number of legitimate uses, such as reproducing someone else's words (*She said, "Fiddlesticks!"*), mentioning a word as a word rather than using it to convey its meaning (*The* New York Times *uses "millenniums," not "millennia"*), and signaling that the writer does not accept the meaning of a word as it is being used by others in this context (*They executed their sister to preserve the family's "honor"*). Squeamishness about one's own choice of words is not among them. Classic style is confident about its own voice. If you're not comfortable using an expression without apologetic quotation marks, you probably shouldn't be using it at all.

And then there's compulsive hedging. Many writers cushion their prose with wads of fluff that imply that they are not willing to stand behind what they are saying, including *almost, apparently, comparatively, fairly, in part, nearly, partially, predominantly, presumably, rather, relatively, seemingly, so to speak, somewhat, sort of, to a certain degree, to some extent,* and the ubiquitous *I would argue* (does this mean that you would argue for your position if things were different, but are not willing to argue for it now?). Consider the "virtually" in the letter of recommendation excerpted above. Did the writer really mean to say that there are some areas the student was interested in where she *didn't* bother to educate herself, or perhaps that she tried to educate herself in those areas but lacked the competence to do so? And then there's the scientist who showed me a picture of her four-year-old daughter and said, beaming, "We virtually adore her."

Writers acquire the hedge habit to conform to the bureaucratic imperative that's abbreviated as CYA, which I'll spell out as Cover Your Anatomy. They hope it will get them off the hook, or at least allow them to plead guilty to a lesser charge, should a critic ever try to prove them wrong. It's the same reason that lawsuit-wary journalists drizzle the words *allegedly* and *reportedly* throughout their copy, as in *The alleged victim was found lying in a pool of blood with a knife in his back.*

There is an alternative slogan to Cover Your Anatomy: So Sue Me. A classic writer counts on the common sense and ordinary charity of his readers, just as in everyday conversation we know when a speaker means "in general" or "all else being equal." If someone tells you that Liz wants to move out of Seattle because it's a rainy city, you don't interpret him as claiming that it rains there twenty-four hours a day seven days a week just because he didn't qualify his statement with *relatively rainy* or *somewhat rainy.* As Thomas and Turner explain, "Accuracy becomes pedantry if it is indulged for its own sake. A classic writer will phrase a subordinate point precisely but without the promise that it is technically accurate. The convention between writer and reader is that the writer is not to be challenged on these points because they are mere scaffolding."[10] Any adversary who is unscrupulous enough to give the least charitable reading to an unhedged statement will find an opening to attack the writer in a thicket of hedged ones anyway.

Sometimes a writer has no choice but to hedge a statement. Better still, the writer can *qualify* the statement, that is, spell out the circumstances in which it does not hold, rather than leaving himself an escape hatch or being coy as to whether he really means it. A statement in a legal document *will* be interpreted adversarially, without the presumption of cooperation that governs an ordinary conversation, so every exception must be spelled out. A scholar who is proposing a hypothesis must go on the record with it in as precise a form as possible at least once so that critics can see exactly what he is claiming and give it their best shot. And if there is a reasonable chance that readers will misinterpret a statistical tendency as an absolute law, a responsible writer will anticipate the oversight and qualify the generalization accordingly. Pronouncements like "Democracies don't fight wars," "Men are better than women at geometry problems," and "Eating broccoli prevents cancer" do not do justice to the reality that these phenomena consist at most of small differences in the means of two overlapping bell curves. Since there are serious consequences to misinterpreting these statements as absolute laws, a responsible writer should insert a qualifier like *on average* or *all things being equal,* together with a *slightly* or *somewhat.* Best of all is to convey the magnitude of the effect and the degree of certainty explicitly, in unhedged statements such as "During the twentieth century, democracies were half as likely to go to war with each other as autocracies were." It's not that good writers never hedge their claims. It's that their hedging is a choice, not a tic.

Paradoxically, intensifiers like *very, highly,* and *extremely* also work like hedges. They not only fuzz up a writer's prose but can undermine his intent. If I'm wondering who pilfered the petty cash, it's more reassuring to hear *Not Jones; he's an honest man* than *Not Jones; he's a very honest man.* The reason is that unmodified adjectives and nouns tend to be interpreted categorically: *honest* means "completely honest," or at least "completely honest in the way that matters here" (just as *Jack drank the bottle of beer* implies that he chugged down all of it, not just a sip or two). As soon as you add an intensifier, you're turning an all-or-none dichotomy into a graduated scale. True, you're trying to place your subject high on the scale—say, an 8.7 out of 10—but it would have been better if the reader were not considering his relative degree of honesty in the first place. That's the basis for the common advice (usually misattributed to Mark Twain) to "substitute *damn* every time you're inclined to write *very;* your editor will delete it and the writing will be just as it should be"—though today the substitution would have to be of a word stronger than *damn.*[11]

Classic prose is a pleasant illusion, like losing yourself in a play. The writer must work to keep up the impression that his prose is a window onto the scene rather than just a mess of words. Like an actor with a wooden delivery, a writer who relies on canned verbal formulas will break the spell. This is the kind of writer who gets the ball rolling in his search for the holy grail, but finds that it's neither a magic bullet nor a slam dunk, so he rolls with the punches and lets the chips fall where they may while seeing the glass as half-full, which is easier said than done.

Avoid clichés like the plague—it's a no-brainer.[12] When a reader is forced to work through one stale idiom after another, she stops converting the language into mental images and slips back into just mouthing the words.[13] Even worse, since a cliché-monger has turned off his own visual brain as he plonks down one dead idiom after another, he will inevitably mix his metaphors, and a reader who does keep her visual brain going will be distracted by the ludicrous imagery. *The price of chicken wings, the company's bread and butter, had risen. Leica had been coasting on its laurels. Microsoft began a low-octane swan song. Jeff is a renaissance man, drilling down to the core issues and pushing the envelope. Unless you bite the bullet, you'll shoot yourself in the foot. No one has yet invented a condom that will knock people's socks off. How low can the team sink? Sky's the limit!*

Even when a shopworn image is the best way to convey an idea, a classic writer can keep his reader engaged by remembering what the idiom literally refers to and playing with the image to keep it in her mind's eye:

When Americans are told about foreign politics, their eyes glaze over.	Ever tried to explain to a New Yorker the finer points of Slovakian coalition politics? I have. He almost needed an adrenaline shot to come out of the coma.[14]
Electronic publication is scholarship on steroids.	With electronic publication, you can see your stuff published just 15 seconds after you write it. It's scholarship on methamphetamines. Publication for speed freaks.[15]

Trying to direct team owners is like herding cats.	To suggest that directing team owners is like herding cats is to give cats a bad name.[16]
Hobbes stripped the human personality for any capacity for love or tenderness or even simple fellow-feeling, leaving instead only fear. He threw out the baby with the bathwater.	Hobbes stripped the human personality for any capacity for love or tenderness or even simple fellow-feeling, leaving instead only fear. The bath was dry, and the baby had vanished.[17]

And if you must use a cliché, why not word it in a way that makes physical sense? When you think about it, the fate of an overlooked item is to fall *through* or *into* the cracks, not *between* them, and the prototypical unrealizable desire is to *eat your cake and have it,* not to *have your cake and eat it* (it's easy to do them in that order). And you'll often be surprised, and your writing will be livelier, if you take a few seconds to look up the original wording of a cliché. *To gild the lily* is not just tired but visually less apt than either of the original metaphors that it scrambles together (from Shakespeare's *King John*), *to paint the lily* and *to gild refined gold,* the latter of which neatly echoes the visual redundancy in the overlap in sound between *gild* and *gold.* For that matter, you could avoid cliché altogether by adapting one of the other images in the full sentence: "To gild refined gold, to paint the lily, to throw a perfume on the violet, to smooth the ice, or add another hue unto the rainbow, or with taper-light to seek the beauteous eye of heaven to garnish, is wasteful and ridiculous excess."

Thoughtless clichés can even be dangerous. I sometimes wonder how much irrationality in the world has been excused by the nonsensical saying "Consistency is the hobgoblin of little minds," a corruption of Ralph Waldo Emerson's remark about "a *foolish* consistency." Recently a White House official referred to the American Israel Political Affairs Committee as "the 800-pound gorilla in the room," confusing *the elephant in the room* (something that everyone pretends to ignore) with *an 800-pound gorilla* (something that is powerful enough to do whatever it wants, from the joke "Where does an 800-pound gorilla sit?"). Given the controversy over whether the Israel lobby is merely undernoticed in American foreign policy or nefariously all-controlling, the meaning of the first cliché is a commonplace; the meaning of the second, incendiary.

Though no writer can avoid idioms altogether—they're part of the English lexicon, just like individual words—good writers reach for fresh similes and metaphors that keep the reader's sensory cortexes lit up. Shakespeare advises against "adding another hue unto the rainbow"; Dickens describes a man "with such long legs that he looked like the afternoon shadow of somebody else"; Nabokov has Lolita plopping into a seat, "her legs splayed, starfish-style."[18] But you don't have to be a great fiction writer to engage a reader's mental imagery. A psychologist explains a computer simulation in which activation builds up in a neuron until it fires "like popcorn in a pan."[19] An editor looking to sign up new talent writes about attending a funeral at which "the concentration of authors was so dense, I felt like an Alaskan grizzly at the foot of a waterfall, poised to pull out salmon by the paw-ful."[20] Even the bassist of the fictional rock band Spinal Tap deserves our admiration, if not for his literary acumen then for his attention to imagery, when he told an interviewer: "We're very lucky in the band in that we have two distinct visionaries, David and Nigel; they're like poets, like Shelley and Byron. . . . It's like fire and ice, basically. I feel my role in the band is to be somewhere in the middle of that, kind of like lukewarm water."

In classic prose the writer is directing the gaze of the reader to something in the world she can see for herself. All eyes are on an agent: a protagonist, a mover and shaker, a driving force. The agent pushes or prods something, and it moves or changes. Or something interesting comes into view, and the reader examines it part by part. Classic style minimizes abstractions, which cannot be seen with the naked eye. This doesn't mean that it avoids abstract *subject matter* (remember Brian Greene's explanation of the multiverse), only that it shows the events making up that subject matter transparently, by narrating an unfolding plot with real characters doing things, rather than by naming an abstract concept that encapsulates those events in a single word. Look at the stuffy passages on the left, which are filled with abstract nouns (underlined), and compare them with the more direct versions on the right:

The researchers found that groups that are typically associated with low alcoholism levels actually have moderate amounts of alcohol intake, yet still have low levels of high intake associated with alcoholism, such as Jews.

The researchers found that in groups with little alcoholism, such as Jews, people actually drink moderate amounts of alcohol, but few of them drink too much and become alcoholics.

I have serious doubts that trying to amend the Constitution would work on an actual level. On the aspirational level, however, a constitutional amendment strategy may be more valuable.

I doubt that trying to amend the Constitution would actually succeed, but it may be valuable to aspire to it.

Individuals with mental health issues can become dangerous. It is important to approach this subject from a variety of strategies, including mental health assistance but also from a law enforcement perspective.

People who are mentally ill can become dangerous. We need to consult mental health professionals, but we also may have to inform the police.

What are the prospects for reconciling a prejudice reduction model of change, designed to get people to like one another more, with a collective action model of change, designed to ignite struggles to achieve intergroup equality?

Should we try to change society by reducing prejudice, that is, by getting people to like one another? Or should we encourage disadvantaged groups to struggle for equality through collective action? Or can we do both?

Could you recognize a "level" or a "perspective" if you met one on the street? Could you point it out to someone else? What about an approach, an assumption, a concept, a condition, a context, a framework, an issue, a model, a process, a range, a role, a strategy, a tendency, or a variable?

These are *metaconcepts:* concepts about concepts. They serve as a kind of packing material in which academics, bureaucrats, and corporate mouthpieces clad their subject matter. Only when the packaging is hacked away does the object come into view. The phrase *on the aspirational level* adds nothing to *aspire,* nor is *a prejudice reduction model* any more sophisticated than *reducing prejudice.* Recall that the winning sentence in the 1998 Bad Writing Contest consisted almost entirely of metaconcepts.

Together with verbal coffins like *model* and *level* in which writers entomb their actors and actions, the English language provides them with a dangerous weapon called nominalization: making something into a noun. The nominalization rule takes a perfectly spry verb and embalms it into a lifeless noun by adding a suffix like *–ance, –ment, –ation,* or *–ing.* Instead of *affirming* an idea, you effect its *affirmation;* rather than *postponing* something, you implement a *postponement.* The writing scholar Helen Sword calls them zombie nouns because they lumber across the scene without a conscious agent directing their motion.[21] They can turn prose into a night of the living dead:

Prevention of neurogenesis diminished social avoidance.	When we prevented neurogenesis, the mice no longer avoided other mice.
Participants read assertions whose veracity was either affirmed or denied by the subsequent presentation of an assessment word.	We presented participants with a sentence, followed by the word TRUE or FALSE.
Comprehension checks were used as exclusion criteria.	We excluded people who failed to understand the instructions.
It may be that some missing genes are more contributive to the spatial deficit.	Perhaps some missing genes contribute to the spatial deficit.

The last example shows that verbs can be drained of life when they are turned into adjectives, too, as when *contribute* becomes *contributive to* or *aspire* becomes *on the aspirational level*. As this cartoon by Tom Toles suggests, zombie nouns and adjectives are one of the signatures of academese:

Any interrogatory verbalizations? But it's not just academics who loose these zombies on the world. In response to a hurricane which threatened the Republican National Convention in 2012, Florida governor Rick Scott told the press, "There is not any anticipation there will be a cancellation," that is, he didn't anticipate that he would have to cancel the convention. And in 2014 Secretary of State John Kerry announced, "The president is desirous of trying to see how we can make our efforts in order to find a way to facilitate," to wit, the president wanted to help. Once again the professional habit has not gone unnoticed by satirists, such as in the MacNelly cartoon on the next page, which appeared when Alexander Haig, the notoriously creative suffixer who served as secretary of state in the Reagan administration, resigned from his post:

When a grammatical construction is associated with politicians you can be sure that it provides a way to evade responsibility. Zombie nouns, unlike the verbs whose bodies they snatched, can shamble around without subjects. That is what they have in common with the passive constructions that also bog down these examples, like *was affirmed* and *were used*. And in a third evasive maneuver, many students and politicians stay away from the pronouns *I, me,* and *you.* The social psychologist Gordon Allport called out these tactics in an "Epistle to Thesis Writers":

> Your anxiety and feeling of insecurity will tempt you to an excessive use of the passive voice:
>
>> On the basis of the analysis which was made of the data which were collected, it is suggested that the null hypothesis can be rejected.
>
> Please, sir; I didn't do it! It was done! Try to conquer your cowardice, and start your concluding chapter with the creative assertion: Lo! I found . . .

You may attempt to defend your enervating use of the passive voice by pointing out that the only alternative is excessive reliance upon the first person personal pronoun or upon the pontifical We. It is safer, you conclude, to choose self-effacement at this critical moment in your career. I reply: even in critical moments I see no harm in saying I if I mean I.[22]

Often the pronouns *I, me,* and *you* are not just harmless but down-right helpful. They simulate a conversation, as classic style recommends, and they are gifts to the memory-challenged reader. It takes a good deal of mental effort to keep track of a cast of characters identified as *he*s, *she*s, and *they*s. But unless one is in the throes of a meditative trance or an ecstatic rapture, one never loses track of oneself or of the person one is addressing (*I, we, you*). That's why guidelines on how to avoid legalese and other turbid professional styles call for using first- and second-person pronouns, inverting passives into actives, and letting verbs be verbs rather than zombie nouns. Here are some examples of discouraged and recommended wordings from the Pennsylvania Plain Language Consumer Contract Act:

If the Buyer defaults and the Seller commences collection through an attorney, the Buyer will be liable for attorney's fees.	If the Buyer is behind in making payments, the Seller may: 1. Hire an attorney to collect the money. 2. Charge the Buyer for the attorney's fees.
If the outstanding balance is prepaid in full, the unearned finance charge will be refunded.	If I pay the whole amount before the due date, you will refund the unearned portion of the finance charge.
The Buyer is obligated to make all payments hereunder.	I will make all payments as they become due.
Membership fees paid prior to the opening of the club will be placed in trust.	If I pay membership fees before the club opens, the club will put the money in a trust account.[23]

A concrete and conversational style does more than make professional verbiage easier to read; it can be a matter of life and death. Take this warning sticker on a portable generator:

> Mild Exposure to CO can result in accumulated damage over time.
> Extreme Exposure to CO may rapidly be fatal without producing significant warning symptoms.
> Infants, children, older adults, and people with health conditions are more easily affected by Carbon Monoxide and their symptoms are more severe.

It's in the third person, and filled with zombie nouns like *Extreme Exposure* and passives like *are more easily affected.* People can read it and not get the feeling that anything terrible will happen. Perhaps as a result, every year more than a hundred Americans inadvertently turn their homes into gas chambers and execute themselves and their families by running generators and combustion heaters indoors. Much better is this sticker found on a recent model:

> Using a generator indoors CAN KILL YOU IN MINUTES.
> Generator exhaust contains carbon monoxide. This is a poison you cannot see or smell.
> NEVER use inside a home or garage, EVEN IF doors and windows are open.
> Only use OUTSIDE and far away from windows, doors, and vents.

In this sticker a concrete verb in the active voice and the use of the second person narrate a concrete event: if you do this, it can kill you. And what is intended as a warning is expressed in the imperative (*NEVER use inside*), just as one would do in a conversation, rather than as an impersonal generalization (*Mild Exposure can result in damage*).

The advice to bring zombie nouns back to life as verbs and to convert passives into actives is ubiquitous in style guides and plain language laws. For the reasons we've just seen, it's often good advice. But it's good advice only when a writer or an editor understands *why* it's being offered. No English construction could have survived in the language for a millennium and a half unless it had continued to serve some purpose, and that includes passives and nominalizations. They may be overused, and often they are badly used, but that does not mean they should not be used at all. Nominalizations, as we will see in chapter 5, can be useful in connecting a sentence to those that came before, keeping the passage coherent. The passive voice, too, has several uses in English. One of them (I'll take up the others in chapters 4 and 5) is indispensable to classic style: the passive allows the writer to direct the reader's gaze, like a cinematographer choosing the best camera angle.

Often a writer needs to steer the reader's attention away from the agent of an action. The passive allows him to do so because the agent can be left unmentioned, which is impossible in the active voice. You can say *Pooh ate the honey* (active voice, actor mentioned), *The honey was eaten by Pooh* (passive voice, actor mentioned), or *The honey was eaten* (passive voice, actor unmentioned)—but not *Ate the honey* (active voice, actor unmentioned). Sometimes the omission is ethically questionable, as when the sidestepping politician admits only that "mistakes were made," omitting the phrase with *by* that would identify who made those mistakes. But sometimes the ability to omit an agent comes in handy because the minor characters in the story are a distraction. As the linguist Geoffrey Pullum has noted, there is nothing wrong with a news report that uses the passive voice to say, "Helicopters were flown in to put out the fires."[24] The reader does not need to be informed that a guy named Bob was flying one of the helicopters.

Even when both the actor and the target of an action are visible in the scene, the choice of the active or passive voice allows the writer to keep the reader focused on one of those characters before pointing out an interesting fact involving that character. That's because the reader's attention usually starts out on the entity named by the subject of the sentence. Actives and passives differ in which character gets to be the subject, and hence which starts out in the reader's mental spotlight. An active construction trains the reader's gaze on someone who is doing something: *See that lady with the shopping bag? She's pelting a mime with zucchini.* The passive trains the reader's gaze on someone who's having something done to him: *See that mime? He's being pelted with zucchini by the lady with the shopping bag.* Using the wrong voice can make the reader crane back and forth like a spectator at a tennis match: *See that lady with the shopping bag? A mime is being pelted with zucchini by her.*

The problem with the passives that bog down bureaucratic and academic prose is that they are not selected with these purposes in mind. They are symptoms of absent-mindedness in a writer who has forgotten that he should be staging an event for the reader. *He* knows how the story turned out, so he just describes the outcome (something was done). But the reader, with no agent in sight, has no way to visualize the event being moved forward by its instigator. She is forced to imagine an effect without a cause, which is as hard to visualize as Lewis Carroll's grin without a cat.

In this chapter I have tried to call your attention to many of the writerly habits that result in soggy prose: metadiscourse, signposting, hedging, apologizing, professional narcissism, clichés, mixed metaphors, metaconcepts, zombie nouns, and unnecessary passives. Writers who want to invigorate their prose could try to memorize that list of don'ts. But it's better to keep in mind the guiding metaphor of classic style: a writer, in conversation with a reader, directs the reader's gaze to something in the world. Each of the don'ts corresponds to a way in which a writer can stray from this scenario.

Classic style is not the only way to write. But it's an ideal that can pull writers away from many of their worst habits, and it works particularly well because it makes the unnatural act of writing seem like two of our most natural acts: talking and seeing.

Chapter 3

THE CURSE OF KNOWLEDGE

THE MAIN CAUSE OF INCOMPREHENSIBLE PROSE IS THE DIFFICULTY OF IMAGINING WHAT IT'S LIKE FOR SOMEONE ELSE NOT TO KNOW SOMETHING THAT YOU KNOW

Why is so much writing so hard to understand? Why must a typical reader struggle to follow an academic article, the fine print on a tax return, or the instructions for setting up a wireless home network?

The most popular explanation I hear is the one captured in this cartoon:

Good start. Needs more gibberish.

According to this theory, opaque prose is a deliberate choice. Bureaucrats and business managers insist on gibberish to cover their anatomy. Plaid-clad tech writers get their revenge on the jocks who kicked sand in their faces and the girls who turned them down for dates. Pseudo-intellectuals spout obscure verbiage to hide the fact that they have nothing to say. Academics in the softer fields dress up the trivial and obvious with the trappings of scientific sophistication, hoping to bamboozle their audiences with highfalutin gobbledygook. Here is Calvin explaining the principle to Hobbes:

Calvin and Hobbes © 1993 Watterson. Reprinted with permission of Universal Uclick. All rights reserved.

I have long been skeptical of the bamboozlement theory, because in my experience it does not ring true. I know many scholars who have nothing to hide and no need to impress. They do groundbreaking work on important subjects, reason well about clear ideas, and are honest, down-to-earth people, the kind you'd enjoy having a beer with. Still, their writing stinks.

People often tell me that academics have no choice but to write badly because the gatekeepers of journals and university presses insist on ponderous language as proof of one's seriousness. This has not been my experience, and it turns out to be a myth. In *Stylish Academic Writing* (no, it is not one of the world's thinnest books), Helen Sword masochistically analyzed the literary style in a sample of five hundred articles in academic journals, and found that a healthy minority in every field were written with grace and verve.[1]

In explaining any human shortcoming, the first tool I reach for is

Hanlon's Razor: Never attribute to malice that which is adequately explained by stupidity.[2] The kind of stupidity I have in mind has nothing to do with ignorance or low IQ; in fact, it's often the brightest and best informed who suffer the most from it. I once attended a lecture on biology addressed to a large general audience at a conference on technology, entertainment, and design. The lecture was also being filmed for distribution over the Internet to millions of other laypeople. The speaker was an eminent biologist who had been invited to explain his recent breakthrough in the structure of DNA. He launched into a jargon-packed technical presentation that was geared to his fellow molecular biologists, and it was immediately apparent to everyone in the room that none of them understood a word. Apparent to everyone, that is, except the eminent biologist. When the host interrupted and asked him to explain the work more clearly, he seemed genuinely surprised and not a little annoyed. This is the kind of stupidity I am talking about.

Call it the Curse of Knowledge: a difficulty in imagining what it is like for someone else not to know something that you know. The term was invented by economists to help explain why people are not as shrewd in bargaining as they could be, in theory, when they possess information that their opposite number does not.[3] A used-car dealer, for example, should price a lemon at the same value as a creampuff of the same make and model, because customers have no way to tell the difference. (In this kind of analysis, economists imagine that everyone is an amoral profit-maximizer, so no one does anything just for honesty's sake.) But at least in experimental markets, sellers don't take full advantage of their private knowledge. They price their assets as if their customers knew as much about their quality as they do.

The curse of knowledge is far more than a curiosity in economic theory. The inability to set aside something that you know but that someone else does not know is such a pervasive affliction of the human mind that psychologists keep discovering related versions of it and giving it new names. There is egocentrism, the inability of children to imagine a simple scene, such as three toy mountains on a tabletop, from another person's vantage point.[4] There's hindsight bias, the tendency of people to think that an outcome they happen to know, such as the confirmation of a disease diagnosis or the outcome of a war, should have been obvious to someone who had to make a prediction about it before the fact.[5] There's false consensus, in which people who make a touchy personal decision (like agreeing to help an experimenter by wearing a sandwich board around campus with the word REPENT) assume that everyone else would make the same decision.[6] There's illusory transparency, in which observers who privately know the backstory to a conversation and thus can tell that a speaker is being sarcastic assume that the speaker's naïve listeners can somehow detect the sarcasm, too.[7] And there's mindblindness, a failure to mentalize, or a lack of a theory of mind, in which a three-year-old who sees a toy being hidden while a second child is out of the room assumes that the other child will look for it in its actual location rather than where she last saw it.[8] (In a related demonstration, a child comes into the lab, opens a candy box, and is surprised to find pencils in it. Not only does the child think that another child entering the lab will know it contains pencils, but the child will say that he himself knew it contained pencils all along!) Children mostly outgrow the inability to separate their own knowledge from someone else's, but not entirely. Even adults *slightly* tilt their guess about where a person will look for a hidden object in the direction of where they themselves know the object to be.[9]

Adults are particularly accursed when they try to estimate other people's knowledge and skills. If a student happens to know the meaning of an uncommon word like *apogee* or *elucidate,* or the answer to a factual question like where Napoleon was born or what the brightest star in the sky is, she assumes that other students know it, too.[10] When experimental volunteers are given a list of anagrams to unscramble, some of which are easier than others because the answers were shown to them beforehand, they rate the ones that are easier for *them* (because they'd seen the answers) to be magically easier for *everyone.*[11] And when experienced cell phone users were asked how long it would take novices to learn to use the phone, they guessed thirteen minutes; in fact, it took thirty-two.[12] Users with less expertise were *more* accurate in predicting the learning curves, though their guess, too, fell short: they predicted twenty minutes. The better you know something, the less you remember about how hard it was to learn.

The curse of knowledge is the single best explanation I know of why good people write bad prose.[13] It simply doesn't occur to the writer that her readers don't know what she knows—that they haven't mastered the patois of her guild, can't divine the missing steps that seem too obvious to mention, have no way to visualize a scene that to her is as clear as day.* And so she doesn't bother to explain the jargon, or spell out the logic, or supply the necessary detail. The ubiquitous experience shown in this *New Yorker* cartoon is a familiar example:

Anyone who wants to lift the curse of knowledge must first appreciate what a devilish curse it is. Like a drunk who is too impaired to realize that he is too impaired to drive, we do not notice the curse

---

* In this chapter, it's the female gender's turn to be the generic writer.

because the curse prevents us from noticing it. This blindness impairs us in every act of communication. Students in a team-taught course save their papers under the name of the professor who assigned it, so I get a dozen email attachments named "pinker.doc." The professors rename the papers, so Lisa Smith gets back a dozen attachments named "smith.doc." I go to a Web site for a trusted-traveler program and have to decide whether to click on GOES, Nexus, GlobalEntry, Sentri, Flux, or FAST—bureaucratic terms that mean nothing to me. A trail map informs me that a hike to a waterfall takes two hours, without specifying whether that means each way or for a round trip, and it fails to show several unmarked forks along the trail. My apartment is cluttered with gadgets that I can never remember how to use because of inscrutable buttons which may have to be held down for one, two, or four seconds, sometimes two at a time, and which often do different things depending on invisible "modes" toggled by still other buttons. When I'm lucky enough to find the manual, it enlightens me with explanations like "In the state of {alarm and chime setting}. Press the [SET] key and the {alarm 'hour' setting}→{alarm 'minute' setting}→{time 'hour' setting}→{time 'minute' setting}→{'year' setting}→{'month' setting}→ {'day' setting} will be completed in turn. And press the [MODE] key to adjust the set items." I'm sure it was perfectly clear to the engineers who designed it.

Multiply these daily frustrations by a few billion, and you begin to see that the curse of knowledge is a pervasive drag on the strivings of humanity, on a par with corruption, disease, and entropy. Cadres of expensive professionals—lawyers, accountants, computer gurus, help-line responders—drain vast sums of money from the economy to clarify poorly drafted text. There's an old saying that for the want of a nail the battle was lost, and the same is true for the want of an adjective: the Charge of the Light Brigade during the Crimean War is only the most famous example of a military disaster caused by vague orders. The nuclear meltdown at Three Mile Island in 1979 has been attributed to poor wording (operators misinterpreted the label on a warning light), as has the deadliest plane crash in history, in which the pilot of a 747 at

Tenerife Airport radioed he was *at takeoff*, by which he meant "taking off," but an air traffic controller interpreted it as "at the takeoff position" and failed to stop him before he plowed his plane into another 747 on the runway.[14] The visually confusing "butterfly ballot" given to Palm Beach voters in the 2000 American presidential election led many supporters of Al Gore to vote for the wrong candidate, which may have swung the election to George W. Bush, changing the course of history.

How can we lift the curse of knowledge? The traditional advice— always remember the reader over your shoulder—is not as effective as you might think.[15] The problem is that just trying harder to put yourself in someone else's shoes doesn't make you a whole lot more accurate in figuring out what that person knows.[16] When you've learned something so well that you forget that other people may not know it, you also forget to *check* whether they know it. Several studies have shown that people are not easily disabused of their curse of knowledge, even when they are told to keep the reader in mind, to remember what it was like to learn something, or to ignore what they know.[17]

But imagining the reader over your shoulder is a start. Occasionally people do learn to discount their knowledge when they are shown how it biases their judgments, and if you've read to this point, perhaps you will be receptive to the warning.[18] So for what it's worth: Hey, I'm talking to *you*. Your readers know a lot less about your subject than you think they do, and unless you keep track of what you know that they don't, you are guaranteed to confuse them.

A better way to exorcise the curse of knowledge is to be aware of specific pitfalls that it sets in your path. There's one that everyone is at least vaguely aware of: the use of jargon, abbreviations, and technical vocabulary. Every human pastime—music, cooking, sports, art, theoretical physics—develops an argot to spare its enthusiasts from having to say or type a long-winded description every time they refer to a familiar concept in each other's company. The problem is that as we become proficient at our job or hobby we come to use these catchwords so often that they flow out of our fingers automatically, and we forget that our readers may not be members of the clubhouse in which we learned them.

Obviously writers cannot avoid abbreviations and technical terms altogether. Shorthand terms are unobjectionable, indeed indispensable, when a term has become entrenched in the community one is writing for. Biologists needn't define *transcription factor* or spell out *mRNA* every time they refer to those things, and many technical terms become so common and are so useful that they eventually cross over into everyday parlance, like *cloning, gene,* and *DNA*. But the curse of knowledge ensures that most writers will overestimate how standard a term has become and how wide the community is that has learned it.

A surprising amount of jargon can simply be banished and no one will be the worse for it. A scientist who replaces *murine model* with *rats and mice* will use up no more space on the page and be no less scientific. Philosophers are every bit as rigorous when they put away Latin expressions like *ceteris paribus, inter alia*, and *simpliciter* and write in English instead: *other things being equal, among other things,* and *in and of itself.* And though nonlawyers might assume that the language of contracts, such as *the party of the first part,* must serve some legal purpose, most of it is superfluous. As Adam Freedman points out in his book on legalese, "What distinguishes legal boilerplate is its combination of archaic terminology and frenzied verbosity, as though it were written by a medieval scribe on crack."[19]

Abbreviations are tempting to thoughtless writers because they can save a few keystrokes every time they have to use the term. The writers forget that the few seconds they add to their own lives come at the cost of many minutes stolen from the lives of their readers. I stare at a table of numbers whose columns are labeled DA DN SA SN, and have to flip back and scan for the explanation: Dissimilar Affirmative, Dissimilar Negative, Similar Affirmative, Similar Negative. Each abbreviation is surrounded by many inches of white space. What possible reason could there have been for the author not to spell them out? Abbreviations that are coined for a single piece of writing are best avoided altogether, to spare the reader from having to engage in the famously tedious memory task called paired-associate learning, in which psychologists force their participants to memorize arbitrary pairs of text like DAX-QOV. Even moderately common abbreviations should be spelled out on first use. As Strunk and White point out, "Not everyone knows that SALT means Strategic Arms Limitation Talks, and even if everyone did, there are babies being born every minute who will someday encounter the name for the first time. They deserve to see the words, not simply the initials."[20] The hazard is not limited to professional prose. Some of us receive annual Christmas letters in which the household spokesperson cheerily writes, "Irwin and I had a great time at the IHRP after dispatching the children to the UNER, and we all continue work on our ECPs at the SFBS."

A considerate writer will also cultivate the habit of adding a few words of explanation to common technical terms, as in "*Arabidopsis,* a flowering mustard plant," rather than the bare "*Arabidopsis*" (which I've seen in many science articles). It's not just an act of magnanimity: a writer who explains technical terms can multiply her readership a thousandfold at the cost of a handful of characters, the literary equivalent of picking up hundred-dollar bills on the sidewalk. Readers will also thank a writer for the copious use of *for example, as in,* and *such as,* because an explanation without an example is little better than no explanation at all. For example: Here's an explanation of the rhetorical term *syllepsis:* "the use of a word that relates to, qualifies, or governs two or more other words but has a different meaning in relation to each." Got that? Now let's say I continue with ". . . such as when Benjamin Franklin said, 'We must all hang together, or assuredly we shall all hang separately.'" Clearer, no? No? Sometimes two examples are better than one, because they allow the reader to triangulate on which aspect of the example is relevant to the definition. What if I add ". . . or when Groucho Marx said, 'You can leave in a taxi, and if you can't get a taxi, you can leave in a huff'"?[21]

And when technical terms are unavoidable, why not choose ones that are easy for readers to understand and remember? Ironically, the field of linguistics is among the worst offenders, with dozens of mystifying technical terms: *themes* that have nothing to do with themes; *PRO* and *pro,* which are pronounced the same way but refer to different things; *stage-level* and *individual-level predicates,* which are just unintuitive ways of saying "temporary" and "permanent"; and *Principles A, B,* and *C,* which could just as easily have been called the Reflexive Principle, the Pronoun Principle, and the Noun Principle. For a long time I got a headache reading papers in semantics that analyzed the two meanings of *some.* In a loose, conversational sense, *some* implies "some, but not all": when I say *Some men are chauvinists,* it's natural to interpret me as implying that others are not. But in a strict, logical sense, *some* means "at least one" and does not rule out "all"; there's no contradiction in saying *Some men are chauvinists; indeed, all of them are.* Many linguists refer to the two meanings as the "upper-bounded" and "lower-bounded" senses, labels borrowed from mathematics, and I could never keep them straight. At last I came across a limpid semanticist who referred to them as the "only" and "at-least" senses, labels from everyday English, and I've followed the literature ever since.

This vignette shows that even belonging to the same professional club as a writer is no protection against her curse of knowledge. I suffer the daily experience of being baffled by articles in my field, my subfield, even my sub-sub-subfield. Take this sentence from an article I just read by two eminent cognitive neuroscientists, which appeared in a journal that publishes brief review articles for a wide readership:

> The slow and integrative nature of conscious perception is con-
> firmed behaviorally by observations such as the "rabbit illusion"
> and its variants, where the way in which a stimulus is ultimately
> perceived is influenced by poststimulus events arising several
> hundreds of milliseconds after the original stimulus.

After I macheted my way through the overgrowth of passives, zombies, and redundancies, I determined that the content of the sentence resided in the term "rabbit illusion," the phenomenon which is supposed to demonstrate "the integrative nature of conscious perception." The authors write as if everyone knows what the "rabbit illusion" is, but I've been in this business for nearly forty years and had never heard of it. Nor does their explanation enlighten. How are we supposed to visualize "a stimulus," "poststimulus events," and "the way in which a stimulus is ultimately perceived"? And what does any of this have to do with rabbits? Richard Feynman once wrote, "If you ever hear yourself saying, 'I think I understand this,' that means you don't." Though the article had been written for the likes of me, the best I could say after reading this explanation was, "I think I understand this."

So I did a bit of digging and uncovered a Cutaneous Rabbit Illusion, in which if you close your eyes and someone taps you a few times on the wrist, then on the elbow, and then on the shoulder, it feels like a string of taps running up the length of your arm, like a hopping rabbit. OK, now I get it—a person's conscious experience of where the early taps fell depends on the location of the later taps. But why didn't the authors just say that, which would have taken no more words than "*stimulus* this" and "*poststimulus* that"?

The curse of knowledge is insidious, because it conceals not only the contents of our thoughts from us but their very form. When we know something well, we don't realize how abstractly we think about it. And we forget that other people, who have lived their own lives, have not gone through our idiosyncratic histories of abstractification.

There are two ways in which thoughts can lose their moorings in the land of the concrete. One is called chunking. Human working memory can hold only a few items at a time. Psychologists used to think that its capacity was around seven items (plus or minus two), but later downsized even that estimate, and today believe it is closer to three or four. Fortunately, the rest of the brain is equipped with a workaround for the bottleneck. It can package ideas into bigger and bigger units, which the psychologist George Miller dubbed "chunks."[22] (Miller was one of the greatest stylists in the history of the behavioral sciences, and it's no coincidence that he co-opted this homey term rather than inventing some technical jargon.)[23] Each chunk, no matter how much information is packed inside it, occupies a single slot in working memory. Thus we can hold in mind just a few of the letters from an arbitrary sequence like M D P H D R S V P C E O I H O P. But if they belong to well-learned chunks such as abbreviations or words, like the ones that pop out when we group the letters as MD PHD RSVP CEO IHOP, five chunks, we can remember all sixteen. Our capacity can be multiplied yet again when we package the chunks into still bigger chunks, such as the story "The MD and the PhD RSVP'd to the CEO of IHOP," which can occupy just one slot, with three or four left over for other stories. Of course this magic depends on one's personal history of learning. To someone who has never heard of the International House of Pancakes, *IHOP* takes up four slots in memory, not one. Mnemonists, the performers who amaze us by regurgitating superhuman amounts of information, have spent a lot of time building up a huge inventory of chunks in their long-term memories.

Chunking is not just a trick for improving memory; it's the lifeblood of higher intelligence. As children we see one person hand a cookie to another, and we remember it as an act of *giving.* One person gives another one a cookie in exchange for a banana; we chunk the two acts of giving together and think of the sequence as *trading.* Person 1 trades a banana to Person 2 for a piece of shiny metal, because he knows he can trade it to Person 3 for a cookie; we think of it as *selling.* Lots of people buying and selling make up a *market.* Activity aggregated over many markets gets chunked into *the economy.* The economy now can be thought of as an entity which responds to actions by central banks; we call that *monetary policy.* One kind of monetary policy, which involves the central bank buying private assets, is chunked as *quantitative easing.* And so on.

As we read and learn, we master a vast number of these abstractions, and each becomes a mental unit which we can bring to mind in an instant and share with others by uttering its name. An adult mind that is brimming with chunks is a powerful engine of reason, but it comes with a cost: a failure to communicate with other minds that have not mastered the same chunks. Many educated adults would be left out of a discussion that criticized the president for not engaging in more "quantitative easing," though they would understand the process if it were spelled out. A high school student might be left out if you spoke about "monetary policy," and a schoolchild might not even follow a conversation about "the economy."

The amount of abstraction that a writer can get away with depends on the expertise of her readership. But divining the chunks that have been mastered by a typical reader requires a gift of clairvoyance with which few of us are blessed. When we are apprentices in our chosen specialty, we join a clique in which, it seems to us, everyone else seems to know so much! And they talk among themselves as if their knowledge were second nature to every educated person. As we settle in to the clique, it becomes our universe. We fail to appreciate that it is a tiny bubble in a vast multiverse of other cliques. When we make first contact with the aliens in other universes and jabber at them in our local code, they cannot understand us without a sci-fi Universal Translator.

Even when we have an inkling that we are speaking in a specialized lingo, we may be reluctant to slip back into plain speech. It could betray to our peers the awful truth that we are still greenhorns, tenderfoots, newbies. And if our readers do know the lingo, we might be insulting their intelligence by spelling it out. We would rather run the risk of confusing them while at least appearing to be sophisticated than take a chance at belaboring the obvious while striking them as naïve or condescending.

It's true that every writer must calibrate the degree of specialization in her language against her best guess of the audience's familiarity with the topic. But in general it's wiser to assume too little than too much. Every audience is spread out along a bell curve of sophistication, and inevitably we'll bore a few at the top while baffling a few at the bottom; the only question is how many there will be of each. The curse of knowledge means that we're more likely to overestimate the average reader's familiarity with our little world than to underestimate it. And in any case one should not confuse clarity with condescension. Brian Greene's explanation of the multiverse in chapter 2 shows how a classic stylist can explain an esoteric idea in plain language without patronizing his audience. The key is to assume that your readers are as intelligent and sophisticated as you are, but that they happen not to know something you know.

Perhaps the best way to remember the dangers of private abbreviation is to recall the joke about a man who walks into a Catskills resort for the first time and sees a group of retired borscht-belt comics telling jokes around a table with their pals. One of them calls out, "Forty-seven!" and the others roar with laughter. Another follows with "A hundred and twelve!" and again the others double over. The newcomer can't figure out what's going on, so he asks one of the old-timers to explain. The man says, "These guys have been hanging around together so long they know all the same jokes. So to save time they've given them numbers, and all they need to do is call out the number." The new fellow says, "That's ingenious! Let me try it." So he stands up and calls out, "Twenty-one!" There is a stony silence. He tries again: "Seventy-two!" Everyone stares at him, and nobody laughs. He sinks back into his seat and whispers to his informant, "What did I do wrong? Why didn't anyone laugh?" The man says, "It's all in how you tell it."

A failure to realize that my chunks may not be the same as your chunks can explain why we baffle our readers with so much shorthand, jargon, and alphabet soup. But it's not the only way we baffle them. Sometimes wording is maddeningly opaque without being composed of technical terminology from a private clique. Even among cognitive scientists, "poststimulus event" is not a standard way to refer to a tap on the arm. A financial customer might be reasonably familiar with the world of investments and still have to puzzle over what a company brochure means by "capital changes and rights." A computer-savvy user trying to maintain his Web site might be mystified by instructions on the maintenance page which refer to "nodes," "content type," and "attachments." And heaven help the sleepy traveler trying to set the alarm clock in his hotel room who must interpret "alarm function" and "second display mode."

Why do writers invent such confusing terminology? I believe the answer lies in another way in which expertise can make our thoughts more idiosyncratic and thus harder to share: as we become familiar with something, we think about it more in terms of the use we put it to and less in terms of what it looks like and what it is made of. This transition, another staple of the cognitive psychology curriculum, is called functional fixity (sometimes functional fixedness).[24] In the textbook experiment, people are given a candle, a book of matches, and a box of thumbtacks, and are asked to attach the candle to the wall so that the wax won't drip onto the floor. The solution is to dump the thumbtacks out of the box, tack the box to the wall, and stick the candle onto the box. Most people never figure this out because they think of the box as a container for the tacks rather than a physical object in its own right, with handy features like a flat surface and perpendicular sides. The blind spot is called functional fixity because people get fixated on an object's function and forget its physical makeup. The toddler who ignores the birthday present and plays with the wrapping paper reminds us of how we lose our appreciation of objects as objects and think of them as means to an end.

Now, if you combine functional fixity with chunking, and stir in the curse that hides each one from our awareness, you get an explanation of why specialists use so much idiosyncratic terminology, together with abstractions, metaconcepts, and zombie nouns. They are not trying to bamboozle us; that's just the way they think. The mental movie of a mouse cowering in the corner of a cage that has another mouse in it gets chunked into "social avoidance." You can't blame the neuroscientist for thinking this way. She's seen the movie thousands of times; she doesn't need to hit the PLAY button in her visual memory and watch the critters quivering every time she talks about whether her experiment worked. But we do need to watch them, at least the first time, to appreciate what actually happened.

In a similar way, writers stop thinking—and thus stop writing—about tangible objects and instead refer to them by the role those objects play in their daily travails. Recall the example from chapter 2 in which a psychologist showed people sentences, followed by the label TRUE or FALSE. He explained what he did as "the subsequent presentation of an assessment word," referring to the label as an "assessment word" because that's why he put it there—so that the participants in the experiment could assess whether it applied to the preceding sentence. Unfortunately, he left it up to us to figure out what an "assessment word" is—while saving no characters, and being less rather than more scientifically precise. In the same way, a tap on the wrist became a "stimulus" and a tap on the elbow became a "poststimulus event," because the writers cared about the fact that one event came after the other and no longer cared about the fact that the events were taps on the arm.

But we readers care. We are primates, with a third of our brains dedicated to vision, and large swaths devoted to touch, hearing, motion, and space. For us to go from "I think I understand" to "I understand," we need to see the sights and feel the motions. Many experiments have shown that readers understand and remember material far better when it is expressed in concrete language that allows them to form visual images, like the sentences on the right:[25]

The set fell off the table.	The ivory chess set fell off the table.
The measuring gauge was covered with dust.	The oil-pressure gauge was covered with dust.
Georgia O'Keeffe called some of her works "equivalents" because their forms were abstracted in a way that gave the emotional parallel of the source experience.	Georgia O'Keeffe's landscapes were of angular skyscrapers and neon thoroughfares, but mostly of the bleached bones, desert shadows, and weathered crosses of rural New Mexico.

Notice how the abstract descriptions on the left leave out just the kind of physical detail that an expert has grown bored with but that a neophyte has to see: ivory chessmen, not just a "set"; an oil-pressure gauge, not just a generic "measuring gauge"; bleached bones, not just "forms." A commitment to the concrete does more than just ease communication; it can lead to better reasoning. A reader who knows what the Cutaneous Rabbit Illusion consists of is in a position to evaluate whether it really does imply that conscious experience is spread over time, or whether it can be explained in some other way.

The profusion of metaconcepts in professional writing—all those levels, issues, contexts, frameworks, and perspectives—also makes sense when you consider the personal history of chunking and functional fixity in the writers. Academics, consultants, policy wonks, and other symbolic analysts really do think about "issues" (they can list them on a page), "levels of analysis" (they can argue about which is most appropriate), and "contexts" (they can use them to figure out why something works in one place but not in another). These abstractions become containers in which they store and handle their ideas, and before they know it they can no longer call anything by its name. Compare the professionalese on the left with the concrete equivalents on the right:

Participants were tested under conditions of good to excellent acoustic isolation.	We tested the students in a quiet room.
Management actions at and in the immediate vicinity of airports do little to mitigate the risk of off-airport strikes during departure and approach.	Trapping birds near an airport does little to reduce the number of times a bird will collide with a plane as it takes off or lands.
We believe that the ICTS approach to delivering integrated solutions, combining effective manpower, canine services and cutting-edge technology was a key differentiator in the selection process.	They chose our company because we protect buildings with a combination of guards, dogs, and sensors.

What we see as "a quiet room" an experimenter sees as "testing conditions," because that's what she was thinking about when she chose the room. For a safety expert at the top of the chain of command, who lives every day with the responsibility for managing risks, the bird traps set out by her underlings are a distant memory. The public-relations hack for a security firm refers to the company's activities in a press statement in terms of the way she thinks about them when selling them to potential clients.

Slicing away the layers of familiar abstraction and showing the reader who did what to whom is a never-ending challenge for a writer. Take the expository chore of describing a correlation between two variables (like smoking and cancer, or video-game playing and violence), which is a staple of public-health and social-science reporting. A writer who has spent a lot of time thinking about correlations will have mentally bubble-wrapped each of the two variables, and will have done the same to the possible ways in which they can be correlated. Those verbal packages are all within arm's reach, and she will naturally turn to them when she has to share some news:

> There is a significant positive correlation between measures of food intake and body mass index.
> Body mass index is an increasing function of food intake.
> Food intake predicts body mass index according to a monotonically increasing relation.

A reader can figure this out, but it's hard work, like hacking through a blister pack to get at the product. If the writer de-thingifies the variables by extracting them from their noun casings, she can refer to them with the language we use for actions, comparisons, and outcomes, and everything becomes clearer:

> The more you eat, the fatter you get.

The curse of knowledge, in combination with chunking and functional fixity, helps make sense of the paradox that classic style is difficult to master. What could be so hard about pretending to open your eyes and hold up your end of a conversation? The reason it's harder than it sounds is that if you are enough of an expert in a topic to have something to say about it, you have probably come to think about it in abstract chunks and functional labels that are now second nature to you but still unfamiliar to your readers—and you are the last one to realize it.

As writers, then, we should try to get into our readers' heads and be mindful of how easy it is to fall back on parochial jargon and private abstractions. But these efforts can take us only so far. None of us has, and few of us would want, a power of clairvoyance that would expose to us everyone else's private thoughts.

To escape the curse of knowledge, we have to go beyond our own powers of divination. We have to close the loop, as the engineers say, and get a feedback signal from the world of readers—that is, show a draft to some people who are similar to our intended audience and find out whether they can follow it.[26] This sounds banal but is in fact profound. Social psychologists have found that we are overconfident, sometimes to the point of delusion, about our ability to infer what other people think, even the people who are closest to us.[27] Only when we ask those people do we discover that what's obvious to us isn't obvious to them. That's why professional writers have editors. It's also why politicians consult polls, why corporations hold focus groups, and why Internet companies use A/B testing, in which they try out two designs on a Web site (versions A and B) and collect data in real time on which gets more clicks.

Most writers cannot afford focus groups or A/B testing, but they can ask a roommate or colleague or family member to read what they wrote and comment on it. Your reviewers needn't even be a representative sample of your intended audience. Often it's enough that they are not you.

This does not mean you should implement every last suggestion they offer. Each commentator has a curse of knowledge of his own, together with hobbyhorses, blind spots, and axes to grind, and the writer cannot pander to all of them. Many academic articles contain bewildering non sequiturs and digressions that the authors stuck in at the insistence of an anonymous reviewer who had the power to reject it from the journal if they didn't comply. Good prose is never written by a committee. A writer should revise in response to a comment when it comes from more than one reader or when it makes sense to the writer herself.

And that leads to another way to escape the curse of knowledge: show a draft to *yourself,* ideally after enough time has passed that the text is no longer familiar. If you are like me you will find yourself thinking, "What did I mean by that?" or "How does this follow?" or, all too often, "Who wrote this crap?"

I am told there are writers who can tap out a coherent essay in a single pass, at most checking for typos and touching up the punctuation before sending it off for publication. You are probably not one of them. Most writers polish draft after draft. I rework every sentence a few times before going on to the next, and revise the whole chapter two or three times before I show it to anyone. Then, with feedback in hand, I revise each chapter twice more before circling back and giving the entire book at least two complete passes of polishing. Only then does it go to the copy editor, who starts another couple of rounds of tweaking.

Too many things have to go right in a passage of writing for most mortals to get them all the first time. It's hard enough to formulate a thought that is interesting and true. Only after laying a semblance of it on the page can a writer free up the cognitive resources needed to make the sentence grammatical, graceful, and, most important, transparent to the reader. The form in which thoughts occur to a writer is rarely the same as the form in which they can be absorbed by a reader. The advice in this and other stylebooks is not so much on how to write as on how to revise.

Much advice on writing has the tone of moral counsel, as if being a good writer will make you a better person. Unfortunately for cosmic justice, many gifted writers are scoundrels, and many inept ones are the salt of the earth. But the imperative to overcome the curse of knowledge may be the bit of writerly advice that comes closest to being sound moral advice: always try to lift yourself out of your parochial mindset and find out how other people think and feel. It may not make you a better person in all spheres of life, but it will be a source of continuing kindness to your readers.

Chapter 4

THE WEB, THE TREE, AND THE STRING

UNDERSTANDING SYNTAX CAN HELP A WRITER AVOID UNGRAMMATICAL, CONVOLUTED, AND MISLEADING PROSE

Kids aren't taught to diagram sentences anymore." Together with "The Internet is ruining the language" and "People write gibberish on purpose," this is the explanation I hear most often for the prevalence of bad writing today.

The plaint about the lost art of diagramming sentences refers to a notation that was invented by Alonzo Reed and Brainerd Kellogg in 1877 and taught in American schools until the 1960s, when it fell victim to the revolt among educators against all things formal.[1] In this system, the words of a sentence are placed along a kind of subway map in which intersections of various shapes (perpendicular, slanted, branching) stand for grammatical relations such as subject-predicate and modifier-head. Here, for instance, is how you would diagram the sentence *In Sophocles' play, Oedipus married his mother*:

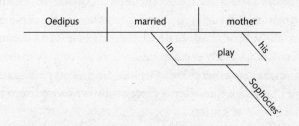

The Reed-Kellogg notation was innovative in its day, but I for one don't miss it. It's just one way to display syntax on a page, and not a particularly good one, with user-unfriendly features such as scrambled word order and arbitrary graphical conventions. But I agree with the main idea behind the nostalgia: literate people should know how to think about grammar.

People already know how to *use* grammar, of course; they've been doing it since they were two. But the unconscious mastery of language that is our birthright as humans is not enough to allow us to write good sentences. Our tacit sense of which words go together can break down when a sentence gets complicated, and our fingers can produce an error we would never accept if we had enough time and memory to take in the sentence at a glance. Learning how to bring the units of language into consciousness can allow a writer to reason his way to a grammatically consistent sentence when his intuitions fail him, and to diagnose the problem when he knows something is wrong with the sentence but can't put his finger on what it is.

Knowing a bit of grammar also gives a writer an entrée into the world of letters. Just as cooks, musicians, and ballplayers have to master some lingo to be able to share their tips and learn from others, so writers can benefit by knowing the names of the materials they work with and how they do their jobs. Literary analysis, poetics, rhetoric, criticism, logic, linguistics, cognitive science, and practical advice on style (including the other chapters in this book) need to refer to things like predicates and subordinate clauses, and knowing what these terms mean will allow a writer to take advantage of the hard-won knowledge of others.

Best of all, grammar is a fascinating subject in its own right, at least when it is properly explained. To many people the very word conjures up memories of choking on chalk dust and cowering in fear of a thwack on the knuckles from a spinster schoolteacher. (Theodore Bernstein, the author of several style manuals, refers to the archetype as Miss Thistlebottom; the writer Kitty Burns Florey, who wrote a history of diagramming sentences, calls her Sister Bernadette.) But grammar should not be thought of as an ordeal of jargon and drudgery, as Skyler does in this *Shoe* cartoon:

SHOE by Jeff MacNelly

It should be thought of instead as one of the extraordinary adaptations in the living world: our species' solution to the problem of getting complicated thoughts from one head into another. Thinking of grammar as the original sharing app makes it much more interesting and much more useful. By understanding how the various features of grammar are designed to make sharing possible, we can put them to use in writing more clearly, correctly, and gracefully.

The three nouns in the chapter title refer to the three things that grammar brings together: the web of ideas in our head, the string of words that comes out of our mouth or fingers, and the tree of syntax that converts the first into the second.

Let's begin with the web. As you wordlessly daydream, your thoughts drift from idea to idea: visual images, odd observations, snatches of melody, fun facts, old grudges, pleasant fantasies, memorable moments. Long before the invention of the World Wide Web, cognitive scientists modeled human memory as a network of nodes. Each node represents a concept, and each is linked to other nodes for words, images, and other concepts.[2] Here is a fragment of this vast, mind-wide web, spotlighting your knowledge of the tragic story brought to life by Sophocles:

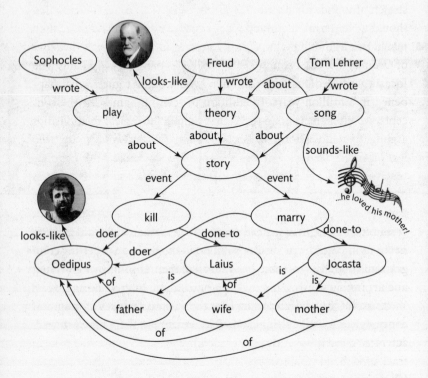

Though I had to place each node somewhere on the page, their positions don't matter, and they don't have any ordering. All that matters is how they're connected. A train of thought might start with any of these concepts, triggered by the mention of a word, by a pulse of activation on an incoming link originating from some other concept far away in the network, or by whatever random neural firings cause an idea to pop into mind unbidden. From there your mind can surf in any direction along any link to any of the other concepts.

Now, what happens if you wanted to share some of those thoughts? One can imagine a race of advanced space aliens who could compress a portion of this network into a zipped file of bits and hum it to each other like two dial-up modems. But that's not the way it's done in *Homo sapiens*. We have learned to associate each thought with a little stretch of sound called a word, and can cause each other to think that thought by uttering the sound. But of course we need to do more than just blurt out individual words. If you were unfamiliar with the story of *Oedipus Rex* and I simply said, "Sophocles play story kill Laius wife Jocasta wed Oedipus father mother," you wouldn't guess what happened in a million years. In addition to reciting names for the concepts, we utter them in an order that signals the logical relationships among them (doer, done-to, is a, and so on): *Oedipus killed Laius, who was his father. Oedipus married Jocasta, who was his mother.* The code that translates a web of conceptual relations in our heads into an early-to-late order in our mouths, or into a left-to-right order on the page, is called syntax.[3] The rules of syntax, together with the rules of word formation (the ones that turn *kill* into *kills, killed,* and *killing*), make up the grammar of English. Different languages have different grammars, but they all convey conceptual relationships by modifying and arranging words.[4]

It's not easy to design a code that can extrude a tangled spaghetti of concepts into a linear string of words. If an event involves several characters involved in several relationships, there needs to be a way to keep track of who did what to whom. *Killed Oedipus married Laius Jocasta,* for example, doesn't make it clear whether Oedipus killed Laius and married Jocasta, Jocasta killed Oedipus and married Laius, Oedipus killed Jocasta and married Laius, and so on. Syntax solves this problem by having adjacent strings of words stand for related sets of concepts, and by inserting one string inside another to stand for concepts that are parts of bigger concepts.

To understand how syntax works, it helps to visualize the ordering of strings-within-strings by drawing them at the ends of the branches of an upside-down tree.

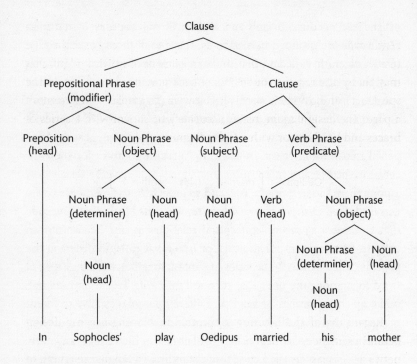

I'll explain the details soon, but for now it's enough to notice that the words at the bottom (like *mother*) are grouped into phrases (like *his mother*), which are grouped into larger phrases (like *married his mother*), which are grouped into a clause (a simple sentence like *Oedipus married his mother*), which in turn may be inserted into a bigger clause (the whole sentence).

Syntax, then, is an app that uses a *tree* of phrases to translate a *web* of thoughts into a *string* of words. Upon hearing or reading the string of words, the perceiver can work backwards, fitting them into a tree and recovering the links between the associated concepts. In this case a hearer can deduce that Sophocles wrote a play in which Oedipus married his mother, rather than that Oedipus wrote a play in which Sophocles married his mother, or just that the speaker is saying something about a bunch of Greeks.

The tree, of course, is only a metaphor. What it captures is that adjacent words are grouped into phrases, that the phrases are embedded inside larger phrases, and that the arrangement of words and phrases may be used to recover the relationships among the characters in the speaker's mind. A tree is simply an easy way to display that design on a page. The design could just as accurately be shown with a series of braces and brackets, or with a Venn diagram:

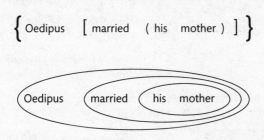

Regardless of the notation, appreciating the engineering design behind a sentence—a linear ordering of phrases which conveys a gnarly network of ideas—is the key to understanding what you are trying to accomplish when you compose a sentence. And that, in turn, can help you understand the menu of choices you face and the things that are most likely to go wrong.

The reason that the task is so challenging is that the main resource that English syntax makes available to writers—left-to-right ordering on a page—has to do two things at once. It's the code that the language uses to convey who did what to whom. But it also determines the sequence of early-to-late processing in the reader's mind. The human mind can do only a few things at a time, and the order in which information comes in affects how that information is handled. As we'll see, a writer must constantly reconcile the two sides of word order: a code for information, and a sequence of mental events.

Let's begin with a closer look at the code of syntax itself, using the tree for the Oedipus sentence as an example.[5] Working upward from the words at the bottom, we see that every word is labeled with a grammatical category. These are the "parts of speech" that should be familiar even to people who were educated after the 1960s:

Nouns (including pronouns)	*man, play, Sophocles, she, my*
Verbs	*marry, write, think, see, imply*
Prepositions	*in, around, underneath, before, until*
Adjectives	*big, red, wonderful, interesting, demented*
Adverbs	*merrily, frankly, impressively, very, almost*
Articles and other determinatives	*the, a, some, this, that, many, one, two, three*
Coordinators	*and, or, nor, but, yet, so*
Subordinators	*that, whether, if, to*

Each word is slotted into a place in the tree according to its category, because the rules of syntax don't specify the order of words but rather the order of categories. Once you have learned that in English the article comes before the noun, you don't have to relearn that order every time you acquire a new noun, such as *hashtag, app,* or *MOOC.* If you've seen one noun, you've pretty much seen them all. There are, to be sure, subcategories of the noun category like proper nouns, common nouns, mass nouns, and pronouns, which indulge in some additional pickiness about where they appear, but the principle is the same: words within a subcategory are interchangeable, so that if you know where the subcategory may appear, you know where every word in that subcategory may appear.

Let's zoom in on one of the words, *married.* Together with its grammatical category, verb, we see a label in parentheses for its grammatical *function,* in this case, head. A grammatical function identifies not what a word *is* in the language but what it *does* in that particular sentence:

how it combines with the other words to determine the sentence's meaning.

The "head" of a phrase is the little nugget which stands for the whole phrase. It determines the core of the phrase's meaning: in this case *married his mother* is a particular instance of marrying. It also determines the grammatical category of the phrase: in this case it is a verb phrase, a phrase built around a verb. A verb phrase is a string of words of any length which fills a particular slot in a tree. No matter how much stuff is packed into the verb phrase—*married his mother; married his mother on Tuesday; married his mother on Tuesday over the objections of his girlfriend*—it can be inserted into the same position in the sentence as the phrase consisting solely of the verb *married*. This is true of the other kinds of phrases as well: the noun phrase *the king of Thebes* is built around the head noun *king,* it refers to an example of a king, and it can go wherever the simpler phrase *the king* can go.

The extra stuff that plumps out a phrase may include additional grammatical functions which distinguish the various roles in the story identified by the head. In the case of marrying, the dramatis personae include the person being married and the person doing the marrying. (Though marrying is really a symmetrical relationship—if Jack married Jill, then Jill married Jack—let's assume for the sake of the example that the male takes the initiative in marrying the female.) The person being married in this sentence is, tragically, the referent of *his mother,* and she is identified as the one being married because the phrase has the grammatical function "object," which in English is the noun phrase following the verb. The person doing the marrying, referred to by the one-word phrase *Oedipus,* has the function "subject." Subjects are special: all verbs have one, and it sits outside the verb phrase, occupying one of the two major branches of the clause, the other being the predicate. Still other grammatical functions can be put to work in identifying other roles. In *Jocasta handed the baby to the servant,* the phrase *the servant* is an oblique object, that is, the object of a preposition. In *Oedipus thought that Polybus was his father,* the clause *that Polybus was his father* is a complement of the verb *thought.*

Languages also have grammatical functions whose job is not to distinguish the cast of characters but to pipe up with other kinds of information. Modifiers can add comments on the time, place, manner, or quality of a thing or an action. In this sentence we have the phrase *In Sophocles' play* as a modifier of the clause *Oedipus married his mother*. Other examples of modifiers include the underlined words in the phrases *walks <u>on four legs</u>*, *<u>swollen</u> feet*, *met him <u>on the road to Thebes</u>*, and *the shepherd <u>whom Oedipus had sent for</u>*.

We also find that the nouns *play* and *mother* are preceded by the words *Sophocles'* and *his,* which have the function "determiner." A determiner answers the question "Which one?" or "How many?" Here the determiner role is filled by what is traditionally called a possessive noun (though it is really a noun marked for genitive case, as I will explain). Other common determiners include articles, as in *<u>the</u> cat* and *<u>this</u> boy*; quantifiers, as in *<u>some</u> nights* and *<u>all</u> people*; and numbers, as in *<u>sixteen</u> tons*.

If you are over sixty or went to private school, you may have noticed that this syntactic machinery differs in certain ways from what you remember from Miss Thistlebottom's classroom. Modern grammatical theories (like the one in *The Cambridge Grammar of the English Language,* which I use in this book) distinguish grammatical categories like noun and verb from grammatical functions like subject, object, head, and modifier. And they distinguish both of these from *semantic* categories and roles like action, physical object, possessor, doer, and done-to, which refer to what the referents of the words are doing in the world. Traditional grammars tend to run the three concepts together.

As a child I was taught, for example, that the words *soap* in *soap flakes* and *that* in *that boy* were adjectives, because they modify nouns. But this confuses the grammatical category "adjective" with the grammatical function "modifier." There's no need to wave a magic wand over the noun *soap* and transmute it into an adjective just because of what it's doing in this phrase. It's simpler to say that sometimes a noun can modify another noun. In the case of *that* in *that boy,* Miss Thistlebottom got the function wrong, too: it's determiner, not modifier. How do we know? Because determiners and modifiers are not interchangeable. You can say *Look at the boy* or *Look at that boy* (determiners), but not *Look at tall boy* (a modifier). You can say *Look at the tall boy* (determiner + modifier), but not *Look at the that boy* (determiner + determiner).

I was also taught that a "noun" is a word for a person, place, or thing, which confuses a grammatical category with a semantic category. The comedian Jon Stewart was confused, too, because on his show he criticized George W. Bush's "War on Terror" by protesting, "*Terror* isn't even a noun!"[6] What he meant was that *terror* is not a concrete entity, in particular a group of people organized into an enemy force. *Terror,* of course, *is* a noun, together with thousands of other words that don't refer to people, places, or things, including the nouns *word, category, show, war,* and *noun,* to take just some examples from the past few sentences. Though nouns are *often* the names for people, places, and things, the noun category can only be defined by the role it plays in a family of rules. Just as a "rook" in chess is defined not as the piece that looks like a little tower but as the piece that is allowed to move in certain ways in the game of chess, a grammatical category such as "noun" is defined by the moves it is allowed to make in the game of grammar. These moves include the ability to appear after a determiner (*the king*), the requirement to have an oblique rather than a direct object (*the king of Thebes,* not *the king Thebes*), and the ability to be marked for plural number (*kings*) and genitive case (*king's*). By these tests, *terror* is certainly a noun: *the terror, terror of being trapped, the terror's lasting impact.*

Now we can see why the word *Sophocles'* shows up in the tree with the category "noun" and the function "determiner" rather than "adjective." The word belongs to the noun category, just as it always has; *Sophocles* did not suddenly turn into an adjective just because it is parked in front of another noun. And its function is determiner because it acts in the same way as the words *the* and *that* and differently from a clear-cut modifier like *famous*: you can say *In Sophocles' play* or *In the play,* but not *In famous play.*

At this point you may be wondering: What's with "genitive"? Isn't that just what we were taught is the possessive? Well, "possessive" is a semantic category, and the case indicated by the suffix *'s* and by pronouns like *his* and *my* needn't have anything to do with possession. When you think about it, there is no common thread of ownership, or any other meaning, across the phrases *Sophocles' play, Sophocles' nose, Sophocles' toga, Sophocles' mother, Sophocles' hometown, Sophocles' era,* and *Sophocles' death.* All that the *Sophocles'*s have in common is that they fill the determiner slot in the tree and help you determine which play, which nose, and so on, the speaker had in mind.

More generally, it's essential to keep an open mind about how to diagram a sentence rather than assuming that everything you need to know about grammar was figured out before you were born. Categories, functions, and meanings have to be ascertained empirically, by running little experiments such as substituting a phrase whose category you don't know for one you do know and seeing whether the sentence still works. Based on these mini-experiments, modern grammarians have sorted words into grammatical categories that sometimes differ from the traditional pigeonholes.

There is a reason why the list on page 84, for example, doesn't have the traditional category called "conjunction," with the subtypes "coordinating conjunction" (words like *and* and *or*) and "subordinating conjunction" (words like *that* and *if*). It turns out that coordinators and subordinators have nothing in common, and there is no category called "conjunction" that includes them both. For that matter, many of the words that were traditionally called subordinating conjunctions, like *before* and *after,* are actually prepositions.[7] The *after* in *after the love has gone,* for example, is just the *after* which appears in *after the dance,* which everyone agrees is a preposition. It was just a failure of the traditional grammarians to distinguish categories from functions that blinded them to the realization that a preposition could take a clause, not just a noun phrase, as its object.

Why does any of this matter? Though you needn't literally diagram sentences or master a lot of jargon to write well, the rest of this chapter will show you a number of ways in which a bit of syntactic awareness can help you out. First, it can help you avoid some obvious grammatical errors, those that are errors according to your own lights. Second, when an editor or a grammatical stickler claims to find an error in a sentence you wrote, but you don't see anything wrong with it, you can at least understand the rule in question well enough to decide for yourself whether to follow it. As we shall see in chapter 6, many spurious rules, including some that have made national headlines, are the result of bungled analyses of grammatical categories like adjective, subordinator, and preposition. Finally, an awareness of syntax can help you avoid ambiguous, confusing, and convoluted sentences. All of this awareness depends on a basic grasp of what grammatical categories are, how they differ from functions and meanings, and how they fit into trees.

Trees are what give language its power to communicate the links between ideas rather than just dumping the ideas in the reader's lap. But they come at a cost, which is the extra load they impose on memory. It takes cognitive effort to build and maintain all those invisible branches, and it's easy for reader and writer alike to backslide into treating a sentence as just one damn word after another.

Let's start with the writer. When weariness sets in, a writer's ability to behold an entire branch of the tree can deteriorate. His field of vision shrinks to a peephole, and he sees just a few adjacent words in the string at a time. Most grammatical rules are defined over trees, not strings, so this momentary tree-blindness can lead to pesky errors.

Take agreement between the subject and the verb: we say *The bridge is crowded,* but *The bridges are crowded.* It's not a hard rule to follow. Children pretty much master it by the age of three, and errors such as *I can has cheezburger* and *I are serious cat* are so obvious that a popular Internet meme (LOLcats) facetiously attributes them to cats. But the "subject" and "verb" that have to agree are defined by branches in the tree, not words in the string:

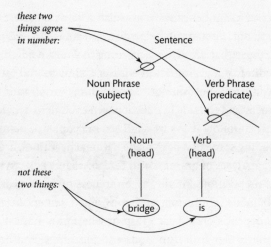

You might be thinking, What difference does it make? Doesn't the sentence come out the same either way? The answer is that it doesn't. If you fatten up the subject by stuffing some words at the end, as in the diagram below, so that *bridge* no longer comes right before the verb, then agreement—defined over the tree—is unaffected. We still say *The bridge to the islands <u>is</u> crowded*, not *The bridge to the islands <u>are</u> crowded*.

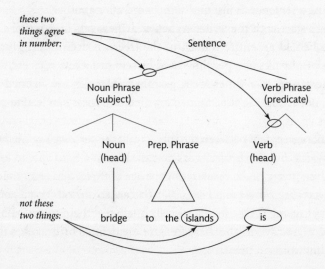

But thanks to tree-blindness, it's common to slip up and type *The bridge to the islands are crowded*. If you haven't been keeping the tree suspended in memory, the word *islands,* which is ringing in your mind's ear just before you type the verb, will contaminate the number you give the verb. Here are a few other agreement errors that have appeared in print:[8]

The <u>readiness</u> of our conventional forces <u>are</u> at an all-time low.
At this stage, the <u>accuracy</u> of the quotes <u>have</u> not been disputed.
The <u>popularity</u> of "Family Guy" DVDs <u>were</u> partly credited with the
  2005 revival of the once-canceled Fox animated comedy.
The <u>impact</u> of the cuts <u>have</u> not hit yet.
The <u>maneuvering</u> in markets for oil, wheat, cotton, coffee and more
  <u>have</u> brought billions in profits to investment banks.

They're easy to miss. As I am writing this chapter, every few pages I see the green wiggly line of Microsoft Word's grammar checker, and usually it flags an agreement error that slipped under my tree-spotting radar. But even the best software isn't smart enough to assign trees reliably, so writers cannot offload the task of minding the tree onto their word processors. In the list of agreement errors above, for example, the last two sentences appear on my screen free of incriminating squiggles.

Wedging an extra phrase into a tree is just one of the ways in which a subject can be separated from its verb. Another is the grammatical process that inspired the linguist Noam Chomsky to propose his famous theory in which a sentence's underlying tree—its deep structure—is transformed by a rule that moves a phrase into a new position, yielding a slightly altered tree called a surface structure.[9] This process is responsible, for example, for questions containing *wh*-words, such as *Who do you love?* and *Which way did he go?* (Don't get hung up on the choice between *who* and *whom* just yet—we'll get to that later.) In the deep structure, the *wh*-word appears in the position you'd expect for an ordinary sentence, in this case after the verb *love,* as in *I love Lucy.* The movement rule then brings it to the front of the sentence, leaving a gap (the underscored blank) in the surface structure. (From here on, I'll keep the trees uncluttered by omitting unnecessary labels and branches.)

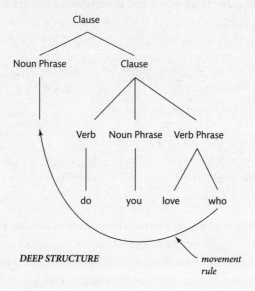

DEEP STRUCTURE

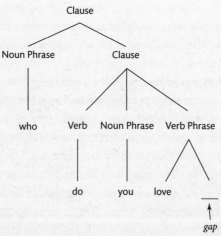

SURFACE STRUCTURE

We understand the question by mentally filling the gap with the phrase that was moved out of it. *Who do you love* __? means "For which person do you love that person?"

The movement rule also generates a common construction called a relative clause, as in *the spy who* __ *came in from the cold* and *the woman I love* __. A relative clause is a clause with a gap in it (*I love* __) which modifies a noun phrase (*the woman*). The position of the gap indicates the role that the modified phrase played in the deep structure; to understand the relative clause, we mentally fill it back in. The first example means "the spy such that the spy came in from the cold." The second means "the woman such that I love the woman."

The long distance between a filler and a gap can be hazardous to writer and reader alike. When we're reading and we come across a filler (like *who* or *the woman*), we have to hold it in memory while we handle all the material that subsequently pours in, until we locate the gap that it is meant to fill.[10] Often that is too much for our thimble-sized memories to handle, and we get distracted by the intervening words:

The impact, which theories of economics predict _____ are bound to be felt sooner or later, could be enormous.

Did you even notice the error? Once you plug the filler *the impact* into the gap after *predict*, yielding *the impact are bound to be felt*, you see that the verb must be *is*, not *are*; the error is as clear as *I are serious cat*. But the load on memory can allow the error to slip by.

Agreement is one of several ways in which one branch of a tree can be demanding about what goes into another branch. This demandingness is called government, and it can also be seen in the way that verbs and adjectives are picky about their complements. We *make plans* but we *do research*; it would sound odd to say that we *do plans* or *make research*. Bad people *oppress their victims* (an object), rather than *oppressing against their victims* (an oblique object); at the same time, they may *discriminate against their victims*, but not *discriminate them*. Something can *be identical to* something else, but must *coincide with* it; the words *identical* and *coincide* demand different prepositions. When phrases are rearranged or separated, a writer can lose track of what requires what else, and end up with an annoying error:

> Among the reasons for his optimism about SARS is the successful <u>research</u> that Dr. Brian Murphy and other scientists have <u>made</u> at the National Institutes of Health.[11]
>
> <u>People</u> who are <u>discriminated</u> based on their race are often resentful of their government and join rebel groups.
>
> The religious holidays <u>to</u> which the exams <u>coincide</u> are observed by many of our students.

One of the commonest forms of tree-blindness consists of a failure to look carefully at each branch of a coordination. A coordination, traditionally called a conjunction, is a phrase composed of two or more phrases which are linked by a coordinator (*the land of the free and the home of the brave; paper or plastic*) or strung together with commas (*Are you tired, run down, listless?*).

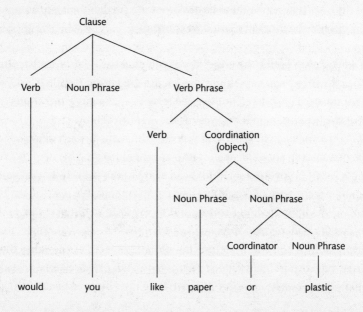

Each of the phrases in a coordination has to work in that position on its own, as if the other phrases weren't there, and they must have the same function (object, modifier, and so on). *Would you like paper or plastic?* is a fine sentence because you can say *Would you like paper?* with *paper* as the object of *like,* and you can also say *Would you like plastic?* with *plastic* as the object of *like. Would you like paper or conveniently?* is ungrammatical, because *conveniently* is a modifier, and it's a modifier that doesn't work with *like;* you would never say *Would you like conveniently?* No one is tempted to make that error, because *like* and *conveniently* are cheek by jowl, which makes the clash obvious. And no one is tempted to say *Would you like paper or conveniently?* because they can mentally block out the intervening *paper* and *or,* whereupon the clash between *like* and *conveniently* becomes just as blatant. That's the basis of the gag title of the comedian Stephen Colbert's 2007 bestseller, intended to flaunt the illiteracy of his on-screen character: *I Am America (And So Can You!).*

When a sentence gets complicated, though, even a literate writer can lose track of how each branch in a coordination harmonizes with the rest of the tree. The writer of the slogan *We get the job done, not make excuses* presumably did not anticipate how customers would wince at the bad coordination. While the phrase *get the job done* is a present-tense predicate that goes with the subject *we,* the phrase *not make excuses* is nontensed and can't go with the subject on its own (*We not make excuses*); it can only be a complement of an auxiliary verb like *do* or *will.* To repair the slogan, one could coordinate two complete clauses (*We get the job done; we don't make excuses*), or one could coordinate two complements of a single verb (*We will get the job done, not make excuses*).

A more subtle kind of off-kilter coordination creeps into writing so often that it is a regular source of mea culpas in newspaper columns in which an editor apologizes to readers for the mistakes that slipped into the paper the week before. Here are a few caught by the *New York Times* editor Philip Corbett for his "After Deadline" feature, together with repaired versions on the right (I've underlined and bracketed the words that were originally miscoordinated):[12]

He said that surgeries and therapy had helped him <u>not only</u> [to recover from his fall], <u>but</u> [had <u>also</u> freed him of the debilitating back pain].

He said that surgeries and therapy had <u>not only</u> [helped him to recover from his fall], <u>but also</u> [freed him of the debilitating back pain].

With Mr. Ruto's appearance before the court, a process began that could influence <u>not only</u> [the future of Kenya] <u>but also</u> [of the much-criticized tribunal].

With Mr. Ruto's appearance before the court, a process began that could influence the future <u>not only</u> [of Kenya] <u>but also</u> [of the much-criticized tribunal].

Ms. Popova, who died at 91 on July 8 in Moscow, was inspired <u>both</u> [by patriotism] <u>and</u> [a desire for revenge].

Ms. Popova was inspired by <u>both</u> [patriotism] <u>and</u> [a desire for revenge]. *Or* Ms. Popova was inspired <u>both</u> [by patriotism] <u>and</u> [by a desire for revenge].

In these examples, the coordinates come in matched pairs, with a quantifier (*both, either, neither, not only*) marking the first coordinate, and a coordinator (*and, or, nor, but also*) marking the second. The markers, underlined in the examples, pair off this way:

    not only . . . but also . . .
    both . . . and . . .
    either . . . or . . .
    neither . . . nor . . .

These coordinations are graceful only when the phrases coming after each marker—the ones enclosed in brackets above—are parallel. Because quantifiers like *both* and *either* have a disconcerting habit of floating around the sentence, the phrases that come after them may end up nonparallel, and that grates on the ear. In the sentence about surgeries, for example, we have *to recover* in the first coordinate (an infinitive) clashing with *freed him* in the second (a participle). The easiest way to repair an unbalanced coordination is to zero in on the second coordinate and then force the first coordinate to match it by sliding its quantifier into a more suitable spot. In this case, we want the first coordinate to be headed by a participle, so that it matches *freed him* in the second. The solution is to pull *not only* two slots leftward, giving us the pleasing symmetry between *helped him* and *freed him*. (Since the first *had* presides over the entire coordination, the second one is now unnecessary.) In the next example, we have a direct object in the first coordinate (*the future of Kenya*) jangling with an oblique object (*of the tribunal*) in the second; by pushing *not only* rightward, we get the neatly twinned phrases *of Kenya* and *of the tribunal*. The final example, also marred by mismatched objects (*by patriotism and a desire for revenge*), can be repaired in either of two ways: by nudging the *both* rightward (yielding *patriotism and a desire for revenge*), or by supplying the second coordinate with a *by* to match the first one (*by patriotism and by a desire for revenge*).

Yet another hazard of tree-blindness is the assignment of case. Case refers to the adornment of a noun phrase with a marker that advertises its typical grammatical function, such as nominative case for subjects, genitive case for determiners (the function mistakenly called "possessor" in traditional grammars), and accusative case for objects, objects of prepositions, and everything else. In English, case applies mainly to pronouns. When Cookie Monster says *Me want cookie* and Tarzan says *Me Tarzan, you Jane*, they are using an accusative pronoun for a subject; everyone else uses the nominative pronoun *I*. The other nominative pronouns are *he, she, we, they*, and *who;* the other accusative pronouns are *him, her, us, them*, and *whom*. Genitive case is marked on pronouns (*my, your, his, her, our, their, whose, its*) and also on other noun phrases, thanks to the suffix spelled *'s*.

Other than Cookie Monster and Tarzan, most of us effortlessly choose the right case whenever a pronoun is found in its usual place in the tree, next to the governing verb or preposition. But when the pronoun is buried inside a coordination phrase, writers are apt to lose sight of the governor and give the pronoun a different case. Thus in casual speech it's common for people to say *Me and Julio were down by the schoolyard;* the *me* is separated from the verb *were* by the other words in the coordination (*and Julio*), and many of us barely hear the clash. Moms and English teachers hear it, though, and they have drilled

children to avoid it in favor of *Julio and I were down by the schoolyard.*
Unfortunately, that leads to the opposite kind of error. With coordination, it's so hard to think in trees that the rationale for the correction
never sinks in, and people internalize a string-based rule, "When you
want to sound correct, say *So-and-so and I* rather than *Me and
so-and-so*." That leads to an error called a hypercorrection, in which
people use a nominative pronoun in an accusative coordination:

> Give Al Gore and I a chance to bring America back.
> My mother was once engaged to Leonard Cohen, which makes my
>   siblings and I occasionally indulge in what-if thinking.
> For three years, Ellis thought of Jones Point as the ideal spot for he
>   and his companion Sampson, a 9-year-old golden retriever, to fish
>   and play.
> Barb decides to plan a second wedding ceremony for she and her
>   husband on Mommies tonight at 8:30 on Channels 7 and 10.

Presumably Bill Clinton, who uttered the first sentence while running
for president in 1992, would never have said *Give I a chance,* because a
noun phrase next to a transitive verb is obviously accusative:

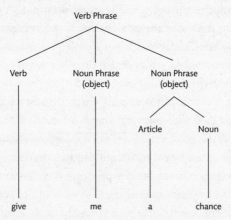

But the words *Al Gore and* separated *give* from *me* in the string, and
the distance between them befuddled his case-selection circuitry:

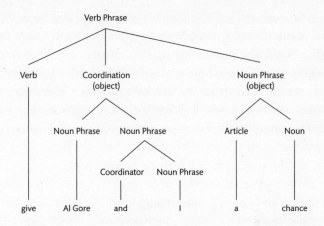

To be fair to the forty-second president, who is by all accounts a linguistically sophisticated speaker (as when he famously testified, "It depends on what the meaning of *is* is"), it's debatable whether he really made an error here. When enough careful writers and speakers fail to do something that a pencil-and-paper analysis of syntax says they should, it may mean that it's the pencil-and-paper analysis that is wrong, not the speakers and writers. In chapter 6 we'll return to this issue when we analyze the despised *between you and I*, a more common example of the alleged error seen in *give Al Gore and I*. But for now, let's assume that the paper-and-pencil analysis is correct. It's the policy enforced by every editor and composition instructor, and you should understand what it takes to please them.

A similar suspension of disbelief will be necessary for you to master another case of tricky case, the difference between *who* and *whom*. You may be inclined to agree with the writer Calvin Trillin when he wrote, "As far as I'm concerned, *whom* is a word that was invented to make everyone sound like a butler." But in chapter 6 we'll see that this is an overstatement. There are times when even nonbutlers need to know their *who* from their *whom*, and that will require you, once again, to brush up on your trees.

At first glance, the difference is straightforward: *who* is nominative, like *I, she, he, we,* and *they*, and is used for subjects; *whom* is accusative, like *me, her, him, us,* and *them,* and is used for objects. So in theory, anyone who laughs at Cookie Monster when he says *Me want cookie* should already know when to use *who* and when to use *whom* (assuming they have opted to use *whom* in the first place). We say *He kissed the bride,* so we ask *Who kissed the bride?* We say *Henry kissed her,* so we ask *Whom did Henry kiss?* The difference can be appreciated by visualizing the *wh*-words in their deep-structure positions, before they were moved to the front of the sentence, leaving behind a gap.[13]

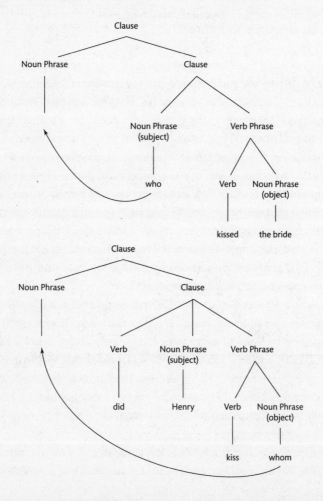

But in practice, our minds can't take in a whole tree at a glance, so when a sentence gets more complicated, any lapse of attention to the link between the *who/whom* and the gap can lead to the wrong one being chosen:[14]

> Under the deal, the Senate put aside two nominees for the National Labor Relations Board <u>who</u> the president appointed ＿ during a Senate recess.
>
> The French actor plays a man <u>whom</u> she suspects ＿ is her husband, missing since World War II.

The errors could have been avoided by mentally moving the *who* or *whom* back into the gap and sounding out the sentence (or, if your intuitions about *who* and *whom* are squishy, inserting *he* or *him* in the gap instead).

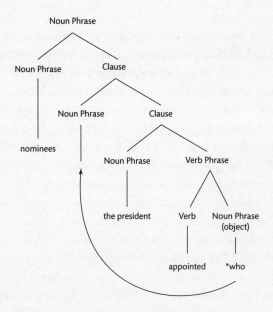

The first replacement yields *the president appointed who*, which corresponds to *the president appointed he*, which sounds entirely wrong; therefore it should be *whom* (corresponding to *him*) instead. (I've inserted an asterisk to remind you that the *who* doesn't belong there.) The second yields *whom is her husband* (or *him is her husband*), which is just as impossible; it should be *who*. Again, I'm explaining the official rules so that you will know how to satisfy an editor or work as a butler; in chapter 6 I'll return to the question of whether the official rules are legitimate and thus whether these really should be counted as errors.

Though tree-awareness can help a writer avoid errors (and, as we shall see, help him make life easy for his readers), I am not suggesting that you literally diagram your sentences. No writer does that. Nor am I even suggesting that you form mental images of trees while you write. The diagrams are just a way to draw your attention to the cognitive entities that are active in your mind as you put together a sentence. The conscious experience of "thinking in trees" does not feel like looking at a tree; it's the more ethereal sensation of apprehending how words are grouped in phrases and zooming in on the heads of those phrases while ignoring the rest of the clutter. For example, the way to avoid the error *The impact of the cuts have not been felt* is to mentally strip the phrase *the impact of the cuts* down to its head, *the impact,* and then imagine it with *have:* the error *the impact have not been felt* will leap right out. Tree-thinking also consists in mentally tracing the invisible filament that links a filler in a sentence to the gap that it plugs, which allows you to verify whether the filler would work if it were inserted there. You un-transform *the research the scientists have made __* back into *the scientists have made the research;* you undo *whom she suspects __ is her husband* and get *she suspects whom is her husband.* As with any form of mental self-improvement, you must learn to turn your gaze inward, concentrate on processes that usually run automatically, and try to wrest control of them so that you can apply them more mindfully.

Once a writer has ensured that the parts of a sentence fit together in a tree, the next worry is whether the reader can *recover* that tree, which she needs to do to make sense of the sentence. Unlike computer programming languages, where the braces and parentheses that delimit expressions are actually typed into the string for everyone to see, the branching structure of an English sentence has to be inferred from the ordering and forms of the words alone. That imposes two demands on the long-suffering reader. The first is to find the correct branches, a process called parsing. The second is to hold them in memory long enough to dig out the meaning, at which point the wording of the phrase may be forgotten and the meaning merged with the reader's web of knowledge in long-term memory.[15]

As the reader works through a sentence, plucking off a word at a time, she is not just threading it onto a mental string of beads. She is also growing branches of a tree upward. When she reads the word *the,* for example, she figures she must be hearing a noun phrase. Then she can anticipate the categories of words that can complete it; in this case, it's likely to be a noun. When the word does come in (say, *cat*), she can attach it to the dangling branch tip.

So every time a writer adds a word to a sentence, he is imposing not one but two cognitive demands on the reader: understanding the word, and fitting it into the tree. This double demand is a major justification for the prime directive "Omit needless words." I often find that when a ruthless editor forces me to trim an article to fit into a certain number of column-inches, the quality of my prose improves as if by magic. Brevity is the soul of wit, and of many other virtues in writing.

The trick is figuring out which words are "needless." Often it's easy. Once you set yourself the task of identifying needless words, it's surprising how many you can find. A shocking number of phrases that drop easily from the fingers are bloated with words that encumber the reader without conveying any content. Much of my professional life consists of reading sentences like this:

> Our study participants show a pronounced tendency to be more
> variable than the norming samples, although this trend may be
> due partly to the fact that individuals with higher measured
> values of cognitive ability are more variable in their responses to
> personality questionnaires.

a pronounced tendency to be more variable: Is there really a difference between "being more variable" (three words in a three-level, seven-branch tree) and "having a pronounced tendency to be more variable" (eight words, six levels, twenty branches)? Even worse, *this trend may be due partly to the fact that* burdens an attentive reader with ten words, seven levels, and more than two dozen branches. Total content? Approximately zero. The forty-three-word sentence can easily be reduced to nineteen, which prunes the number of branches even more severely:

> Our participants are more variable than the norming samples,
> perhaps because smarter people respond more variably to
> personality questionnaires.

Here are a few other morbidly obese phrases, together with leaner alternatives that often mean the same thing:[16]

make an appearance with	appear with
is capable of being	can be
is dedicated to providing	provides
in the event that	if
it is imperative that we	we must
brought about the organization of	organized
significantly expedite the process of	speed up
on a daily basis	daily
for the purpose of	to
in the matter of	about
in view of the fact that	since
owing to the fact that	because
relating to the subject of	regarding
have a facilitative impact	help
were in great need of	needed
at such time as	when
It is widely observed that X	X

Several kinds of verbiage are perennial targets for the delete key. Light verbs such as *make, do, have, bring, put,* and *take* often do nothing but create a slot for a zombie noun, as in *make an appearance* and *put on a performance.* Why not just use the verb that spawned the zombie in the first place, like *appear* or *perform*? A sentence beginning with *It is* or *There is* is often a candidate for liposuction: *There is competition between groups for resources* works just fine as *Groups compete for resources.* Other globs of verbal fat include the metaconcepts we suctioned out in chapter 2, including *matter, view, subject, process, basis, factor, level,* and *model.*

Omitting needless words, however, does *not* mean cutting out every single word that is redundant in context. As we shall see, many omissible words earn their keep by preventing the reader from making a wrong turn as she navigates her way through the sentence. Others fill out a phrase's rhythm, which can also make the sentence easier for the reader to parse. Omitting such words is taking the prime directive too far. There is a joke about a peddler who decided to train his horse to get by without eating. "First I fed him every other day, and he did just fine.

Then I fed him every third day. Then every fourth day. But just I was getting him down to one meal a week, he died on me!"

The advice to omit needless words should not be confused with the puritanical edict that all writers must pare every sentence down to the shortest, leanest, most abstemious version possible. Even writers who prize clarity don't do this. That's because the difficulty of a sentence depends not just on its word count but on its *geometry*. Good writers often use very long sentences, and they garnish them with words that are, strictly speaking, needless. But they get away with it by arranging the words so that a reader can absorb them a phrase at a time, each phrase conveying a chunk of conceptual structure.

Take this excerpt from a 340-word soliloquy in a novel by Rebecca Goldstein.[17] The speaker is a professor who has recently achieved professional and romantic fulfillment and is standing on a bridge on a cold, starry night trying to articulate his wonder at being alive:

Here it is then: the sense that existence is just such a *tremendous* thing, one comes into it, astonishingly, here one is, formed by biology and history, genes and culture, in the midst of the contingency of the world, here one is, one doesn't know how, one doesn't know why, and suddenly one doesn't know where one is either or who or what one is either, and all that one knows is that one is a part of it, a considered and conscious part of it, generated and sustained in existence in ways one can hardly comprehend, all the time conscious of it, though, of existence, the fullness of it, the reaching expanse and pulsing intricacy of it, and one wants to live in a way that at least begins to do justice to it, one wants to expand one's reach of it as far as expansion is possible and even beyond that, to live one's life in a way commensurate with the privilege of being a part of and conscious of the whole reeling glorious infinite sweep, a sweep that includes, so improbably, a psychologist of religion named Cass Seltzer, who, moved by powers beyond himself, did something more improbable than all the improbabilities constituting his improbable existence could have entailed, did something that won him someone else's life, a better life, a more brilliant life, a life beyond all the ones he had wished for in the pounding obscurity of all his yearnings.

For all its length and lexical exuberance, the sentence is easy to follow, because the reader never has to keep a phrase suspended in memory for long while new words pour in. The tree has been shaped to spread the cognitive load over time with the help of two kinds of topiary. One is a flat branching structure, in which a series of mostly uncomplicated clauses are concatenated side by side with *and* or with commas. The sixty-two words following the colon, for example, consist mainly of a very long clause which embraces seven self-contained clauses (shown as triangles) ranging from three to twenty words long:

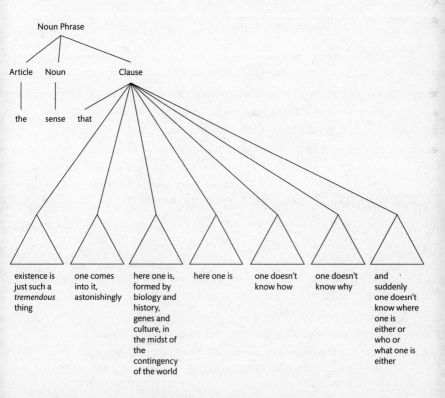

The longest of these embedded clauses, the third and the last, are also flattish trees, each composed of simpler phrases joined side by side with commas or with *or*.

Even when the sentence structure gets more complicated, a reader can handle the tree, because its geometry is mostly *right-branching*. In a right-branching tree, the most complicated phrase inside a bigger phrase comes at the end of it, that is, hanging from the rightmost branch. That means that when the reader has to handle the complicated phrase, her work in analyzing all the other phrases is done, and she can concentrate her mental energy on that one. The following twenty-five-word phrase is splayed along a diagonal axis, indicating that it is almost entirely right-branching:

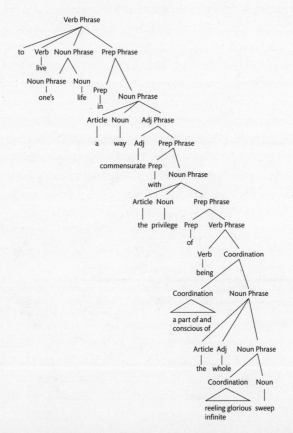

The only exceptions, where the reader has to analyze a downstairs phrase before the upstairs phrase is complete, are the two literary flourishes marked by the triangles.

English is predominantly a right-branching language (unlike, say, Japanese or Turkish), so right-branching trees come naturally to its writers. The full English menu, though, offers them a few left-branching options. A modifier phrase can be moved to the beginning, as in the sentence *In Sophocles' play, Oedipus married his mother* (the tree on page 82 displays the complicated left branch). These front-loaded modifiers can be useful in qualifying a sentence, in tying it to information mentioned earlier, or simply in avoiding the monotony of having one right-branching sentence after another. As long as the modifier is short, it poses no difficulty for the reader. But if it starts to get longer it can force a reader to entertain a complicated qualification before she has any idea what it is qualifying. In the following sentence, the reader has to parse thirty-four words before she gets to the part that tells her what the sentence is about, namely *policymakers*:[18]

> Because most existing studies have examined only a single stage
> of the supply chain, for example, productivity at the farm, or
> efficiency of agricultural markets, in isolation from the rest of the
> supply chain, <u>policymakers</u> have been unable to assess how
> problems identified at a single stage of the supply chain compare
> and interact with problems in the rest of the supply chain.

Another common left-branching construction consists of a noun modified by a complicated phrase that precedes it:

Ringling Bros. and Barnum & Bailey Circus
Failed password security question answer attempts limit
The US Department of the Treasury Office of Foreign Assets Control
Ann E. and Robert M. Bass Professor of Government Michael Sandel

> T-fal Ultimate Hard Anodized Nonstick Expert Interior Thermo-Spot Heat Indicator Anti-Warp Base Dishwasher Safe 12-Piece Cookware Set

Academics and bureaucrats concoct them all too easily; I once came up with a monstrosity called the *relative passive surface structure acceptability index*. If the left branch is slender enough, it is generally understandable, albeit top-heavy, with all those words to parse before one arrives at the payoff. But if the branch is bushy, or if one branch is packed inside another, a left-branching structure can give the reader a headache. The most obvious examples are iterated possessives such as *my mother's brother's wife's father's cousin*. Left-branching trees are a hazard of headline writing. Here's one that reported the death of a man who achieved fifteen minutes of fame in 1994 for hatching a plot to get Tonya Harding onto the US Olympic skating team by clubbing her main rival on the knee:

ADMITTED OLYMPIC SKATER NANCY KERRIGAN ATTACKER
BRIAN SEAN GRIFFITH DIES

A blogger posted a commentary entitled "Admitted Olympic Skater Nancy Kerrigan Attacker Brian Sean Griffith Web Site Obituary Headline Writer Could Have Been Clearer." The lack of clarity in the original headline was the result of its left-branching geometry: it has a ramified left branch (all the material before *Dies*), which itself contains a ramified left branch (all the material before *Brian Sean Griffith*), which in turn contains a ramified left branch (all the material before *Attacker*):[19]

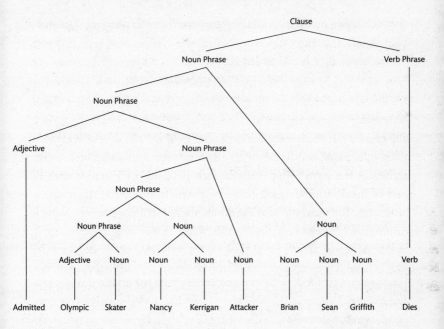

Linguists call these constructions "noun piles." Here are few others that have been spotted by contributors to the forum *Language Log:*

> NUDE PIC ROW VICAR RESIGNS
> TEXTING DEATH CRASH PEER JAILED
> BEN DOUGLAS BAFTA RACE ROW HAIRDRESSER JAMES BROWN "SORRY"
> FISH FOOT SPA VIRUS BOMBSHELL
> CHINA FERRARI SEX ORGY DEATH CRASH

My favorite explanation of the difference in difficulty between flat, right-branching, and left-branching trees comes from Dr. Seuss's Fox in Socks, who takes a flat clause with three branches, each containing a short right-branching clause, and recasts it as a single left-branching noun phrase: "When beetles fight these battles in a bottle with their paddles and the bottle's on a poodle and the poodle's eating noodles, they call this a muddle puddle tweetle poodle beetle noodle bottle paddle battle."

As much of a battle as left-branching structures can be, they are nowhere near as muddled as center-embedded trees, those in which a phrase is jammed into the middle of a larger phrase rather than fastened to its left or right edge. In 1950 the linguist Robert A. Hall wrote a book called *Leave Your Language Alone.* According to linguistic legend, it drew a dismissive review entitled "Leave Leave Your Language Alone Alone." The author was invited to reply, and wrote a rebuttal called—of course—"Leave Leave Leave Your Language Alone Alone Alone."

Unfortunately, it's only a legend; the recursive title was dreamed up by the linguist Robin Lakoff for a satire of a linguistics journal.[20] But it makes a serious point: a multiply center-embedded sentence, though perfectly grammatical, cannot be parsed by mortal humans.[21] Though I'm sure you can follow an explanation on why the string *Leave Leave Leave Your Language Alone Alone Alone* has a well-formed tree, you could never recover it from the string. The brain's sentence parser starts to thrash when faced with the successive *leave*s at the beginning, and it crashes altogether when it gets to the pile of *alone*s at the end.

Center-embedded constructions are not just linguistic in-jokes; they are often the diagnosis for what we sense as "convoluted" or "tortuous" syntax. Here is an example from a 1999 editorial on the Kosovo crisis (entitled "Aim Straight at the Target: Indict Milosevic") by the senator and former presidential candidate Bob Dole:[22]

> The view that beating a third-rate Serbian military that for the third time in a decade is brutally targeting civilians is hardly worth the effort is not based on a lack of understanding of what is occurring on the ground.

As with *Leave Leave Leave Your Language Alone Alone Alone,* this sentence ends bafflingly, with three similar phrases in a row: *is brutally targeting civilians, is hardly worth the effort, is not based on a lack of understanding.* Only with a tree diagram can you figure it out:

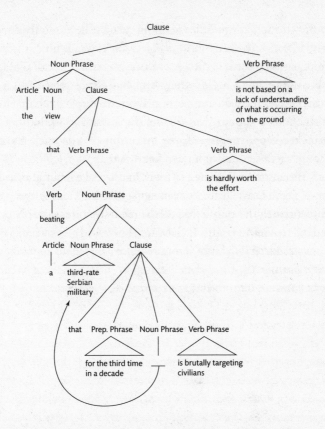

The first of the three *is*-phrases, *is brutally targeting civilians,* is the most deeply embedded one; it is part of a relative clause that modifies *third-rate Serbian military.* That entire phrase (the military that is targeting the civilians) is the object of the verb *beating.* That still bigger phrase (beating the military) is the subject of a sentence whose predicate is the second *is*-phrase, *is hardly worth the effort.* That sentence in turn belongs to a clause which spells out the content of the noun *view.* The noun phrase containing *view* is the subject of the third *is*-phrase, *is not based on a lack of understanding.*

In fact, the reader's misery begins well before she plows into the pile of *is*-phrases at the end. Midway through the sentence, while she is parsing the most deeply embedded clause, she has to figure out what the *third-rate Serbian military* is doing, which she can only do when she gets to the gap before *is brutally targeting civilians* nine words later (the link between them is shown as a curved arrow). Recall that filling gaps is a chore which arises when a relative clause introduces a filler noun and leaves the reader uncertain about what role it is going to play until she finds a gap for it to fill. As she is waiting to find out, new material keeps pouring in (*for the third time in a decade*), making it easy for her to lose track of how to join them up.

Can this sentence be saved? If you insist on keeping it as a single sentence, a good start is to disinter each embedded clause and place it side by side with the clause that contained it, turning a deeply center-embedded tree into a relatively flat one. This would give us *For the third time in a decade, a third-rate Serbian military is brutally targeting civilians, but beating it is hardly worth the effort; this view is not based on a lack of understanding of what is occurring on the ground.*

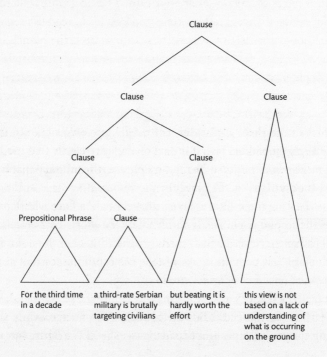

It's still not a great sentence, but now that the tree is flatter one can see how to lop off entire branches and make them into separate sentences. Splitting in two (or three or four) is often the best way to tame a sentence that has grown unruly. In the following chapter, which is about sequences of sentences rather than individual sentences, we'll see how to do that.

How does a writer manage to turn out such tortuous syntax? It happens when he shovels phrase after phrase onto the page in the order in which each one occurs to him. The problem is that the order in which thoughts occur to the writer is different from the order in which they are easily recovered by a reader. It's a syntactic version of the curse of knowledge. The writer can see the links among the concepts in his internal web of knowledge, and has forgotten that a reader needs to build an orderly tree to decipher them from his string of words.

In chapter 3 I mentioned two ways to improve your prose—showing a draft to someone else, and revisiting it after some time has passed—and both can allow you to catch labyrinthine syntax before inflicting it on your readers. There's a third time-honored trick: read the sentence aloud. Though the rhythm of speech isn't the same as the branching of a tree, it's related to it in a systematic way, so if you stumble as you recite a sentence, it may mean you're tripping on your own treacherous syntax. Reading a draft, even in a mumble, also forces you to anticipate what your readers will be doing as they understand your prose. Some people are surprised by this advice, because they think of the claim by speed-reading companies that skilled readers go directly from print to thought. Perhaps they also recall the stereotype from popular culture in which unskilled readers move their lips when they read. But laboratory studies have shown that even skilled readers have a little voice running through their heads the whole time.[23] The converse is not true—you might zip through a sentence of yours that everyone else finds a hard slog—but prose that's hard for you to pronounce will almost certainly be hard for someone else to comprehend.

Earlier I mentioned that holding the branches of a tree in memory is one of the two cognitive challenges in parsing a sentence. The other is growing the right branches, that is, inferring how the words are supposed to join up in phrases. Words don't come with labels like "I'm a noun" or "I'm a verb." Nor is the boundary where one phrase leaves off and the next one begins marked on the page. The reader has to guess, and it's up to the writer to ensure that the guesses are correct. They aren't always. A few years ago a member of a consortium of student groups at Yale put out this press release:

> I'm coordinating a huge event for Yale University which is titled "Campus-Wide Sex Week."
>
> The week involves a faculty lecture series with topics such as transgender issues: where does one gender end and the other begin, the history of romance, and the history of the vibrator. Student talks on the secrets of great sex, hooking up, and how to be a better lover and a student panel on abstainance.... A faculty panel on sex in college with four professors. a movie film festival (sex fest 2002) and a concert with local bands and yale bands....
>
> The event is going to be huge and all of campus is going to be involved.

One recipient, the writer Ron Rosenbaum, commented, "One of my first thoughts on reading this was that before Yale (my beloved alma mater) had a Sex Week it ought to institute a gala Grammar and Spelling Week. In addition to 'abstainance' (unless it was a deliberate mistake in order to imply that 'Yale puts the stain in abstinence') there was that intriguing 'faculty panel on sex in college with four professors,' whose syntax makes it sound more illicit than it was probably intended to be."[24]

The student coordinator had blundered into the problem of syntactic ambiguity. In the simpler case of lexical ambiguity, an individual word has two meanings, as in the headlines SAFETY EXPERTS SAY SCHOOL BUS PASSENGERS SHOULD BE BELTED and NEW VACCINE MAY CONTAIN RABIES. In syntactic ambiguity, there may be no single word that is ambiguous, but the words can be interconnected into more than one tree. The organizer of Sex Week at Yale intended the first tree, which specifies a panel with four professors: Rosenbaum parsed it with the second tree, which specifies sex with four professors:

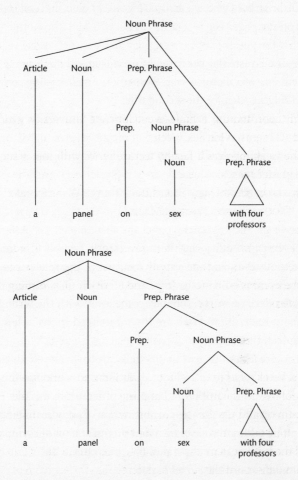

Syntactic ambiguities are the source of frequently emailed bloopers in newspaper headlines (LAW TO PROTECT SQUIRRELS HIT BY MAYOR), medical reports (*The young man had involuntary seminal fluid emission when he engaged in foreplay for several weeks*), classified ads (*Wanted: Man to take care of cow that does not smoke or drink*), church bulletins (*This week's youth discussion will be on teen suicide in the church basement*), and letters of recommendation (*I enthusiastically recommend this candidate with no qualifications whatsoever*).[25] These Internet memes may seem too good to be true, but I've come across a few on my own, and colleagues have sent me others:

> Prosecutors yesterday confirmed they will appeal the "unduly lenient" sentence of a motorist who escaped prison after being convicted of killing a cyclist for the second time.
>
> THE PUBLIC VALUES FAILURES OF CLIMATE SCIENCE IN THE US
>
> A teen hunter has been convicted of second-degree manslaughter for fatally shooting a hiker on a popular Washington state trail he had mistaken for a bear.
>
> MANUFACTURING DATA HELPS INVIGORATE WALL STREET[26]
>
> THE TROUBLE WITH TESTING MANIA

For every ambiguity that is inadvertently funny or ironic, there must be thousands that are simply confusing. The reader has to scan the sentence several times to figure out which of two meanings the writer intended, or worse, she may come away with the wrong meaning without realizing it. Here are three I noticed in just a few days of reading:

> The senator plans to introduce legislation next week that fixes a critical flaw in the military's handling of assault cases. The measure would replace the current system of adjudicating sexual assault by taking the cases outside a victim's chain of command. [Is it the *new* measure that takes the cases outside the chain of command, or is it the *current* system?]

> China has closed a dozen websites, penalized two popular social media sites, and detained six people for circulating rumors of a coup that rattled Beijing in the middle of its worst high-level political crisis in years. [Did the coup rattle Beijing, or did rumors?]

Last month, Iran abandoned preconditions for resuming
international negotiations over its nuclear programs that the
West had considered unacceptable. [Were the preconditions
unacceptable, or the negotiations, or the programs?]

And for every ambiguity that yields a coherent (but unintended)
interpretation of the whole sentence, there must be thousands which
trip up the reader momentarily, forcing her to backtrack and re-parse
a few words. Psycholinguists call these local ambiguities "garden
paths," from the expression "to lead someone up the garden path," that
is, to mislead him. They have made an art form out of grammatical yet
unparsable sentences:[27]

The horse raced past the barn fell. [= "The horse that was raced (say,
    by a jockey) past the barn was the horse that fell."]
The man who hunts ducks out on weekends.
Cotton clothing is made from is grown in Egypt.
Fat people eat accumulates.
The prime number few.
When Fred eats food gets thrown.
I convinced her children are noisy.
She told me a little white lie will come back to haunt me.
The old man the boat.
Have the students who failed the exam take the supplementary.

Most garden paths in everyday writing, unlike the ones in textbooks, don't bring the reader to a complete standstill; they just delay
her for a fraction of a second. Here are a few I've collected recently, with
an explanation of what led me astray in each case:

During the primary season, Mr. Romney opposed the Dream Act,
proposed legislation that would have allowed many young illegal
immigrants to remain in the country. [Romney opposed the Act
and also proposed some legislation? No, the Act is a piece of
legislation that had been proposed.]

Those who believe in the necessity of nuclear weapons as a deterrent tool fundamentally rely on the fear of retaliation, whereas those who don't focus more on the fear of an accidental nuclear launch that might lead to nuclear war. [Those who don't focus? No, those who don't believe in the necessity of a nuclear deterrent.]

The data point to increasing benefits with lower and lower LDL levels, said Dr. Daniel J. Rader. [Is this sentence about a data point? No, it's about data which point to something.]

But the Supreme Court's ruling on the health care law last year, while upholding it, allowed states to choose whether to expand Medicaid. Those that opted not to leave about eight million uninsured people who live in poverty without any assistance at all. [Opted not to leave? No, opted not to expand.]

Garden paths can turn the experience of reading from an effortless glide through a sentence to a tedious two-step of little backtracks. The curse of knowledge hides them from the writer, who therefore must put some effort into spotting and extirpating them. Fortunately, garden-pathing is a major research topic in psycholinguistics, so we know what to look for. Experimenters have recorded readers' eye movements and brainwaves as they work their way through sentences, and have identified both the major lures that lead readers astray and the helpful signposts that guide them in the right direction.[28]

Prosody. Most garden paths exist only on the printed page. In speech, the prosody of a sentence (its melody, rhythm, and pausing) eliminates any possibility of the hearer taking a wrong turn: *The man who HUNTS . . . ducks out on weekends; The PRIME . . . number few.* That's one of the reasons a writer should mutter, mumble, or orate a draft of his prose to himself, ideally after enough time has elapsed that it is no longer familiar. He may find himself trapped in his own garden paths.

Punctuation. A second obvious way to avoid garden paths is to punctuate a sentence properly. Punctuation, together with other graphical indicators such as italics, capitalization, and spacing, developed over the history of printed language to do two things. One is to provide the reader with hints about prosody, thus bringing writing a bit closer to speech. The other is to provide her with hints about the major divisions of the sentence into phrases, thus eliminating some of the ambiguity in how to build the tree. Literate readers rely on punctuation to guide them through a sentence, and mastering the basics is a nonnegotiable requirement for anyone who writes.

Many of the silliest ambiguities in the Internet memes come from newspaper headlines and magazine tag lines precisely because they have been stripped of all punctuation. Two of my favorites are MAN EATING PIRANHA MISTAKENLY SOLD AS PET FISH and RACHAEL RAY FINDS INSPIRATION IN COOKING HER FAMILY AND HER DOG. The first is missing the hyphen that bolts together the pieces of the compound word that was supposed to remind readers of the problem with piranhas, *man-eating*. The second is missing the commas that delimit the phrases making up the list of inspirations: *cooking, her family, and her dog*.

Generous punctuation would also take the fun out of some of the psycholinguists' garden path sentences, such as *When Fred eats food gets thrown*. And the press release on Sex Week at Yale would have been easier to parse had the student authors spent less time studying the history of the vibrator and more time learning how to punctuate. (Why is the history of romance a transgender issue? What are the secrets of how to be a student panel?)

Unfortunately, even the most punctilious punctuation is not informative enough to eliminate all garden paths. Modern punctuation has a grammar of its own, which corresponds neither to the pauses in speech nor to the boundaries in syntax.[29] It would be nice, for example, if we could clear things up by writing *Fat people eat, accumulates,* or *I convinced her, children are noisy.* But as we shall see in chapter 6, using a comma to separate a subject from its predicate or a verb from one of its complements is among the most grievous sins of mispunctuation. You can get away with it when the need for disambiguation becomes an emergency, as in George Bernard Shaw's remark "He who can, does; he who cannot, teaches" (and in Woody Allen's addendum "And he who cannot teach, teaches gym"). But in general the divisions between the major parts of a clause, such as subject and predicate, are comma-free zones, no matter how complex the syntax.

Words that signal syntactic structure. Another way to prevent garden paths is to give some respect to the apparently needless little words which don't contribute much to the meaning of a sentence and are in danger of ending up on the cutting-room floor, but which can earn their keep by marking the beginnings of phrases. Foremost among them are the subordinator *that* and relative pronouns like *which* and *who,* which can signal the beginning of a relative clause. In some phrases, these are "needless words" that can be deleted, as in *the man [whom] I love* and *things [that] my father said,* sometimes taking *is* or *are* with them, as in *A house [which is] divided against itself cannot stand.* The deletions are tempting to a writer because they tighten up a sentence's rhythm and avoid the ugly sibilance of *which.* But if the *which*-hunt is prosecuted too zealously, it may leave behind a garden path. Many of the textbook examples become intelligible when the little words are restored: *The horse which was raced past the barn fell; Fat which people eat accumulates.*

Oddly enough, one of the most easily overlooked disambiguating words in English is the most frequent word in the language: the lowly definite article *the.* The meaning of *the* is not easy to state (we'll get to it in the next chapter), but it could not be a clearer marker of syntax: when a reader encounters it, she has indubitably entered a noun phrase. The definite article can be omitted before many nouns, but the result can feel claustrophobic, as if noun phrases keep bumping into you without warning:

If selection pressure on a trait is strong, then alleles of large effect are likely to be common, but if selection pressure is weak, then existing genetic variation is unlikely to include alleles of large effect.	If the selection pressure on a trait is strong, then alleles of large effect are likely to be common, but if the selection pressure is weak, then the existing genetic variation is unlikely to include alleles of large effect.

| Mr. Zimmerman talked to police repeatedly and willingly. | Mr. Zimmerman talked to <u>the</u> police repeatedly and willingly. |

This feeling that a definite noun phrase without *the* does not properly announce itself may underlie the advice of many writers and editors to avoid the journalese construction on the left below (sometimes called the false title) and introduce the noun phrase with a dignified *the*, even if it is semantically unnecessary:

| People who have been interviewed on the show include novelist Zadie Smith and cellist Yo-Yo Ma. | People who have been interviewed on the show include <u>the</u> novelist Zadie Smith and <u>the</u> cellist Yo-Yo Ma. |
| As linguist Geoffrey Pullum has noted, sometimes the passive voice is necessary. | As <u>the</u> linguist Geoffrey Pullum has noted, sometimes the passive voice is necessary. |

Though academic prose is often stuffed with needless words, there is also a suffocating style of technical writing in which the little words like *the*, *are*, and *that* have been squeezed out. Restoring them gives the reader some breathing space, because the words guide her into the appropriate phrase and she can attend to the meaning of the content words without simultaneously having to figure out what kind of phrase she is in:

| Evidence is accumulating that most previous publications claiming genetic associations with behavioral traits are false positives, or at best vast overestimates of true effect sizes. | Evidence is accumulating that most <u>of</u> <u>the</u> previous publications <u>that</u> claimed genetic associations with behavioral traits are false positives, or at best <u>are</u> vast overestimates of <u>the</u> true effect sizes. |

Another tradeoff between brevity and clarity may be seen in the placement of modifiers. A noun can be modified either by a prepositional phrase on the right or by a naked noun on the left: *data on manufacturing* versus *manufacturing data*, *strikes by teachers* versus *teacher strikes*, *stockholders in a company* versus *company stockholders*. The little preposition can make a big difference. The headline MANUFAC-TURING DATA HELPS INVIGORATE WALL STREET could have used one, and a preposition would also have come in handy in TEACHER STRIKES

IDLE KIDS and TEXTRON MAKES OFFER TO SCREW COMPANY STOCK-HOLDERS.

Frequent strings and senses. Yet another lure into a garden path comes from the statistical patterns of the English language, in which certain words are likely to precede or follow others.[30] As we become fluent readers we file away in memory tens of thousands of common word pairs, such as *horse race, hunt ducks, cotton clothing, fat people, prime number, old man,* and *data point.* These pairs pop out of the text at us, and when they belong to the same phrase they can lubricate the parsing process, allowing the words to be joined up quickly. But when they coincidentally find themselves rubbing shoulders despite belonging to different phrases, the reader will be derailed. That's what makes the garden paths in the textbook examples so seductive, together with my real-word example that begins with the words *The data point.*

The textbook examples also stack the deck by taking advantage of a second way in which readers go with statistical patterns in the English language: when faced with an ambiguous word, readers favor the more frequent sense. The textbook garden paths trip up the reader because they contain ambiguous words in which the less frequent sense is the correct one: *race* in the transitive version of *race the horse* (rather than the intransitive *the horse raced*), *fat* as a noun rather than as an adjective, *number* as a verb rather than a noun, and so on. This can lead to garden paths in real life, too. Consider the sentence *So there I stood, still as a glazed dog.* I stumbled when I first read it, thinking that the writer continued to be a glazed dog (the frequent sense of *still* as an adverb), rather than that he was as motionless as a glazed dog (the infrequent sense of *still* as an adjective).

Structural parallelism. A bare syntactic tree, minus the words at the tips of its branches, lingers in memory for a few seconds after the words are gone, and during that time it is available as a template for the reader to use in parsing the next phrase.[31] If the new phrase has the same structure as the preceding one, its words can be slotted into the waiting tree, and the reader will absorb it effortlessly. The pattern is called structural parallelism, and it is one of the oldest tricks in the book for elegant (and often stirring) prose:

> He maketh me to lie down in green pastures; he leadeth me beside the still waters.

> We shall fight on the beaches, we shall fight on the landing grounds, we shall fight in the fields and in the streets, we shall fight in the hills; we shall never surrender.

> I have a dream that one day on the red hills of Georgia the sons of former slaves and the sons of former slave owners will be able to sit down together at the table of brotherhood. . . . I have a dream that my four little children will one day live in a nation where they will not be judged by the color of their skin but by the content of their character.

Structural parallelism works not just in poetic and hortatory passages but also in ordinary expository prose. Here is Bertrand Russell using it to explain the movement called romanticism:

> The romantic movement is characterized, as a whole, by the substitution of aesthetic for utilitarian standards. The earth-worm is useful, but not beautiful; the tiger is beautiful, but not useful. Darwin (who was not a romantic) praised the earth-worm; Blake praised the tiger.

Go back to the four passages of good writing in chapter 1 and you'll find example after example of structural parallelism, so many of them that after I called your attention to the first few I stopped pointing them out.

Although neophyte writers may repeat a simple sentence structure to the point of inanity, most writers go to the opposite extreme and vary their syntax capriciously. This can keep the reader off balance, luring her into wrong guesses about a sentence's structure. Take this entry on noun plurals, from, of all books, *The New York Times Manual of Style and Usage:*

> Nouns derived from foreign languages form plurals in different ways. Some use the original, foreign plurals: *alumnae; alumni; data; media; phenomena.* But form the plurals of others simply by adding *s: curriculums; formulas; memorandums; stadiums.*

Were you stopped short, as I was, by "form the plurals"? The passage begins with two indicative sentences whose subjects refer to foreign nouns, and whose predicates comment on how those nouns "form" or "use" the plural. Then, without warning, the third sentence shifts to the imperative mood and we are supposed to have the *reader,* not the nouns, forming plurals in a certain way.

And here's an all-too-typical example from academic prose, where the author felt that he had to vary his syntax from clause to clause and ended up with a big fat garden path:

> The authors propose that distinct selection pressures have influenced cognitive abilities and personality traits, and that intelligence differences are the result of mutation-selection balance, while balancing selection accounts for personality differences.

To be fair, it's not the author's fault that the technical term *balancing selection* looks like a verb phrase (to balance a selection) but is really a noun phrase (one of several kinds of natural selection). But to encourage the reader to parse it as a noun phrase, he should have set up a context in which the reader indeed expects to see a noun phrase. Instead he threw us off by ping-ponging from a cause-effect order in the first clause (*have influenced*) to an effect-cause order in the second (*are the result of*) and then back to a cause-effect order in the third (*accounts for*). And while he was at it, he varied his vocabulary from one sentence to the next, again for no good reason: *cognitive abilities* in the first clause refers to the same thing that *intelligence* does in the second. Recasting the sentence with parallel syntax and consistent terminology makes it intelligible even to readers who are not familiar with the technical terms:

The authors propose that distinct selection pressures have influenced cognitive abilities and personality traits: mutation-selection balance accounts for differences in cognitive ability, whereas balancing selection accounts for differences in personality traits.

Note, too, how parallel syntax can allow a reader to make sense of even the most unintelligible of the garden path sentences: *Though the horse guided past the barn walked with ease, the horse raced past the barn fell.*

Attachment to the phrase next door. Finally, we get to the panel on sex with four professors. Here we have a bias that is mainly geometrical. Go back to the trees on page 117. Why is the tree on the bottom, with the unintended meaning, the one the reader arrived at? The difference is in where the phrase *with four professors* is attached. When given a choice, readers tend to attach phrases lower in the tree rather than higher. Another way of putting it is that they like to absorb words into the phrase they are working on for as long they can, rather than closing off the phrase and figuring out somewhere else to place the incoming words.

Since readers tend to link a phrase to the words that came just before it, they will misunderstand a sentence when the writer had a more remote association in mind. Together with the sex with professors, this bias explains the foreplay of several weeks' duration, the cow that does not smoke or drink, the job candidate with no qualifications, the cyclist who was killed twice, the trail that was mistaken for a bear, and the coup that rattled Beijing.

Many authors of stylebooks, such as Strunk and White, try to protect writers against this accidental hilarity with the advice to "keep related words together." Unfortunately, the advice is unhelpful because it is stated in terms of strings rather than trees. In *a panel on sex with four professors,* trying to keep related words together won't help: they already are together. The mischievous phrase *on sex* is smack-dab next to the related phrase *a panel* on the left, where it belongs—but it's also

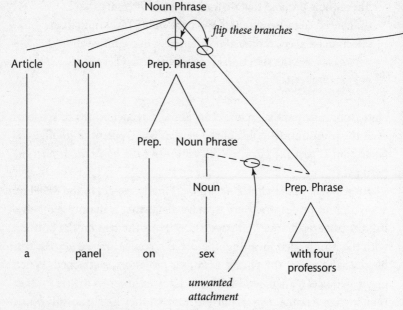

AMBIGUOUS VERSION

smack-dab next to the unrelated phrase *four professors* on the right, where it doesn't. What the writer has to worry about is connectedness in the tree (*a panel on sex* versus *sex with four professors*), not just adjacency in the string. In fact the obvious way to clarify the sentence— flipping the order of the two phrases, yielding *a panel with four professors on sex*—pulls related words apart (*a panel* and *on sex*) rather than keeping them together, at least in the string. As the diagrams on pages 128 and 129 show, the related words are still connected in the tree, just in a different order.

The advice is better stated as "pull unrelated (but mutually attracted) phrases apart." If the panel had been about controlled substances rather than amorous interactions, the opposite order would be safer: A *panel with four professors on drugs* promises as interesting an evening as the panel on sex with four professors, but the writer would be better off wording it as *a panel on drugs with four professors*. That's because of

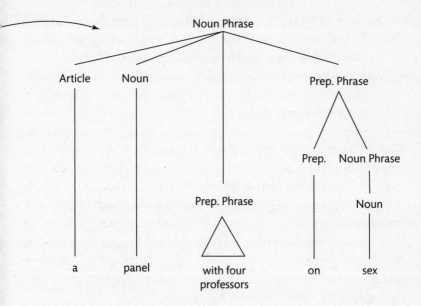

UNAMBIGUOUS VERSION

the effect of statistically frequent word sequences: the pair *sex with* attracts the phrase on the right; the pair *on drugs* attracts the phrase on the left. Writers need to look in both directions, and shunt phrases around to keep them from dangerous liaisons with an inappropriate next-door neighbor. Here are some reorderings of the examples from pages 117–18, with the ambiguities eliminated:

> For several weeks the young man had involuntary seminal fluid emission when he engaged in foreplay.
> Wanted: Man that does not smoke or drink, to take care of cow.
> This week's youth discussion in the church basement will be on teen suicide.
> I enthusiastically recommend, with no qualifications whatsoever, this candidate.

Prosecutors yesterday confirmed they will appeal the "unduly lenient" sentence of a motorist who escaped prison after being convicted for the second time of killing a cyclist.

A teen hunter has been convicted of second-degree manslaughter for fatally shooting a hiker he had mistaken for a bear on a popular Washington state trail.

The guideline to move a phrase close to the words it belongs with, and away from those it doesn't belong with, is useful only insofar as the rules of English syntax allow a phrase to be moved. Our language puts us at a disadvantage here. In many other languages, such as Latin and Russian, writers have the freedom to scramble the order of words to suit their rhetorical purposes, because case markers on the nouns, or agreement markers on the verbs, will keep the relationships straight in the reader's mind. English, which has a rudimentary system of case and agreement, must be more tyrannical about order.

This puts the writer in a bind. The rules of English syntax force him to put the subject before the verb, and the verb before the object. But he may not want the reader to *think* about the content of the subject before she thinks about the contents of the verb and object.

Why should a writer want to control the order in which the reader thinks her thoughts? Preventing unwanted attachments, as we have just seen, is one reason. There are two others, and each is a monumental principle of composition.

Save the heaviest for last. The Scottish prayer asks the Lord to deliver us from "ghoulies and ghosties and long-leggedy beasties and things that go bump in the night"—not from "things that go bump in the night and long-leggedy beasties and ghoulies and ghosties." The order fits with our cognitive processes: it's taxing to work on a big heavy phrase (*things that go bump in the night*) while you are holding in memory an incomplete bigger phrase it's part of (in this case, the four-part coordination embracing *things, beasties, ghoulies,* and *ghosties*). A big heavy phrase is easier to handle if it comes at the end, when your work assembling the overarching phrase is done and nothing else is on your mind. (It's another version of the advice to prefer right-branching trees over left-branching and center-embedded ones.) Light-before-heavy is one of the oldest principles in linguistics, having been discovered in the fourth century BCE by the Sanskrit grammarian Pāṇini.[32] It often guides the intuitions of writers when they have to choose an order for items in a list, as in *life, liberty, and the pursuit of happiness; The Wild, The Innocent, and The E Street Shuffle;* and *Faster than a speeding bullet! More powerful than a locomotive! Able to leap tall buildings in a single bound!*

Topic, then comment. Given, then new. These are more precise versions of the Strunkian advice to "put the emphatic words of a sentence at the end." Paul McCartney was mindful of the advice when he sang, "So may I introduce to you, the act you've known for all these years: Sergeant Pepper's Lonely Hearts Club Band!" Once he had the listeners' attention, and reminded them that they were there to be introduced to someone, he used the end of the sentence to provide the newsworthy information; he did not sing, "Sergeant Pepper's Lonely Hearts Club Band, the act you've known for all these years; may I introduce them to you?"[33] Once again, it's good cognitive psychology: people learn by integrating new information into their existing web of knowledge. They don't like it when a fact is hurled at them from out of the blue and they have to keep it levitating in short-term memory until they find a relevant background to embed it in a few moments later. Topic-then-comment and given-then-new orderings are major contributors to coherence, the feeling that one sentence flows into the next rather than jerking the reader around.

English syntax demands subject before object. Human memory demands light before heavy. Human comprehension demands topic before comment and given before new. How can a writer reconcile these irreconcilable demands about where the words should go in a sentence?

Necessity is the mother of invention, and over the centuries the English language has developed workarounds for its rigid syntax. They consist of alternative constructions that are more or less synonymous but that place the participants in different positions in the left-to-right ordering of the string, which means they appear at different times in the early-to-late processing in a reader's mind. Fluent writers have these constructions at their fingertips to simultaneously control the content of a sentence *and* the sequencing of its words.

Foremost among them is the unfairly maligned passive voice: *Laius was killed by Oedipus,* as opposed to *Oedipus killed Laius.* In chapter 2 we saw one of the benefits of the passive, namely that the agent of the event, expressed in the *by*-phrase, can go unmentioned. This is handy for mistake-makers who are trying to keep their names out of the spotlight and for narrators who want you to know that helicopters were used to put out some fires but don't think you need to know that it was a guy named Bob who flew one of the helicopters. Now we see the other major benefit of the passive: it allows the doer to be mentioned later in the sentence than the done-to. That comes in handy in implementing the two principles of composition when they would otherwise be stymied by the rigid word order of English. The passive allows a writer to postpone the mention of a doer that is heavy, old news, or both. Let's look at how this works.

Consider this passage from the Wikipedia entry for *Oedipus Rex,* which (spoiler alert) reveals the terrible truth about Oedipus's parentage.

> A man arrives from Corinth with the message that Oedipus's father has died. . . . It emerges that this messenger was formerly a shepherd on Mount Cithaeron, and that he was given a baby. . . . The baby, he says, was given to him by another shepherd from the Laius household, who had been told to get rid of the child.

It contains three passives in quick succession (*was given a baby; was given to him; had been told*), and for good reason. First we are introduced to a messenger; all eyes are upon him. If he figures in any subsequent news, he should be mentioned first. And so he is, thanks to the passive voice, even though the news does not involve his doing anything: *He* (old information) was given *a baby* (new information).

Now that we've been introduced to a baby, the baby is on our minds. If there's anything new to say about him, the news should begin with a mention of that baby. Once again the passive voice makes that possible, even though the baby didn't do anything: *The baby, he says, was given to him by another shepherd.* The shepherd in question is not just newsworthy but also heavy: he is being singled out with the big, hairy phrase *another shepherd from the Laius household, who had been told to get rid of the child.* That's a lot of verbiage for a reader to handle while figuring out the syntax of the sentence, but the passive voice allows it to come at the end, when all of the reader's other work is done.

Now imagine that an editor mindlessly followed the common advice to avoid the passive and altered the passage accordingly:

> A man arrives from Corinth with the message that Oedipus's
> father has died. . . . It emerges that this messenger was formerly a
> shepherd on Mount Cithaeron, and that someone gave him a
> baby. . . . Another shepherd from the Laius household, he says,
> whom someone had told to get rid of the child, gave the baby to
> him.

Active, shmactive! This is what happens when a heavy phrase with new information is forced into the beginning of a sentence just because it happens to be the agent of the action and that's the only place an active sentence will let it appear.

The original passage had a third passive—*who had been told to get rid of the child*—which the copy editor of my nightmares has also turned into an active: *whom someone had told to get rid of the child.* This highlights yet another payoff of the passive voice: it can unburden memory by shortening the interval between a filler and a gap. When an item is modified by a relative clause, and its role inside the clause is the object of the verb, the reader is faced with a long span between the filler and the gap.[34] Look at the tree at the top of the next page, which has a relative clause in the active voice:

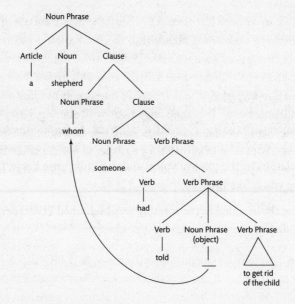

You can see a long arrow between the filler *whom* and the gap after *told*, which spans three words and three newly introduced phrases. That's the material a reader must hold in mind between the time she

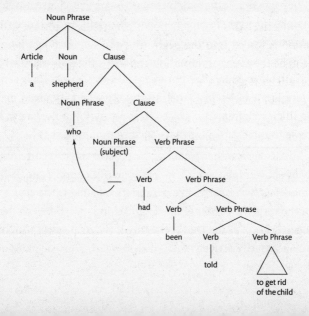

encounters *whom* and the time she can figure out what the *whom* is doing. Now look at the second tree, where the relative clause has been put in the passive. A puny arrow connects the filler *who* with a gap right next door, and the reader gets instant gratification: no sooner does she come across *who* than she knows what it's doing. True, the passive phrase itself is heavier than the active, with four levels of branching rather than three, but it comes at the end, where there's nothing else to keep track of. That's why well-written prose puts object relative clauses in the passive voice, and difficult prose keeps them in the active voice, like this:

> Among those called to the meeting was Mohamed ElBaradei,
> <u>the former United Nations diplomat</u> protesters demanding Mr.
> Morsi's ouster have tapped ___ as one of their negotiators over a
> new interim government, Reuters reported, citing unnamed
> official sources.

This sentence is encumbered, among other things, by a long stretch between the filler of the relative clause, *the former United Nations diplomat,* and the gap after *tapped* seven words later. Though the sentence may be beyond salvation, passivizing the relative clause would be a place to start: *the former United Nations diplomat who has been tapped by protesters demanding Mr. Morsi's ouster.*

The passive voice is just one of the gadgets that the English language makes available to rearrange phrases while preserving their semantic roles. Here are a few others that are handy when the need arises to separate illicit neighbors, to place old information before new, to put fillers close to their gaps, or to save the heaviest for last:[35]

Basic order:	Preposing:
Oedipus met Laius on the road to Thebes.	On the road to Thebes, Oedipus met Laius.

Basic order:	Postposing:
The servant left the baby whom Laius had condemned to die on the mountaintop.	The servant left on the mountaintop the baby whom Laius had condemned to die.

Double-object dative:
Jocasta handed her servant the infant.

Prepositional dative:
Jocasta handed the infant to her servant.

Basic construction:
A curse was on the kingdom.

Existential:
There was a curse on the kingdom.

Clause as subject:
That Oedipus would learn the truth was inevitable.

Extraposed clause:
It was inevitable that Oedipus would learn the truth.

Basic construction:
Oedipus killed Laius.

Cleft:
It was Oedipus who killed Laius.
It was Laius whom Oedipus killed.

Basic construction:
Oedipus killed Laius.

Pseudo-cleft:
What Oedipus did was kill Laius.

The versions on the right are a bit longer, wordier, or more formal than the ones on the left, and the last four, with their needless words (*there, it, what*), are often good candidates for replacement by their snappier near-synonyms. But by now you can see why they're sometimes useful: they give the writer additional freedom in ordering phrases in the tree.

Preposing allows the writer to move a modifying phrase leftward, which can separate it from a pesky little phrase to which it might otherwise attach itself (as with the young man who had involuntary seminal emissions if he engaged in foreplay for several weeks). The next four constructions allow a writer to shift a phrase rightward when it is too heavy or too newsworthy to be taking up space in the middle of a sentence. The last two allow a writer an additional lever of control over what the reader will treat as given and what she will treat as new. The cleft inverts the usual ordering: the new information is thrust into the spotlight early, and the given information, which serves as its background, comes at the end. The pseudo-cleft retains the usual order (given-to-new), but both kinds of clefting add an important twist: the given information is not old news, in the sense of having been mentioned earlier in the discussion, but *presupposed:* the reader is asked to accept it as true, and is now being informed what it is true of. *It was Oedipus who killed Laius,* for example, takes it for granted that *someone* killed Laius, the only question being who; the main clause of the sentence informs us who the who is.

Another major resource that English puts at a writer's disposal is the choice of verb. Some verbs have a counterpart which narrates the same scenario but fills its grammatical slots (subject, object, oblique object) with different role-players (the mover, the thing moved, the source, or the recipient):

Jocasta gave the infant to her servant.	The servant received the infant from Jocasta.
She robbed her uncle of a cigar.	She stole a cigar from her uncle.
Morris sold a watch to Zak.	Zak bought a watch from Morris.
I substituted margarine for the lard.	I replaced the lard with margarine.
The vandals fled the police.	The police chased the vandals.
The goalie sustained an injury from the onrushing forward.	The onrushing forward inflicted an injury on the goalie.

Like the menu of constructions, the menu of verbs can give a writer several options on where to place a given, new, light, or heavy phrase. Holding the crime constant, the verb *rob* places the ill-gotten gains at the end (*She robbed her uncle of an expensive hand-rolled Cuban cigar*); the verb *steal* places the victim at the end (*She stole a cigar from her greedy lascivious uncle*).

Good writers may have no explicit awareness of how these constructions and verb types work, and they certainly don't know their names. The words and structures lie waiting in memory, bearing little tags like "here's a way to delay mentioning a modifier" or "my direct object is the thing being transferred." Accomplished wordsmiths identify a need while writing, or spot a problem in a sentence while revising, and when all goes well the suitable word or construction pops into mind.

Just below the surface of these inchoate intuitions, I believe, is a tacit awareness that the writer's goal is to encode a web of ideas into a string of words using a tree of phrases. Aspiring wordsmiths would do well to cultivate this awareness. It can help rid their writing of errors, dead ends, and confusing passages. And it can take the fear and boredom out of grammar, because it's always more inviting to master a system when you have a clear idea of what it is designed to accomplish.

Chapter 5

ARCS OF COHERENCE

HOW TO ENSURE THAT READERS WILL GRASP THE
TOPIC, GET THE POINT, KEEP TRACK OF THE PLAYERS,
AND SEE HOW ONE IDEA FOLLOWS FROM ANOTHER

So many things can go wrong in a passage of prose. The writing can be bloated, self-conscious, academic; these are habits that classic style, which treats prose as a window onto the world, is designed to break. The passage can be cryptic, abstruse, arcane; these are symptoms of the curse of knowledge. The syntax can be defective, convoluted, ambiguous; these are flaws that can be prevented by an awareness of the treelike nature of a sentence.

This chapter is about yet another thing that can go wrong in writing. Even if every sentence in a text is crisp, lucid, and well formed, a *succession* of them can feel choppy, disjointed, unfocused—in a word, incoherent. Consider this passage:

The northern United States and Canada are places where herons live and breed. Spending the winter here has its advantages. Great Blue Herons live and breed in most of the northern United States. It's an advantage for herons to avoid the dangers of migration. Herons head south when the cold weather arrives. The earliest herons to arrive on the breeding grounds have an advantage. The winters are relatively mild in Cape Cod.

The individual sentences are clear enough, and they obviously pertain to a single topic. But the passage is incomprehensible. By the second sentence we're wondering about where *here* is. The third has us puzzling over whether great blue herons differ from herons in general, and if they do, whether these herons live only in the northern United States, unlike the other herons, who live in Canada as well. The fourth sentence seems to come out of the blue, and the fifth seems to contradict the fourth. The paragraph is then rounded out with two non sequiturs.

Now, I doctored this passage to make it bewilderingly incoherent, just to dramatize the topic of this chapter. But lesser failures of coherence are among the commonest flaws in writing. Consider some of the clumsy sentences I fixed in earlier chapters, repeated here in their improved versions:

> The researchers found that in groups with little alcoholism, such as Jews, people actually drink moderate amounts of alcohol, but few of them drink too much and become alcoholics.

> For the third time in a decade, a third-rate Serbian military is brutally targeting civilians, but beating it is hardly worth the effort; this view is not based on a lack of understanding of what is occurring on the ground.

Even with the syntax repaired, the sentences are difficult to understand, and the original contexts don't make them any clearer. The problem is coherence: we don't know why one clause follows another. No further tinkering with the syntax will help. We need a context that leads the reader to understand why the writer felt the need to assert what she is now asserting:

One might think that the reason some ethnic groups have high rates of alcoholism is that drinking is common in the group. According to this hypothesis, drinking even moderate amounts of alcohol puts people at risk of drinking too much and becoming alcoholics. If so, we should find that the groups with the lowest rates of alcoholism are those in which drinking of any kind is forbidden, such as Mormons or Muslims. But that's not what the researchers discovered. . . .

Many policy analysts write as if the obvious way to deal with armies that commit human rights violations is to invade them with our vastly superior military forces. Anyone who opposes a military invasion, they argue, must be ignorant of the atrocities taking place. But that's not why I and other statesmen favor a different strategy for ending this crisis. Make no mistake: . . .

Whenever one sentence comes after another, readers need to see a connection between them. So eager are readers to seek coherence that they will often supply it when none exists. One category of frequently emailed bloopers consists of sequences which are amusing not because of problems in syntax but because of problems in coherence:[1]

Miss Charlene Mason sang, "I Will Not Pass This Way Again," giving obvious pleasure to the congregation.

The sermon this morning: "Jesus Walks on the Water." The sermon tonight will be "Searching for Jesus."

Dog for sale: Eats anything and is fond of children.

We do not tear your clothing with machinery. We do it carefully by hand.

The patient has been depressed ever since she began seeing me in 2008.

In fact, it's the hunger for coherence that drives the entire process of understanding language. Suppose a reader has successfully parsed a sentence and now has an understanding of who did what to whom or what is true of what. Now he must integrate it with the rest of his knowledge, because a factoid floating around in the brain unlinked to anything else is as useless as a book filed on a random shelf in a library or a Web site with no links to it. This linking must be repeated with each sentence in the text. That is how the content of a passage of text becomes integrated into the reader's web of knowledge.

This chapter is about the sense of style in passages longer than a sentence—a paragraph, a blog post, a review, an article, an essay, or a book. Some of the principles of style that apply within a sentence, such as building an orderly tree and placing given before new information, apply to extended passages as well. But as we shall see, coherent discourse also uses devices that differ from the branching of a tree, and our metaphors must expand accordingly.

At first glance, the organization of a text really does seem like a tree, with passages of language embedded in still larger passages of language. Several clauses are joined or embedded in a sentence; several sentences make up a paragraph; several paragraphs make up a section, several sections a chapter, several chapters a book. A text with this hierarchical structure is easy for a reader to assimilate because at any level of granularity, from clauses to chapters, the passage can be represented in the reader's mind as a single chunk, and the reader never has to juggle more than a few chunks at a time as he figures out how they are related.

To compose a passage with this orderly structure, a writer must organize the content she hopes to convey into a neat hierarchy. Sometimes she may be lucky enough to begin with a firm grasp of the hierarchical organization of her material, but more often she will have an unruly swarm of ideas buzzing in her head and must get them to settle down into an orderly configuration. The time-honored solution is to create an outline, which is just a tree lying on its side, its branches marked by indentations, dashes, bullets, or Roman and Arabic numerals, rather than by forking line segments. One way to fashion an outline is to jot your ideas on a page or on index cards more or less at random and then look for ones that seem to belong together. If you reorder the items with the clusters of related ideas placed near one another, then arrange the clusters that seem to belong together in larger clusters, group those into still larger clusters, and so on, you'll end up with a treelike outline.

But now you face a major difference between the syntactic tree of a sentence and the outline tree of a text. When it comes to putting the units into a left-to-right order, the rules of English syntax leave writers with only a few possibilities. The object, for example, pretty much has to come after the verb. But if you're writing an essay on mammals, it's up to you whether to write first about the rodents, then the primates, then the bats, and so on, or first the primates, then the felines, then the whales and dolphins, or any of the other 403,291,461,126,605,635,584, 000,000 logically possible orderings of the twenty-six subgroups. The writer's challenge is to come up with a scheme to order these units of text—to turn a dangly mobile into a rigid tree.

Often an author will pick an order more or less arbitrarily and use verbal signposts or numbered headings to guide the reader on his journey through the text (*Part II Section C Subsection 4 Paragraph b*, or *Section 2.3.4.2*). But in many genres, numbered headings are not an option, and as we saw in chapter 2, excessive signposting can bore and confuse a reader. And regardless of how many headings or signposts you use, it's always best to lay an intuitive trail through the territory: a scheme for stringing the units into a natural order that allows readers to anticipate what they will encounter next. There is no algorithm for doing this, but let me give you a couple of examples.

I once had the challenge of explaining an unruly literature on the neurobiology and genetics of language, which embraces a vast range of topics, including case studies of neurological patients, computer simulations of neural networks, and neuroimaging of the brain areas that are active during language processing. The first temptation was to order the studies historically, which is how textbooks do it, but this would have been an indulgence in professional narcissism: my readers were interested in the brain, not in the history of the doctors and professors who study the brain. It dawned on me that a clearer trajectory through this morass would consist of zooming in from a bird's-eye view to increasingly microscopic components. From the highest vantage point you can make out only the brain's two big hemispheres, so I began with studies of split-brain patients and other discoveries that locate language in the left hemisphere. Zooming in on that hemisphere, one can see a big cleft dividing the temporal lobe from the rest of the brain, and the territory on the banks of that cleft repeatedly turns up as crucial for language in clinical studies of stroke patients and brain scans of intact subjects. Moving in closer, one can distinguish various regions—Broca's area, Wernicke's area, and so on—and the discussion can turn to the more specific language skills, such as recognizing words and parsing them into a tree, that have been tied to each area. Now we can switch from the naked eye to a microscope and peer into models of neural networks. From there we can crank the microscope one more turn to the level of genes, which is an opportunity to review studies of dyslexia and other inherited language disorders. All the research fell into place along a single global-to-local continuum. I had my ordering.

The ways to order material are as plentiful as the ways to tell a story. On another occasion I had to review research on English, French, Hebrew, German, Chinese, Dutch, Hungarian, and Arapesh, a language spoken in New Guinea. English was the natural starting point, but in what order should I bring up the others? I suppose I could have reviewed them in terms of how familiar they are to me or to American readers, or the order in which the studies were done, or even alphabetically. But instead I marched backwards in time to older and older (and more and more inclusive) language families: first the languages begotten by Germanic tribes who lived about 2,000 years ago, including Dutch and German; then to other Indo-European tribes, such as the Italic people who split from their Germanic brethren about 3,500 years ago, which brings in French; then to the Uralic tribes, which probably coexisted with the Indo-Europeans about 7,000 years ago and left us with Hungarian; and so on, back through history and outward in language families.

There are many other ordering schemes: leading the reader on a trek across a geographical territory; narrating the travails of a hero who must overcome obstacles on his way to achieving a goal; mimicking a debate in which the two sides present their positions, rebut each other, sum up their cases, and await a verdict; and, sometimes, recounting the history of discovery that culminated in our current understanding.

Appreciating the treelike nature of a text can also help you understand one of the few devices available in nontechnical prose to visually mark the structure of discourse: the paragraph break. Many writing guides provide detailed instructions on how to build a paragraph. But the instructions are misguided, because there is no such thing as a paragraph. That is, there is no item in an outline, no branch of a tree, no unit of discourse that consistently corresponds to a block of text delimited by a blank line or an indentation. What does exist is the paragraph *break:* a visual bookmark that allows the reader to pause, take a breather, assimilate what he has read, and then find his place again on the page.

Paragraph breaks generally coincide with the divisions between branches in the discourse tree, that is, cohesive chunks of text. But the same little notch must be used for divisions between branches of every size, whether it's the end of a minor digression, the end of a major summation, or anything in between. Sometimes a writer should cleave an intimidating block of print with a paragraph break just to give the reader's eyes a place to alight and rest. Academic writers often neglect to do this and trowel out massive slabs of visually monotonous text. Newspaper journalists, mindful of their readers' attention spans, sometimes go to the other extreme and dice their text into nanoparagraphs consisting of a sentence or two apiece. Inexperienced writers tend to be closer to academics than to journalists and use too few paragraph breaks rather than too many. It's always good to show mercy to your readers and periodically let them rest their weary eyes. Just be sure not to derail them in the middle of a train of thought. Carve the notch above a sentence that does not elaborate or follow from the one that came before.

For all the cognitive benefits of hierarchical organization, not all texts have to be organized into a tree. A skilled writer can interleave multiple story lines, or deliberately manipulate suspense and surprise, or engage the reader with a chain of associations, each topic shunting the reader to the next. But no writer can leave the macroscopic organization of a text to chance.

Whether or not a text is organized to fit into a hierarchical outline, the tree metaphor goes only so far. No sentence is an island; nor is a paragraph, a section, or a chapter. All of them contain links to other chunks of text. A sentence may elaborate, qualify, or generalize the one that came before. A theme or topic may run through a long stretch of writing. People, places, and ideas may make repeat appearances, and the reader must keep track of them as they come and go. These connections, which drape themselves from the limbs of one tree to the limbs of another, violate the neatly nested, branch-within-branch geometry of a tree.[2] I'll call them arcs of coherence.

Like the mass of cables drooping behind a desk, the conceptual connections from one sentence to another have a tendency to get gnarled up in a big, snaggly tangle. That's because the links connected to any idea in our web of knowledge run upwards, downwards, and sideways to other ideas, often spanning long distances. Inside the writer's brain, the links between ideas are kept straight by the neural code that makes memory and reasoning possible. But out there on the page, the connections have to be signaled by the lexical and syntactic resources of the English language. The challenge to the writer is to use those resources so that the reader can graft the information in a series of sentences into his web of knowledge without getting tangled up in either.

Coherence begins with the writer and reader being clear about the *topic*. The topic corresponds to the small territory within the vast web of knowledge into which the incoming sentences should be merged. It may seem obvious that a writer should begin by laying her topic on the table for the reader to see, but not all writers do. A writer might think that it's unsubtle to announce the topic in so many words, as in "This paper is about hamsters." Or she herself may discover her topic only after she has finished laying her ideas on paper, and forget to go back and revise the opening to let the reader in on her discovery.

A classic experiment by the psychologists John Bransford and Marcia Johnson shows why it's essential to let the reader in on the topic early.[3] They asked participants to read and remember the following passage:

> The procedure is actually quite simple. First you arrange things into different groups depending on their makeup. Of course, one pile may be sufficient depending on how much there is to do. If you have to go somewhere else due to lack of facilities that is the next step, otherwise you are pretty well set. It is important not to overdo any particular endeavor. That is, it is better to do too few things at once than too many. In the short run this may not seem important, but complications from doing too many can easily arise. A mistake can be expensive as well. The manipulation of the appropriate mechanisms should be self-explanatory, and we need not dwell on it here. At first the whole procedure will seem complicated. Soon, however, it will become just another facet of life. It is difficult to foresee any end to the necessity for this task in the immediate future, but then one never can tell.

Needless to say, the passage made little sense to them, as I expect it made little sense to you, and they could remember few of the sentences. Another group of people got the same passage but with a new tidbit slipped into the instructions: "The paragraph you will hear will be about washing clothes." The level of recall doubled. A third group was given the topic *after* reading the story; it didn't help them at all. The moral for a writer is obvious: a reader must know the topic of a text in order to understand it. As newspaper editors say: Don't bury the lede (*lede* being journalist jargon for "lead," which might otherwise be misread as the heavy metal).

Now, you might object that the experimenters stacked the deck by writing a passage about a concrete physical activity in vague and abstract language. But they also ran a study in which almost every sentence referred to a concrete object or action:

> A newspaper is better than a magazine.
> A seashore is a better place than the street.
> At first it is better to run than to walk.
> You may have to try several times.
> It takes some skill but it's easy to learn.
> Even young children can enjoy it.
> Once successful, complications are minimal.
> Birds seldom get too close.
> Rain, however, soaks in very fast.
> Too many people doing the same thing can also cause problems.
> One needs lots of room.
> If there are no complications, it can be very peaceful.
> A rock will serve as an anchor.
> If things break loose from it, however, you will not get a second chance.

Make sense? How about with this clue: "The sentences are about making and flying a kite." Stating the topic is necessary because even the most explicit language can touch on only a few high points of a story. The reader has to fill in the background—to read between the lines, to connect the dots—and if he doesn't know which background is applicable, he will be mystified.

Together with the topic of a text, the reader usually needs to know its *point*. He needs to know what the author is trying to accomplish as she explores the topic. Human behavior in general is understandable only once you know the actor's goals. When you see someone waving her arms, the first thing you want to know is whether she is trying to attract attention, shoo away flies, or exercise her deltoids. That is also true of writing. The reader needs to know whether a writer is rabbiting on about a topic in order to explain it, convey interesting new facts about it, advance an argument about it, or use it as an example of an important generalization. In other words, a writer has to have both something to talk about (the topic) and something to say (the point).

Writers often resist telegraphing their point at the outset. Sometimes they feel it would spoil the suspense. Sometimes they are victims of professional narcissism and write as if the reader were interested in every blind alley, fool's errand, and wild-goose chase they engaged in while exploring the topic. Most often, they themselves don't know the point of their essay until they have written a first draft, and never go back to reshape the essay so that the point is clear at the beginning. An old cartoon captioned "The PhD thesis" shows a little boy firing an arrow into the air, seeing where it lands, walking over to it, and painting a target around that spot. It's not how science should work, but it's sometimes how writing must work.

Some genres, such as the scholarly journal article, force an author to lay out her point in a summary, an abstract, or a synopsis. Others, such as magazines and newspapers, help the reader with a tag line (an explanation beneath the cutesy title) or a pull quote (an illustrative sentence displayed in a box). Some style guides, such as Joseph Williams's excellent *Style: Toward Clarity and Grace,* provide a formula. Williams advises writers to structure every section as an "issue" (the topic) followed by a "discussion," and to state the point of the text at the end of the issue.

The exact place in which the point of a text is displayed is less important than the imperative to divulge it somewhere not too far from the beginning. There are, to be sure, stand-up comedians, shaggy-dog raconteurs, consummate essayists, and authors of mystery novels who can build up curiosity and suspense and then resolve it all with a sudden revelation. But everyone else should strive to inform, not dumbfound, and that means that writers should make it clear to their readers what they are trying to accomplish.

As a reader works his way through a text, the next challenge is to keep track of the ideas that run through it and to discern the logical relationship between one idea and the next. Let's work through a simple text in which the author makes it easy.

My model of coherent discourse is the original version of the text that I doctored for the opening of the chapter. It comes from a weekly feature in a local tabloid, *The Cape Codder,* called "Ask the Bird Folks." The Bird Folks actually consist of one bird folk, Mike O'Connor, who owns the Bird Watcher's General Store in Orleans, Massachusetts. Soon after opening the store O'Connor found himself fielding so many questions from curious customers that he tried his hand at writing a column. In this one, he responded to a reader worried about a heron which showed up at a bog near her house and was unable to feed because the bog had frozen over.[4] After reassuring her that herons can survive a few days without eating, he provides the backstory to this pathetic scene:

Great Blue Herons live and breed just about anywhere in the northern United States and most of Canada. When the cold weather arrives, the herons head south. A few come to Cape Cod where the winters usually aren't too bad. Most of these herons are either inexperienced young birds or lost adult males too stubborn to ask for directions south. Spending the winter here has its advantages, and I'm not talking about the free off-season parking in Provincetown. Herons are able to avoid the dangers of migration, plus they can be one of the earliest to arrive on the breeding grounds.

However, there is a risk with staying this far north. Yes, our winters are often mild and pleasant. Then there is this winter, the winter that never ends. Snow, ice and cold are not kind to birds and I'd bet many herons won't be booking a visit to Cape Cod next year.

Herons have one thing in their favor: they are excellent hunters and are total opportunists. When the fish are frozen out, they'll eat other things, including crustaceans, mice, voles and small birds. One hungry heron was seen chowing down a litter of feral kittens. I know, I know, I too was upset to read about the herons eating small birds.

Herons also have one odd behavior that is not in their favor. In the winter they seem to choose and defend a favorite fishing hole. When these areas become frozen solid, some herons don't seem to catch on and often will stand over a frozen stream for days waiting for the fish to return. Boy, talk about stubborn.

The primary lifeline between an incoming sentence and a reader's web of knowledge is the topic. The word "topic" in linguistics actually has two meanings.[5] In this chapter we have been looking at the topic of a *discourse* or text, namely the subject matter of a series of connected sentences. In chapter 4 we looked at the topic of a *sentence*, namely what that sentence is about. In most English sentences, the topic is the grammatical subject, though it can also be introduced in a separate phrase, like *As for fruit, I prefer blueberries,* or *Speaking of ducks, have you heard the one about the man who walked into a bar with a duck on his head?* In that chapter we saw that in a coherent passage the topic of the discourse is aligned with the topic of the sentence. Now let's see how O'Connor uses this principle over an extended discussion.

The topic of the column is obviously "herons in winter"; that's what the reader asked about. The point of the column is to explain why a heron might stand over a frozen bog. The topic of the first sentence, namely the subject, is also the topic of the column: "Great Blue Herons live and breed . . ." Imagine that it had begun with something like my doctored version, "Canada is a place where herons live and breed." It would knock the reader off balance, because he has no reason at this moment to be thinking about Canada.

As the passage proceeds, O'Connor keeps the herons in subject position. Here is a list of the subjects in order, with the ones referring to herons in the left column, the ones referring to something else in the right column, and horizontal lines separating the paragraphs:

Great Blue Herons live
the herons head
A few come
Most of these herons are

                          Spending the winter here has

Herons are able to avoid

---

                          there is a risk
                          our winters are
                          there is this winter
                          Snow, ice and cold are not kind

Herons have one thing
they are excellent hunters
they'll eat
One hungry heron was seen

                          I too was upset

Herons also have
they seem to choose
some herons don't seem to catch on

                          [You] talk about

Putting aside the interjections at the ends of the last two paragraphs, in which the author addresses the reader directly for humorous effect (*I know, I know, I too was upset* and *Talk about stubborn*), the subjects (and hence the sentence topics) are remarkably consistent. In the first, third, and fourth paragraphs, every subject but one consists of herons. The consistent string of sentence topics, all related to the column topic, forms a satisfying arc of coherence over the passage.

Better still, the herons are not just any old subjects. They are actors who do things. They migrate, they avoid danger, they hunt, they eat, they stand. That is a hallmark of classic style, or for that matter any good style. It's always easier for a reader to follow a narrative if he can keep his eyes on a protagonist who is moving the plot forward, rather than on a succession of passively affected entities or zombified actions.

It's worth looking at a couple of tricks that allow O'Connor to keep this unblinking focus on his protagonists. He strategically slips in a passive sentence: *One hungry heron was seen,* as opposed to *Birdwatchers saw one hungry heron.* Though the heron is merely being observed by an unidentified birdwatcher at this point in the passage, the passive voice keeps it in the reader's spotlight of attention. And O'Connor frequently moves temporal modifiers to the front of the sentence: *When the cold weather arrives; When the fish are frozen out; In the winter; When these areas become frozen solid.* This preposing avoids the monotony of a long string of similar sentences, even though herons are the grammatical subjects of every one.

Those temporal modifiers all have something to do with cold weather, and that is also a deliberate choice. The new information in each sentence is about how the herons react to cold weather. So in each of these sentences, some aspect of cold weather (mentioned in the modifier at the beginning) sets the stage for an announcement of what herons do about it (mentioned in the main clause that follows). Given always precedes new.

In the second paragraph, cold weather takes its turn on the stage as a topic in its own right. The transition is orderly. The switch of topic is announced in the penultimate sentence of the first paragraph (*Spending the winter here has its advantages*), and it is maintained consistently in the second, where two of the sentences have cold things as their subjects, and the other two have them in complements to *There is,* which are like subjects. We have a second arc of coherence spanning the text, which links all the manifestations of cold weather.

The arc linking the sentences about herons and the arc linking the sentences about cold weather are two instances of what Williams calls topic strings: they keep the reader focused on a single topic as he proceeds from sentence to sentence. Let's turn now to another arc of coherence, which connects the different appearances of an entity on the reader's mental stage as they come and go over the course of a passage.

The noun system of English provides a writer with ways to distinguish entities the reader is being introduced to for the first time from the entities he already knows about. This is the major distinction between the indefinite article, *a,* and the definite article, *the.*[6] When a character makes his first appearance on stage, he is introduced with *a.* When we are subsequently told about him, we already know who he is, and he is mentioned with *the:*

> An Englishman, a Frenchman, and a Jew are sitting in a doctor's waiting room and each is told he has twenty-four hours to live. They are asked how they plan to spend their final day. The Englishman says, "I'm going to my club to smoke my pipe, sip some sherry, and chat with the blokes." The Frenchman says, "I'm going to call my mistress for a sumptuous dinner, a bottle of the finest wine, and a night of passionate lovemaking." The Jew says, "I'm going to see another doctor."

A (or *an*) and *the* are not the only way that the English language distinguishes indefinite from definite nouns. Indefinite plurals and mass nouns can be introduced with the article *some* (*Some mud was on the floor; Some marbles were on the floor*), and they can also appear without an article at all (*Mud was on the floor; Marbles were on the floor*). Definiteness can be marked by other *th*-words such as *this, that, these,* and *those,* or with a genitive noun, as in *Claire's knee* or *Jerry's kids.*

The distinction between a first appearance on stage and subsequent appearances can also be marked by the use of names or indefinite nouns on the one hand and pronouns on the other. Pronouns such as *he, she, they,* and *it* do more than save keystrokes. They tell the reader, "You've already met this guy; no need to stop and think about a new kid in town."

<u>Stanley Goldfarb</u> died and <u>his</u> relatives and the congregation gathered for an evening of prayers and mourning. When the time came for the mourners to come up and eulogize <u>him</u>, no one stirred. After several minutes, the rabbi was getting anxious. "Someone must have something nice to say about <u>him</u>," he implored. More silence. Finally a voice piped up from the back of the room: "<u>His</u> brother was worse."

Helping a reader keep track of the entities that make repeated appearances in a text is a tricky business. Repeating a name or an indefinite noun can confuse readers by making them think that someone new has walked onto the stage.[7] (Imagine *Stanley Goldfarb died and Stanley Goldfarb's relatives gathered for an evening of mourning.*) On the other hand, if new characters walk into the scene in the interim, or enough time has passed that the first entrance is a distant memory, a pronoun or definite noun can leave them wondering who the *he* or *the man* is. Bloopers make the danger plain:[8]

> Guilt, vengeance, and bitterness can be emotionally destructive to you and your children. You must get rid of them.
> After Governor Baldwin watched the lion perform, he was taken to Main Street and fed 25 pounds of raw meat in front of the Cross Keys Theater.
> The driver had a narrow escape, as a broken board penetrated his cabin and just missed his head. This had to be removed before he could be released.
> My mother wants to have the dog's tail operated on again, and if it doesn't heal this time, she'll have to be put away.

Now let's go back to the herons and see how O'Connor refers to them. He introduces them with an indefinite noun phrase: <u>*Great Blue Herons* live</u>. Now that they are on stage, he switches to a definite noun phrase: <u>*the herons* head</u>. At this point he wants to refer to a subset of those herons, so he introduces just these ones with the indefinite article: *A few come to Cape Cod*. He refers to that subset a second time, and so it's time to switch back to the definite: *Most of these herons*. Then he makes a rare slip: he tells us that *herons*—indefinite—can avoid the dangers of migration. Since these are herons he introduced us to a few sentences ago, the ones who stop in Cape Cod rather than continuing farther south, I say it should be *The herons* or *These herons*.

After the interlude of the paragraph whose topic is winter, which introduces yet another subset of herons (the hypothetical ones who aren't booking a return trip), we need a reset, and so it's indefinite *Herons* again; on next mention they can safely be identified with the pronoun *they*. The kitten-eating heron is different from the rest, and he's introduced with indefinite *One hungry heron*, followed by a reference back to the little-bird-eating herons; we've already met them, so they're *the herons*, their identity further pinpointed by a reduced relative clause *[that were] eating small birds*.

Pay attention as well to what O'Connor does *not* do as he repeatedly refers to the herons. Other than shifting from *Great Blue Herons* to *herons*, he doesn't strain for new ways of referring to the birds. The herons are herons; they don't turn into *Ardea herodias*, long-legged waders, azure airborne avians, or sapphire sentinels of the skies. Many style experts warn against the compulsion to name things with different words when they are mentioned multiple times. Henry Fowler, author of *Modern English Usage* (next to Strunk and White, the most influential style manual of the twentieth century), sarcastically stigmatized the practice as "elegant variation." Theodore Bernstein called it monologophobia, the fear of using the same word twice, and synonymomania, the "compulsion to call a spade successively *a garden implement* and *an earth-turning tool*." Newspaper editors sometimes warn their writers that if they obey the opposing guideline "Don't use a word twice on one page" they are likely to slip into journalese, peppering their prose with words that journalists use but that people never say, such as the nouns *blaze, eatery, moniker, vehicle, slaying,* and *white stuff* (snow), and the verbs *pen, quaff, slate, laud, boast* (have), and *sport* (wear).

In fairness to journalists and other synonymomaniacs, there are times when a writer really does need to avoid repeating words in close succession. Take the second sentence in the preceding paragraph, in which I switched from *herons* to *birds*. The alternative would have been "Other than shifting from *Great Blue Herons* to *herons,* he doesn't strain for new ways of referring to the herons." That third "herons" is clunky, even confusing, for the same reason that repeating the name *Stanley Goldfarb* in the funeral joke would have been confusing. Or consider the sentence from the Wikipedia entry on Oedipus: *The baby, he says, was given to him by another shepherd from the Laius household, who had been told to get rid of the child.* The entry uses "the child" because a second mention of "the baby" would not have worked. When a noun is repeated in quick succession, readers may assume that the second mention refers to a different individual and fruitlessly scan the stage for him. They do this because the natural way to refer to an individual a second time is with a pronoun, the word that signals, "You know who this guy is." But sometimes a pronoun doesn't work—in the Oedipus sentence, *get rid of him* would have left it unclear who *him* was referring to—and in that case a generic definite noun phrase like *the child* or *the birds* can serve as an honorary pronoun.

So which guideline should a writer follow, "Avoid elegant variation" or "Don't use a word twice on one page"? Traditional style guides don't resolve the contradiction, but psycholinguistics can help.[9] Wording should not be varied capriciously, because in general people assume that if someone uses two different words they're referring to two different things. And as we shall soon see, wording should *never* be varied when a writer is comparing or contrasting two things. But wording *should* be varied when an entity is referred to multiple times in quick succession and repeating the name would sound monotonous or would misleadingly suggest that a new actor had entered the scene.

When wording is varied, only certain variations will be easy for the reader to track. The second label is acting as a pseudo-pronoun, so it should be pronounish in two ways. First, it should be more generic than the original noun, applying to a larger class of entities; that's why the first of these two sequences (which were used in an experiment on understanding stories) is easier to understand than the second:

A bus came roaring around a corner. The vehicle nearly flattened a pedestrian.

A vehicle came roaring around a corner. The bus nearly flattened a pedestrian.

Also, the second label should easily call to mind the first one, so that readers don't have to rack their brains figuring out who or what the writer is talking about. A bus is a typical example of a vehicle, so the backward association from *vehicle* to *bus* is effortless. But if the first sentence had been *A tank came roaring around the corner,* which refers to an atypical example of a vehicle, a reader would have had a harder time making the connection. One of the reasons that O'Connor avoided referring to the herons as *birds* is that a heron is not a typical example of a bird, so readers would not have readily thought "heron" when they saw the word *bird*. It would be another thing if the column had been about sparrows.

In chapter 2 I promised to explain what zombie nouns like *anticipation* and *cancellation* (as opposed to *anticipate* and *cancel*) are doing in the English language. The main answer is that they serve the same role as the pronouns, definite articles, and generic synonyms we have just examined: they allow a writer to refer to something a second time (in this case a situation or an event rather than a person or a thing) without tedium or confusing repetition. Suppose we begin a passage with *The governor canceled the convention today.* At this point it's more coherent to continue it with *The cancellation was unexpected* than with *It was unexpected that the governor would cancel the convention* or *The fact that the governor canceled the convention was unexpected.* So zombie nouns do have their place in the language. The problem with them is that knowledge-cursed writers use them on first mention because they, the writers, have already been thinking about the event, so it's old hat to them and is conveniently summarized by a noun. They forget that their readers are encountering the event for the first time and need to see it enacted with their own eyes.

In addition to a consistent thread of sentence topics and an orderly way of referring to repeated appearances, there is a third arc of coherence spanning sentences, and that is the logical relationship between one proposition and another. Let's go back to some examples from the chapter opening. What's so confusing about this sequence?

> It's an advantage for herons to avoid the dangers of migration. Herons head south when the cold weather arrives.

And what's so funny about these?

> The patient has been depressed ever since she began seeing me in 2008.
> Miss Charlene Mason sang, "I Will Not Pass This Way Again," giving obvious pleasure to the congregation.

In the doctored passage about herons, the second sentence is a non sequitur: we can't understand why the author is telling us that the birds migrate south just after saying that herons should avoid the dangers of migration. In the original passage, the two statements appeared in the opposite order, and the author connected them with the sentence noting that a few herons come to Cape Cod, where the winters are not too cold. That sentence lays out two arcs of logical coherence: Cape Cod is an *example* of southward migration, and the fact that its winters are not too cold is an *explanation* of why some herons end up there. Readers might still expect herons to choose a warmer destination than Cape Cod—it may not be as cold as some places, but it's a lot colder than others—so in his next sentence O'Connor acknowledges this *violated expectation* and supplies two explanations for the anomaly. One is that some herons (the young and inexperienced ones) may arrive on Cape Cod by accident. The other is that wintering at a relatively northern latitude has advantages that make up for the disadvantage of its coldness. O'Connor then *elaborates* on this explanation (that there are compensating advantages) with two specific advantages: it's safer not to travel far, and the local herons have first dibs on the breeding grounds come spring.

Now let's turn to the bloopers. The psychiatrist who wrote the first blooper presumably intended his second clause to convey a *temporal sequence* between two events: the patient saw the doctor, and since that time she has been depressed. We interpret it as a *cause-and-effect* sequence: she saw the doctor, and that made her depressed. In the second blooper, the problem does not lie in the relationship between clauses— it's cause-and-effect in both interpretations—but in exactly what causes what. In the intended reading, the pleasure is caused by the singing; in the unintended one, it's caused by the not-passing-this-way-again.

Examples, explanations, violated expectations, elaborations, sequences, causes, and effects are arcs of coherence that pinpoint how one statement follows from another. They are not so much components of language as components of *reason,* identifying the ways in which one idea can lead to another in our train of thought. You might think there are hundreds or even thousands of ways in which one thought can lead to another, but in fact the number is far smaller. David Hume, in his 1748 book, *An Enquiry Concerning Human Understanding,* wrote, "There appear to be only three principles of connections among ideas, namely *Resemblance, Contiguity* in time or place, and *Cause* or *Effect.*"[10] The linguist Andrew Kehler argues that Hume basically got it right, though he and other linguists have subdivided Hume's Big Three into about a dozen more specific kinds of connection.[11] And more to the point for the language of coherence, they have shown how the connections among ideas are expressed as connections among sentences. The key linguistic couplers are connective words like *because, so,* and *but.* Let's take a look at the logic of the coherence relations and how they're typically expressed.

In a resemblance relation, a statement makes a claim that overlaps in content with the one that came before it. The most obvious two are similarity and contrast:

Coherence Relation	Example	Typical Connectives
Similarity	Herons live in the northern United States. Herons live in most of Canada.	*and, similarly, likewise, too*
Contrast	Herons have one thing in their favor: they are opportunistic hunters. Herons have one thing not in their favor: they defend a fishing hole even when it is frozen.	*but, in contrast, on the other hand, alternatively*

Similarity and contrast link two propositions that are similar in most ways but different in at least one way. They call the reader's attention either to the similarities or to the difference. These relations may be conveyed without even using a connective word: all the writer has to do is write the statements using parallel syntax and vary only the words that indicate the difference. Unfortunately, many writers blow the opportunity and capriciously vary their wording as they compare two things, a pernicious kind of synonymomania which flummoxes the reader because he doesn't know whether the writer is directing his attention to the difference between the contrasting things or to some difference between the synonyms. Imagine that O'Connor had written *Herons are opportunistic hunters, but great blues defend a fishing hole even when it's frozen.* The reader would wonder whether it's only great blue herons that defend frozen fishing holes, or all herons.

It's always surprising to me to see how often scientists thoughtlessly use synonyms in comparisons, because the cardinal principle of experimental design is the Rule of One Variable. If you want to see the effects of a putative causal variable, manipulate that variable alone while holding everything else constant. (If you want to see whether a drug lowers blood pressure, don't enroll your participants in an exercise program at the same time, because if their blood pressure does go down, you'll never know whether it was the drug or the exercise.)

Parallel syntax is just the Rule of One Variable applied to writing: if you want readers to appreciate some variable, manipulate the expression of that variable alone while keeping the rest of the language unchanged. On the left below are two examples—the first expressing similarity, the second expressing contrast—in which scientists do in their prose what they would never do in the lab. On the right are the more rigorously controlled alternatives:

In the ten nations with the largest online populations, non-domestic news sites represent less than 8% of the 50 most visited news sites, while in France, 98% of all visits to news sources are directed to domestic sites.	In the ten nations with the largest online populations, non-domestic news sites represent less than 8% of the 50 most visited news sites; in France, the figure is just 2%.
Children's knowledge of how to use tools could be a result of experience, but also object affordances defined by shape and manipulability may provide cues such that humans do not require much time experimenting with an object in order to discover how it functions.	Children's knowledge of how to use a tool could be a result of their experience with the tool; alternatively, it could be a result of their perceiving the tool's affordances from shape and manipulability cues.

The first sentence, which says that most Internet users go to news sites in their own country, subverts its attempt to express a resemblance relation in three ways. It inverts the syntax (*news sites represent* versus *visits to news sources*), it flips the measurement scale (from the percentage of visits to *non*-domestic sites to the percentage of visits to *domestic* sites), and it uses a connective that is perversely ambiguous. If *while* is used in a temporal sense ("at the same time"), it implies similarity; if it is used in a logical sense ("although"), it suggests contrast. Rereading the passage a few times reveals that the authors meant similarity.

The second example also trips over its message. It upends the syntax from one proposition to the other (*Children know how to use tools from experience* and *Object affordances provide cues [to children about tools]*), and it uses the connective *also* in a confusing way. *Also* implies similarity or elaboration (another resemblance relation, which we'll get to soon), and the author uses it here to mean that there are at least two hypotheses for how children know how to use tools (rather than the single hypothesis that they know from experience). But he is actually trying to *contrast* the two hypotheses, so *also* pulls the reader in the wrong direction (the author presumably chose it because there is "also" another hypothesis on the table for scientists to consider). The author seems to realize the problem as he proceeds, so he tacks on *such that* to signal that he is contrasting the two hypotheses after all. But it would have been better to rewrite the sentence to convey the contrast from the start, using an unambiguous connective such as *alternatively*. (*Affordance*, by the way, is a psychologist's term for the aspect of an object's appearance that suggests what you can do to it, such as its lift-ability or its squeezability.)

Similarity and contrast are not the only resemblance relations. In *elaboration,* a single event is first described in a generic way and then in specific detail. Then there are four relations that fall into two neat pairs, depending on which event the author wishes to mention first. There's *exemplification* (a generalization, followed by one or more examples) and *generalization* (one or more examples, followed by a generalization). And there's the opposite, *exception,* which can be introduced either generalization first or exception first.

Coherence Relation	Example	Typical Connectives
Elaboration	Herons have one thing in their favor: they are total opportunists.	: (colon), *that is, in other words, which is to say, also, furthermore, in addition, notice that, which*
Exemplification	Herons are total opportunists. When the fish are frozen out, they'll eat other things, including crustaceans, mice, voles, and small birds.	*for example, for instance, such as, including*

Coherence Relation	Example	Typical Connectives
Generalization	When the fish are frozen out, herons will eat other things, including crustaceans, mice, voles, and small birds. They are total opportunists.	*in general, more generally*
Exception: generalization first	Cape Cod winters are often mild and pleasant. Then there is this winter, the winter that never ends.	*however, on the other hand, then there is*
Exception: exception first	This winter seems like it will never end. Nonetheless, Cape Cod winters are often mild and pleasant.	*nonetheless, nevertheless, still*

The second of Hume's family of relations is contiguity: a before-and-after sequence, usually with some connection between the two events. Here, too, the English language gives us the means to mention the events in either order while holding the meaning constant.

Coherence Relation	Example	Typical Connectives
Sequence: before-and-after	The cold weather arrives and then the herons head south.	*and, before, then*
Sequence: after-and-before	The herons head south when the cold weather arrives.	*after, once, while, when*

The language gives writers a second way of controlling the order in which two events are mentioned. Not only can they choose between *before* and *after*, but they can also choose whether to prepose a temporal modifier or leave it in its place: *After the cold weather arrives, the herons head south* versus *The herons head south after the cold weather arrives.*

But here the language may be a bit too clever for its own users. Though English cleanly distinguishes the order in which two things happened in the world from the order in which they are mentioned in a text, English *speakers* tend to be more concrete, and naturally assume that the order in which events are mentioned is the order in which they took place (as in the old wisecrack *They got married and had a baby, but not in that order*). All things being equal, it's good for a writer to work with the ongoing newsreel in readers' minds and describe events in chronological order: *She showered before she ate* is easier to understand than *She ate after she showered.* For the same reason, *After she showered, she ate* is easier than *Before she ate, she showered.*[12] Of course, things are not always equal. If the spotlight of attention has been lingering on a later event, and now the writer must introduce an earlier one, the imperative to mention given before new trumps the imperative to mention early before late. For example, if you had been staring at the wet footprints leading to the breakfast table and were seeking an explanation, it would be more helpful to hear *Before Rita ate, she showered* than *After Rita showered, she ate.*

And this brings us to Hume's third category of connections, cause and effect. Here again the English language is mathematically elegant and provides the writer with a neat group of symmetries. She can state the cause first or the effect first, and the causal force can either make something happen or prevent it from happening.

Coherence Relation	Example	Typical Connectives
Result (cause-effect)	Young herons are inexperienced, so some of them migrate to Cape Cod.	*and, as a result, therefore, so*
Explanation (effect-cause)	Some herons migrate to Cape Cod, because they are young and inexperienced.	*because, since, owing to*

Coherence Relation	Example	Typical Connectives
Violated expectation (preventer-effect)	Herons have a tough time when the ponds freeze over. However, they will hunt and eat many other things.	*but, while, however, nonetheless, yet*
Failed prevention (effect-preventer)	Herons will hunt and eat many things in winter, even though the ponds are frozen over.	*despite, even though*

One other major coherence relation doesn't easily fit into Hume's trichotomy, *attribution:* so-and-so believes such-and-such. Attribution is typically indicated by connectives like *according to* and *stated that.* It's important to get it right. In many written passages it's unclear whether the author is arguing for a position or is explaining a position that someone else is arguing for. This is one of the many problems in Bob Dole's sentence about intervening in Serbia (page 112).

There are a few other coherence relations, such as anticipations of a reaction by the reader (*yes; I know, I know*). There are also gray areas and various ways to lump and split the relations, which give linguists plenty of things to argue about.[13] But these dozen or so cover most of the territory. A coherent text is one in which the reader always knows which coherence relation holds between one sentence and the next. In fact, coherence extends beyond individual sentences and also applies to entire branches in the discourse tree (in other words, to items in an essay outline). Several propositions may be interconnected by a set of coherence relations, and the resulting chunk is in turn connected to others. For example, the heron chowing down feral kittens was *similar* to the herons eating crustaceans, mice, and small birds. The entire set of these meals is now united as a single block of text which serves as an *exemplification* of herons eating things other than fish. And their ability to eat nonfishy meals is, in turn, an *elaboration* of their being opportunistic hunters.

Coherence relations among sets of sentences need not be perfectly treelike. They also drape across long stretches of text. The odd behavior of defending a frozen fishing hole connects all the way back to the reader's question at the beginning of the column. It is an *explanation,* a cause of the effect she was asking about.

As a writer bangs out sentences, she needs to ensure that her readers can reconstruct the coherence relations she has in mind. The obvious way to do this is to use the appropriate connectives. The "typical" connectives in the charts, however, are only typical, and writers can leave them out when the connection is obvious to the reader. It's an important choice. Too many connectives can make it seem as if an author is belaboring the obvious or patronizing the reader, and it can give prose a pedantic feel. Just imagine the sequence *Herons live in the northern United States; similarly, herons live in most of Canada.* Or *Herons have one thing in their favor. . . . In contrast, herons have one thing not in their favor.* Too few connectives, on the other hand, can leave the reader puzzled as to how one statement follows from the last.

Even more challenging, the optimal number of connectives depends on the expertise of the reader.[14] Readers who are familiar with the subject matter will already know a lot about what is similar to what else, what causes what else, and what tends to accompany what else, and they don't need to have these connections spelled out in so many words. They may even get confused if the writer spells out the obvious ones: they figure that she must have a good reason to do so and therefore that she must really be making some *other* claim, one that isn't so obvious, which they then waste time trying to discern. In the case of where herons live, most readers know that the northern United States is contiguous to Canada and that the two have similar ecosystems, so they don't need a *similarly.* If the author had mentioned less familiar birds and territories—say, that crested honey buzzards live in Yakutsk and Shenyang—the reader might appreciate being told whether the territories are similar, which would imply that the species is adapted to a specific ecosystem, or dissimilar, implying that it is widespread and flexible.

Figuring out the right level of explicitness for coherence relations is a major reason that a writer needs to think hard about the state of knowledge of her readers and show a few of them a draft to see whether she got it right. It's an aspect of the art of writing which depends on intuition, experience, and guesswork, but there is also an overarching guideline. Humans are cursed with attributing too much of their own knowledge to others (chapter 3), which means that overall there is a greater danger of prose being confusing because it has too few connectives than pedantic because it has too many. When in doubt, connect.

If you do indicate a connection, though, do it just once. Prose becomes stuffy when an insecure writer hammers the reader over the head with redundant indicators of a connection, as if unsure that one would be enough.

Perhaps <u>the reason</u> so many people are in the dark is <u>because</u> they want it that way. [explanation]	Perhaps the reason so many people are in the dark is that they want it that way.
There are many biological influences of psychological traits <u>such as</u> cognitive ability, conscientiousness, impulsivity, risk aversion, <u>and the like</u>. [exemplification]	There are many biological influences of psychological traits such as cognitive ability, conscientiousness, impulsivity, and risk aversion.
We <u>separately</u> measured brainwide synchronization in local <u>versus</u> long-range channel pairs. [contrast]	We separately measured brainwide synchronization in local and long-range channel pairs.

The first redundancy, *the reason is because,* is widely disliked, because the word *reason* already implies that we are dealing with an explanation, and we don't need a *because* to remind us. (Some purists also frown on *the reason why,* but it has been used by good writers for centuries and should be no more exceptionable than *the place where* or *the time when.*) Gratuitous redundancy makes prose difficult not just because readers have to duplicate the effort of figuring something out, but because they naturally assume that when a writer says two things she means two things, and fruitlessly search for the nonexistent second point.

Coherence connectives are the unsung heroes of lucid prose. They aren't terribly frequent—most of them occur just a handful of times every 100,000 words—but they are the cement of reasoning and one of the most difficult yet most important tools of writing to master. A recent analysis of underperforming high school students showed that many of them, even those who read well, were stymied by the challenge of writing a coherent passage.[15] One student, asked to write an essay on Alexander the Great, managed to come up with "I think Alexander the Great was one of the best military leaders," then turned to her mother and said, "Well, I got a sentence down. What now?" A failure to command coherence connectives turned out to be among the skills that most sharply differentiated the struggling students from their successful peers. When these students were asked to read *Of Mice and Men* and complete a sentence beginning with "Although George," many were stumped. A few wrote, "Although George and Lenny were friends." The teachers introduced a program that explicitly trained the students to construct coherent arguments, with a focus on the connections between successive ideas. It was a radical shift from the kind of assignment that dominates high school writing instruction today, in which students are asked to write memoirs and personal reflections. The students showed dramatic improvements in their test scores in several subjects, and many more of them graduated from high school and applied to college.

It's no coincidence that we use the word "coherent" to refer both to concrete passages of text and to abstract lines of reasoning, because the logical relations that govern them—implication, generalization, counterexample, denial, causation—are the same. Though the claim that good prose leads to good thinking is not always true (brilliant thinkers can be clumsy writers, and slick writers can be glib thinkers), it may be true when it comes to the mastery of coherence. If you try to repair an incoherent text and find that no placement of *therefore*s and *moreover*s and *however*s will hold it together, that is a sign that the underlying argument may be incoherent, too.

———

Coherence depends on more than mechanical decisions such as keeping the topic in subject position and choosing appropriate connectives. It depends as well on impressions that build up in a reader over the course of reading many paragraphs and that depend on the author's grasp of the text as a whole.

Let me explain what I mean by sharing my reaction to another passage, this one much loftier in tone and ambition than "Ask the Bird Folks." It is the opening of John Keegan's 1993 magnum opus, *A History of Warfare*:

> War is not the continuation of policy by other means. The world would be a simpler place to understand if this dictum of Clausewitz's were true. Clausewitz, a Prussian veteran of the Napoleonic wars who used his years of retirement to compose what was destined to become the most famous book on war—called *On War*—ever written, actually wrote that war is the continuation "of political intercourse" (*des politischen Verkehrs*) "with the intermixing of other means" (*mit Einmischung anderer Mittel*). The original German expresses a more subtle and complex idea than the English words in which it is so frequently quoted. In either form, however, Clausewitz's thought is incomplete. It implies the existence of states, of state interests and of rational calculation about how they may be achieved. Yet war antedates the state, diplomacy and strategy by many millennia. Warfare is almost as old as man himself, and reaches into the most secret places of the human heart, places where self dissolves rational purpose, where pride reigns, where emotion is paramount, where instinct is king. "Man is a political animal," said Aristotle. Clausewitz, a child of Aristotle, went no further than to say that a political animal is a warmaking animal. Neither dared confront the thought that man is a thinking animal in whom the intellect directs the urge to hunt and the ability to kill.[16]

Keegan is among the most esteemed military historians who ever lived, and *A History of Warfare* was a critically acclaimed bestseller. Several reviews singled out the quality of his writing for praise. Certainly the mechanics here are sound, and at first glance, so is the coherence. The topics are war and Clausewitz, and we have a number of connectives, like *however* and *yet*. Nonetheless, I found this paragraph barely coherent.

The problems begin in the first sentence. Why is a book on warfare starting out by telling us what war is *not*? I recognized the dictum from Clausewitz, but it was hardly uppermost in my mind as I began a book on war, if for no other reason than that I always found it obscure—an impression confirmed by Keegan's equivocating explanation in the third and fourth sentences. If Clausewitz's dictum is so subtle, complex, and misunderstood, how is the reader being enlightened by being told it is false? And if even the people who are familiar with the dictum don't know what it means, how could the world be "simpler" if it were true? For that matter, *is* the dictum false? Keegan now tells us that it's merely "incomplete." Should he have begun, "War is not *just* the continuation of policy by other means"?

OK, I tell myself, I'll wait for the rest of the explanation. Soon we are told that war reaches into a place where emotion is paramount, where instinct is king. But two sentences later we're told that the instinct to hunt and kill is directed by the intellect. These can't both be true: kings don't take orders, so instinct cannot be a king *and* be directed by the intellect. Let's go with the last thing we were told and assume it's the intellect that's in charge. So what part of this thought did Clausewitz and Aristotle (and what's *he* suddenly doing in this conversation?) fail to confront: the fact that man is a thinking animal, or the fact that what he thinks about is how to hunt and kill?

The confusing opening of *A History of Warfare* provides us with an opportunity to look at three other contributors to coherence, which are conspicuous here by their absence: clear and plausible negation, a sense of proportion, and thematic consistency.

The first problem is Keegan's maladroit use of negation. Logically speaking, a sentence with a naysaying word like *not, no, neither, nor,* or *never* is just the mirror image of an affirmative sentence. Saying that the integer 4 is not odd is logically the same as saying that it is even. If something is not alive, then it's dead, and vice versa. But psychologically speaking, a negative statement and an affirmative statement are fundamentally different.[17]

More than three centuries ago, Baruch Spinoza pointed out that the human mind cannot suspend disbelief in the truth or falsity of a statement and leave it hanging in logical limbo awaiting a "true" or "false" tag to be hung on it.[18] To hear or read a statement is to believe it, at least for a moment. For us to conclude that something is *not* the case, we must take the extra cognitive step of pinning the mental tag "false" on a proposition. Any statement that is untagged is treated as if it is true. As a result, when we have a lot on our minds, we can get confused about where the "false" tag belongs, or can forget it entirely. In that case what is merely mentioned can become true. Richard Nixon did not allay suspicions about his character when he declared, "I am not a crook," nor did Bill Clinton put rumors to rest when he said, "I did not have sexual relations with that woman." Experiments have shown that when jurors are told to disregard the witness's remarks, they never do, any more than you can follow the instruction "For the next minute, try not to think about a white bear."[19]

The cognitive difference between believing that a proposition is true (which requires no work beyond understanding it) and believing that it is false (which requires adding and remembering a mental tag) has enormous implications for a writer. The most obvious is that a negative statement such as *The king is not dead* is harder on the reader than an affirmative one like *The king is alive.*[20] Every negation requires mental homework, and when a sentence contains many of them the reader can be overwhelmed. Even worse, a sentence can have more negations than you think it does. Not all negation words begin with *n*; many have the concept of negation tucked inside them, such as *few, little, least, seldom, though, rarely, instead, doubt, deny, refute, avoid,* and *ignore.*[21] The use of multiple negations in a sentence (like the ones on the left below) is arduous at best and bewildering at worst:

According to the latest annual report on violence, Sub-Saharan Africa for the first time is <u>not</u> the world's <u>least</u> peaceful region.	According to the latest annual report on violence, Sub-Saharan Africa for the first time is not the world's most violent region.
The experimenters found, <u>though</u>, that the infants did <u>not</u> respond as predicted to the appearance of the ball, but <u>instead</u> did <u>not</u> look significantly longer than they did when the objects were <u>not</u> swapped.	The experimenters predicted that the infants would look longer at the ball if it had been swapped with another object than if it had been there all along. In fact, the infants looked at the balls the same amount of time in each case.
The three-judge panel issued a ruling <u>lifting</u> the <u>stay</u> on a district judge's injunction to <u>not</u> enforce the <u>ban</u> on same-sex marriages.	The three-judge panel issued a ruling that allows same-sex marriages to take place. There had been a ban on such marriages, and a district judge had issued an injunction not to enforce it, but a stay had been placed on that injunction. Today the panel lifted the stay.

As the Duchess in *Alice in Wonderland* explained, "The moral of that is—'Be what you would seem to be'—or, if you'd like it put more simply—'Never imagine yourself not to be otherwise than what it might appear to others that what you were or might have been was not otherwise than what you had been would have appeared to them to be otherwise.'"

It's not just readers who are confused by negations. Writers themselves can lose track and put too many of them into a word or sentence, making it mean the opposite of what they intended. The linguist Mark Liberman calls them misnegations, and points out that "they're easy to fail to miss".[22]

After a couple of days in Surry County, I found myself no less closer
   to unraveling the riddle.

No head injury is too trivial to ignore.

It is difficult to underestimate Paul Fussell's influence.

Patty looked for an extension cord from one of the many still unpacked
   boxes.

You'll have to unpeel those shrimp yourself.

Can you help me unloosen this lid?

The difficulty posed by negations has long been noted in style manuals.
Dave Barry's "Ask Mr. Language Person" satirized their typical advisory:

> WRITING TIP FOR PROFESSIONALS: To make your writing more
> appealing to the reader, avoid "writing negatively." Use positive
> expressions instead.
> WRONG: "Do not use this appliance in the bathtub."
> RIGHT: "Go ahead and use this appliance in the bathtub."

The satire makes a serious point. Like most advice on style that is
couched as a commandment rather than an explanation, the flat directive to avoid negations is almost useless. As Mr. Language Person implies,
sometimes a writer really does need to express a negation. How long
could you go in a day without using the words *no* and *not*? The sarcastic question "What part of 'NO' don't you understand?" reminds us that
negation is perfectly easy for people to handle in everyday speech. Why
should it be so hard in writing?

The answer is that negation is easy to understand when the proposition being negated is plausible or tempting.[23] Compare the negations
in these two columns:

A whale is not a fish.	A herring is not a mammal.
Barack Obama is not a Muslim.	Hillary Clinton is not a Muslim.
Vladimir Nabokov never won a Nobel Prize.	Vladimir Nabokov never won an Oscar.

The sentences in the left-hand column all deny a proposition that it would be reasonable for readers to entertain. A whale looks like a big fish; Obama has been the subject of rumors about his religion; Nabokov was denied the Nobel Prize in Literature that many critics thought he deserved. Experiments have shown that statements like the ones in the left column, which deny a plausible belief, are easier to understand than statements in the right column, which deny an implausible belief. The first reaction to reading a sentence on the right is, "Who would ever have thought it was?" (Or she was? Or he did?) Negative sentences are easy when the reader already has an affirmative in mind or can create one on short notice; all he has to do is pin a "false" tag onto it. But concocting a statement that you have trouble believing in the first place (such as "A herring is a mammal"), and then negating it, requires two bouts of cognitive heavy lifting rather than one.

And now we see why the opening to *A History of Warfare* is so puzzling. Keegan began by denying a proposition that was not particularly compelling to the reader in the first place (and which became no more compelling upon further explanation). The same is true for the two baffling sentences I used on page 140, the ones about moderate drinkers and Serbian intervention. In all these cases, the reader is apt to think, "Who ever thought it was?" When an author has to negate something that a reader doesn't already believe, she has to set it up as a plausible belief on his mental stage before she knocks it down. Or, to put it more positively, when a writer wants to negate an unfamiliar proposition, she should unveil the negation in two stages:

1. You might think . . .
2. But no.

That's what I did in repairing the sentences on page 141.

The other feature of negation that Keegan mishandled is making the negation unambiguous, which requires nailing down two things: its *scope* and its *focus*.[24] The scope of a logical operator such as *not, all,* or *some* consists of the exact proposition it pertains to. When the

Boston–New York train arrives at smaller stations along the route, the conductor announces, "All doors will not open." I momentarily panic, thinking that we're trapped. Of course what he means is that not all doors will open. In the intended reading, the negation operator *not* has scope over the universally quantified proposition "All doors will open." The conductor means, "It is <u>not</u> the case that [<u>all</u> doors will open]." In the unintended reading, the universal quantifier *all* has scope over the negated proposition "Doors will not open." Claustrophobic passengers hear it as "For <u>all</u> doors, it is the case that [the door will <u>not</u> open]."

The conductor is not making a grammatical error. It's common in colloquial English for a logical word like *all, not,* or *only* to cling to the left of the verb even when its scope encompasses a different phrase.[25] In the train announcement, the *not* has no logical business being next to *open;* its logical scope is *All doors will open,* so it really belongs outside the clause, before *All.* But English is more flexible than what a logician would have designed, and the context generally makes it clear what the speaker means. (No one on the train but me seemed in any way alarmed.) Similarly, a logician might say that the song "I Only Have Eyes for You" should be retitled "I Have Eyes for Only You," because the singer has more than just eyes, and he uses those eyes for more than ogling someone; it's just that when he does ogle someone with those eyes, it's you he ogles. Likewise, the logician would argue, *You only live once* should be rewritten as *You live only once,* with *only* next to the thing it quantifies, *once.*

This logician would be unbearably pedantic, but there is a grain of good taste in the pedantry. Writing is often clearer and more elegant when a writer pushes an *only* or a *not* next to the thing that it quantifies. In 1962 John F. Kennedy declared, "We choose to go to the moon not because it is easy but because it is hard."[26] That sounds a lot classier than "We don't choose to go to the moon because it is easy but because it is hard." Not only is it classier; it's clearer. Whenever a sentence has a *not* and a *because,* and the *not* remains stuck to the auxiliary verb, readers may be left in the dark about the scope of the negation and hence about what the sentence means. Suppose that Kennedy had said,

"We don't choose to go to the moon because it is easy." Listeners would not have known whether Kennedy was choosing to scuttle the moon program (because it was too easy) or whether he was choosing to go ahead with the moon program (but for some reason other than how easy it was). Pushing the *not* next to the phrase it negates eliminates the scope ambiguity. Here's a rule: Never write a sentence of the form "X not Y because Z," such as *Dave is not evil because he did what he was told*. It should be either *Dave is not evil, because he did what he was told*, where the comma keeps the *because* outside the scope of the *not*, or *Dave is evil not because he did what he was told* (but for some other reason), where the *because* occurs next to the *not*, indicating that it *is* within its scope.

When a negative element has wide scope (that is, when it applies to the whole clause), it is not literally ambiguous, but it can be maddeningly vague. The vagueness lies in the *focus* of the negation—which phrase the writer had in mind as falsifying the whole sentence. Take the sentence *I didn't see a man in a gray flannel suit*. It could mean:

I didn't see him; Amy did.
I *didn't* see him; you just thought I did.
I didn't *see* him; I was looking away.
I didn't see *him*; I saw a different man.
I didn't see a *man* in a gray suit; it was a woman.
I didn't see a man in a *gray* flannel suit; it was brown.
I didn't see a man in a gray *flannel* suit; it was polyester.
I didn't see a man in a gray flannel *suit*; he was wearing a kilt.

In conversation, we can stress the phrase we wish to deny, and in writing we can use italics to do the same thing. More often, the context makes it clear which affirmative statement was plausible in the first place, and hence which one the writer is going to the trouble of denying. But if the subject matter is unfamiliar and has many parts, and if the writer doesn't set the reader up by focusing on one of those parts as a fact worth taking seriously, the reader may not know what he should no longer be thinking. That is the problem with Keegan's puzzling speculation about the multipart thought that Clausewitz and Aristotle dared not confront, that man is a thinking animal in whom the intellect directs the urge to hunt and the ability to kill: were they spooked by the possibility that man thinks, that he's an animal, or that he thinks about hunting and killing?

Now let's give Keegan a chance to explain the thought. He does so in the book's second paragraph, which I'll use to illustrate, by its absence, another principle of coherence—a sense of proportion:

This is not an idea any easier for modern man to confront than it was for a Prussian officer, born the grandson of a clergyman and raised in the spirit of the eighteenth-century Enlightenment. For all the effect that Freud, Jung and Adler have had on our outlook, our moral values remain those of the great monotheistic religions, which condemn the killing of fellow souls in all but the most constrained circumstances. Anthropology tells us and archaeology implies that our uncivilised ancestors could be red in tooth and claw; psychoanalysis seeks to persuade us that the savage in all of us lurks not far below the skin. We prefer, none the less, to recognise human nature as we find it displayed in the everyday behaviour of the civilised majority in modern life—imperfect, no doubt, but certainly cooperative and frequently benevolent. Culture to us seems the great determinant of how human beings conduct themselves; in the relentless academic debate between "nature and nurture," it is the "nurture" school which commands greater support from the bystanders. We are cultural animals and it is the richness of our culture which allows us to accept our undoubted potentiality for violence but to believe nevertheless that its expression is a cultural aberration. History lessons remind us that the states in which we live, their institutions, even their laws, have come to us through conflict, often of the most bloodthirsty sort. Our daily diet of news brings us reports of the shedding of blood, often in regions quite close to our homelands, in circumstances that deny our conception of cultural normality altogether. We succeed, all the same, in consigning the lessons both of history and of reportage to a special and separate category of "otherness" which invalidate our expectations of how our own world will be tomorrow and the day after not at all. Our institutions and our laws, we tell ourselves, have set the human potentiality for violence about with such restraints that violence in everyday life will be punished as criminal by our laws, while its use by our institutions of state will take the particular form of "civilised warfare."[27]

I think I see what Keegan is getting at—humans have innate impulses toward violence, yet today we try to deny it—but the momentum of his presentation pushes in the other direction. Most of this passage says the opposite: that we *couldn't help* but be aware of humanity's dark side. Keegan loads us up with reminders of the dark side, including Freud, Jung, Adler, anthropology, archaeology, psychoanalysis, the savage in all of us, our undoubted potentiality for violence, history lessons about conflict, bloodthirsty violence, our daily diet of news, reports of the shedding of blood, the human potentiality for violence, and violence in everyday life. The reader starts to think, Who is this "we" who fail to appreciate them?

The problem here is a lack of balance, of proportionality. An important principle in composition is that the amount of verbiage one devotes to a point should not be too far out of line with how central it is to the argument. If a writer believes that 90 percent of the evidence and argument supports a position, then something like 90 percent of the discussion should be devoted to the reasons for believing it. If a reader is spending only 10 percent of his time on why it's a good idea, and fully 90 percent on why he might reasonably think it's a bad idea—while the writer insists all along that it really is a good idea—then the reader's mounting impressions will be at cross-purposes with the author's intent. The author then must furiously try to minimize what she has been saying, which only arouses the reader's suspicions. Keegan tries to dig himself out from under his own heap of counterevidence by repeatedly issuing pronouncements about what an unidentified "we" stubbornly and defensively believe—which only prompts the reader to think, "Speak for yourself!" The reader gets the feeling that he's being bullied rather than persuaded.

Of course, responsible writers have to deal with counterarguments and counterevidence. But if there are enough of them to merit an extended discussion, they deserve a section of their own, whose stated point is to examine the contrary position. A fair-minded examination of the counterevidence can then occupy as much space as it needs, because its bulk will reflect its importance *within that section*. This divide-and-conquer strategy is better than repeatedly allowing counterexamples to intrude into the main line of an argument while browbeating readers into looking away.

After a page-long digression on pacifism, Christianity, and the Roman Empire, Keegan returns to what is wrong with Clausewitz's dictum and with the modern understanding of war it captures. The passage will help us appreciate a third principle of text-wide coherence:

[Clausewitz's dictum] certainly distinguished sharply between the lawful bearer of arms and the rebel, the freebooter and the brigand. It presupposed a high level of military discipline and an awesome degree of obedience by subordinates to their lawful superiors. . . . It assumed that wars had a beginning and an end. What it made no allowance for at all was war without beginning or end, the endemic warfare of non-state, even pre-state peoples, in which there was no distinction between lawful and unlawful bearers of arms, since all males were warriors; a form of warfare which had prevailed during long periods of human history and which, at the margins, still encroached on the life of civilised states and was, indeed, turned to their use through the common practice of recruiting its practitioners as "irregular" light cavalry and infantrymen. . . . During the eighteenth century the expansion of such forces—Cossacks, "hunters," Highlanders, "borderers," Hussars—had been one of the most noted contemporary military developments. Over their habits of loot, pillage, rape, murder, kidnap, extortion and systematic vandalism their civilised employers chose to draw a veil.[28]

This is all quite fascinating, but over the next six pages the paragraphs jump around between descriptions of the Cossacks' way of war and still more exegesis of Clausewitz. Like the "we" of the second paragraph, who supposedly see plenty of violence while denying its importance, the hapless "Clausewitz" character in this narrative shows plenty of awareness of the Cossacks' cruel and cowardly ways, but, according to Keegan, he still failed to come to grips with them. Once again the bulk of the verbiage pushes in one direction while the content of the author's argument pushes in the other. Keegan concludes the section:

> It is at the cultural level that Clausewitz's answer to his question, What is war?, is defective. . . . Clausewitz was a man of his times, a child of the Enlightenment, a contemporary of the German Romantics, an intellectual, a practical reformer. . . . Had his mind been furnished with just one extra intellectual dimension . . . he might have been able to perceive that war embraces much more than politics: that it is always an expression of culture, often a determinant of cultural forms, in some societies the culture itself.[29]

Now, wait a minute! Didn't Keegan tell us in the second paragraph that the problem with Clausewitz and his heirs is that they all put *too much* stock in culture? Didn't he say that it's our culture which allows us to believe that violence is an aberration, and that the primitive warfare we choose to ignore is a manifestation of nature, biology, and instinct? Then how can Clausewitz's problem be that he didn't put *enough* stock in culture? For that matter, how can Clausewitz be a product both of the Enlightenment *and* of the German Romantic movement, which arose in reaction to the Enlightenment? And while we're at it, how can his being the grandson of a clergyman, and our moral values being those of the monotheistic religions, be reconciled with all of us being children of the Enlightenment, which *opposed* the monotheistic religions?

To be fair to Keegan, after reading his book I don't think he is quite as confused as the first few pages suggest. If you put aside the slaphappy allusions to grand intellectual movements, you can see that he does have a point, namely that the disciplined warfare of modern states is a departure from the opportunistic rapacity of traditional tribes, that traditional warfare has always been more common, and that it has never gone away. Keegan's problem is that he flouts another principle of coherence in writing, the last one we will visit in this chapter.

Joseph Williams refers to the principle as *consistent thematic strings,* thematic consistency for short.[30] A writer, after laying out her topic, will introduce a large number of concepts which explain, enrich, or comment on that topic. These concepts will center on a number of themes which make repeated appearances in the discussion. To keep the text coherent, the writer must allow the reader to keep track of these themes by referring to each in a consistent way or by explaining their connection. We looked at a version of this principle when we saw that to help the reader keep track of a single entity across multiple mentions, a writer should not flip-flop between unnecessary synonyms. Now we can generalize the principle to *sets* of related concepts, that is, to themes. The writer should refer to each theme in a consistent way, one that allows the reader to know which is which.

Here, then, is the problem. Keegan's topic is the history of warfare—that part is clear enough. His themes are the primitive form of warfare and the modern form of warfare. But he discusses the two themes by traipsing among a set of concepts that are only loosely related to the theme and to one another, each in a way that caught Keegan's eye but that is obscure to the whipsawed reader. With the benefit of hindsight, we can see that the concepts fall into two loose clusters, each corresponding to one of Keegan's themes:

| Clausewitz, modern warfare, states, political calculations, strategy, diplomacy, military discipline, "we," the intellect, Aristotle, the pacifist aspect of monotheistic religions, the criminal justice system, civilized constraints on warfare, the intellectualizing aspect of the Enlightenment, the ways in which culture constrains violence | Primitive warfare, tribes, clans, irregulars, freebooters, brigands, Cossacks, looting and pillaging, instinct, nature, Freud, the emphasis on instinct in psychoanalysis, anthropological evidence for violence, archaeological evidence for violence, conflict in history, crime in the news, the ways in which culture encourages violence |

We can also reconstruct why each term might have reminded him of some other term. But it's better when the common threads are made explicit, because in the vast private web of a writer's imagination, anything can be similar to anything else. Jamaica is like Cuba; both are Caribbean island nations. Cuba is like China; both are led by regimes that call themselves communist. But a discussion of "countries like Jamaica and China" which fails to identify their commonality—being similar in some way to Cuba—is bound to be incoherent.

How might an author have presented these themes in a more coherent way? In *The Remnants of War*, the political scientist John Mueller covers the same territory as Keegan and picks up where Keegan left off. He argues that modern war is becoming obsolete, leaving primitive, undisciplined warfare as the major kind of war remaining in the world today. But Mueller's exposition of the two themes is a model of coherence:

> Broadly speaking, there seem to be two methods for developing combat forces—for successfully cajoling or coercing collections of men into engaging in the violent, profane, sacrificial, uncertain, masochistic, and essentially absurd enterprise known as war. The two methods lead to two kinds of warfare, and the distinction can be an important one.
>
> Intuitively, it might seem that the easiest (and cheapest) method for recruiting combatants would be to ... enlist those

who revel in violence and routinely seek it out or who regularly employ it to enrich themselves, or both. We have in civilian life a name for such people—criminals. . . . Violent conflicts in which people like that dominate can be called criminal warfare, a form in which combatants are induced to wreak violence primarily for the fun and material profit they derive from the experience.

Criminal armies seem to arise from a couple of processes. Sometimes criminals—robbers, brigands, freebooters, highwaymen, hooligans, thugs, bandits, pirates, gangsters, outlaws—organize or join together in gangs or bands or mafias. When such organizations become big enough, they can look and act a lot like full-blown armies.

Or criminal armies can be formed when a ruler needs combatants to prosecute a war and concludes that the employment or impressment of criminals and thugs is the most sensible and direct method for accomplishing this. In this case, criminals and thugs essentially act as mercenaries.

It happens, however, that criminals and thugs tend to be undesirable warriors. . . . To begin with, they are often difficult to control. They can be troublemakers: unruly, disobedient, and mutinous, often committing unauthorized crimes while on (or off) duty that can be detrimental or even destructive of the military enterprise. . . .

Most importantly, criminals can be disinclined to stand and fight when things become dangerous, and they often simply desert when whim and opportunity coincide. Ordinary crime, after all, preys on the weak—on little old ladies rather than on husky athletes—and criminals often make willing and able executioners of defenseless people. However, if the cops show up they are given to flight. The motto for the criminal, after all, is not a variation of "Semper fi," "All for one and one for all," "Duty, honor, country," "Banzai," or "Remember Pearl Harbor," but "Take the money and run." . . .

These problems with the employment of criminals as combatants have historically led to efforts to recruit ordinary men as combatants—people who, unlike criminals and thugs, commit violence at no other time in their lives. . . .

   The result has been the development of disciplined warfare in which men primarily inflict violence not for fun and profit but because their training and indoctrination have instilled in them a need to follow orders; to observe a carefully contrived and tendentious code of honor; to seek glory and reputation in combat; to love, honor, or fear their officers; to believe in a cause; to fear the shame, humiliation, or costs of surrender; or, in particular, to be loyal to, and to deserve the loyalty of, their fellow combatants.[31]

There's no mistaking what the themes of Mueller's discussion are; he tells us in so many words. One of them he calls criminal warfare, and he then explores it in five consecutive paragraphs. He starts by reminding us what a criminal is, and explaining how criminal warfare works. The next two paragraphs elaborate on each of the ways in which criminal armies may form, and the two after that explain the two problems that criminal armies pose for their leaders, one problem per paragraph. These problems naturally lead Mueller to his second theme, disciplined warfare, and he explains that theme in the two consecutive paragraphs.

   The discussion of each theme coheres not just because it is localized in a string of consecutive paragraphs but because it refers to the theme using a set of transparently related terms. In one thematic string we have terms like *criminals, criminal warfare, crime, fun, profit, gangs, mafias, thugs, mercenaries, troublemakers, preys on the weak, executioners, violence, desertion, flight, whim, opportunity,* and *run.* In the other we have *ordinary men, training, indoctrination, honor, glory, reputation, shame, loyalty, code,* and *believe in a cause.* We don't have to puzzle over what the words in each cluster have to do with one another, as we did for Keegan's *Clausewitz, culture, states, policy, Enlightenment, political animal, criminal justice, monotheistic religions, Aristotle,* and so on. The threads that connect them are obvious.

   The thematic coherence in Mueller's exposition is a happy consequence of his use of classic style, particularly the imperative to show rather than tell. As soon as we see the thugs preying on little old ladies and fleeing when the cops show up, we appreciate how an army composed of such men would operate. We also see how the leader of a modern state would seek a more reliable way to deploy muscle to advance its interests, namely by developing a well-trained modern army. We can even understand how, for these modern states, war can become the continuation of policy by other means.

In all of my previous examples of bad writing I picked on easy marks: deadline-pressured journalists, stuffy academics, corporate hacks, the occasional inexperienced student. How could a seasoned author like John Keegan, a man who shows frequent flashes of writerly flair, serve as a model of incoherent writing, comparing badly with a guy who sells birdseed on Cape Cod? Part of the answer is that male readers will put up with a lot in a book called *A History of Warfare*. But most of the problem comes from the very expertise that made Keegan so qualified to write his books. Immersed as he was in the study of war, he became a victim of professional narcissism, and was apt to confuse the History of Warfare with the History of a Man in My Field Who Gets Quoted a Lot about Warfare. And after a lifetime of scholarship he was so laden with erudition that his ideas came avalanching down faster than he could organize them.

There is a big difference between a coherent passage of writing and a flaunting of one's erudition, a running journal of one's thoughts, or a published version of one's notes. A coherent text is a designed object: an ordered tree of sections within sections, crisscrossed by arcs that track topics, points, actors, and themes, and held together by connectors that tie one proposition to the next. Like other designed objects, it comes about not by accident but by drafting a blueprint, attending to details, and maintaining a sense of harmony and balance.

Chapter 6

TELLING RIGHT
FROM WRONG

HOW TO MAKE SENSE OF THE RULES OF CORRECT
GRAMMAR, WORD CHOICE, AND PUNCTUATION

Many people have strong opinions on the quality of language today. They write books and articles deploring it, fire off letters to the editor, and call in to radio talk shows with their criticisms and complaints. I have found that few of these objections single out clarity or grace or coherence. Their concern is *correct usage*—rules of proper English such as these:

- The word *less* may not be used for countable items, as in the sign over the supermarket express lane which restricts customers to TEN ITEMS OR LESS; the sign should read TEN ITEMS OR FEWER.
- A modifier may not contain a dangling participle, such as *Lying in bed, everything seemed so different,* where the implicit subject of the participle *lying* (*I*) is different from the subject of the main clause (*everything*).
- The verb *aggravate* does not mean "annoy"; it means "make worse."

The purists who call out these errors see them as symptomatic of a decline in the quality of communication and reasoning in our culture today. As one columnist put it, "I'm concerned about a country that's not quite sure what it's saying and doesn't seem to care."

It's not hard to see how these worries arose. There is a kind of writer who makes issues of usage impossible to ignore. These writers are incurious about the logic and history of the English language and the ways in which it has been used by its exemplary stylists. They have a tin ear for its nuances of meaning and emphasis. Too lazy to crack open a dictionary, they are led by gut feeling and intuition rather than attention to careful scholarship. For these writers, language is not a vehicle for clarity and grace but a way to signal their membership in a social clique.

Who are these writers? You might think I'm referring to Twittering teenagers or Facebooking freshmen. But the writers I have in mind are the purists—also known as sticklers, pedants, peevers, snobs, snoots, nitpickers, traditionalists, language police, usage nannies, grammar Nazis, and the Gotcha! Gang. In their zeal to purify usage and safeguard the language, they have made it difficult to think clearly about felicity in expression and have muddied the task of explaining the art of writing.

The goal of this chapter is to allow you to reason your way to avoiding the major errors of grammar, word choice, and punctuation. In announcing this goal shortly after making fun of the language police, I might seem to be contradicting myself. If this is your reaction, you are a victim of the confusion sown by the sticklers. The idea that there are exactly two approaches to usage—all the traditional rules must be followed, or else anything goes—is the sticklers' founding myth. The first step in mastering usage is to understand why the myth is wrong.

The myth goes like this:

Once upon a time, people cared about using language properly. They consulted dictionaries to look up correct information about word meanings and grammatical constructions. The makers of these dictionaries were Prescriptivists: they prescribed correct usage. Prescriptivists uphold standards of excellence and a respect for the best of our civilization, and are a bulwark against relativism, vulgar populism, and the dumbing down of literate culture.

In the 1960s an opposing school emerged, inspired by academic linguistics and theories of progressive education. The ringleaders of this school are Descriptivists: they describe how language actually is used rather than prescribing how it ought to be used. Descriptivists believe that the rules of correct usage are nothing more than the secret handshake of the ruling class, designed to keep the masses in their place. Language is an organic product of human creativity, say the Descriptivists, and people should be allowed to write however they please.

The Descriptivists are hypocrites: they adhere to standards of correct usage in their own writing but discourage the teaching and dissemination of those standards to others, thereby denying the possibility of social advancement to the less privileged.

The Descriptivists had their way with the publication of *Webster's Third New International Dictionary* in 1961, which accepted such errors as *ain't* and *irregardless*. This created a backlash that led to Prescriptivist dictionaries such as *The American Heritage Dictionary of the English Language*. Ever since then, Prescriptivists and Descriptivists have been doing battle over whether writers should care about correctness.

What's wrong with this fairy tale? Pretty much everything. Let's begin with the very idea of objective correctness in language.

What does it mean to say that it is incorrect to end a sentence with a preposition, or to use *decimate* to mean "destroy most of" rather than "destroy a tenth of"? After all, these are not logical truths that one could prove like theorems, nor are they scientific discoveries one could make in the lab. And they are certainly not the stipulations of some governing body, like the rules of Major League Baseball. Many people assume that there is such a governing body, namely the makers of dictionaries, but as chair of the Usage Panel of the famously prescriptive *American Heritage Dictionary* (*AHD*), I am here to tell you that this assumption is false. When I asked the editor of the dictionary how he and his colleagues decide what goes into it, he replied, "We pay attention to the way people use language."

That's right: when it comes to correct English, there's no one in charge; the lunatics are running the asylum. The editors of a dictionary read a lot, keeping their eyes open for new words and senses that are used by many writers in many contexts, and the editors add or change the definitions accordingly. Purists are often offended when they learn that this is how dictionaries are written. In his famous 1962 smackdown of *Webster's Third,* the literary critic Dwight Macdonald declared that even if nine-tenths of English speakers were to use a word incorrectly (say, *nauseous* meaning "nauseated" rather than "nauseating"), the remaining tenth would be correct (he did not say by what criterion or on whose authority), and the dictionaries should back them up.[1] But no lexicographer could carry out Macdonald's mandate. A dictionary that instructed its users to write in a way that guaranteed they would be misunderstood would be as useless as the Hungarian–English phrasebook in the Monty Python sketch which translated "Can you direct me to the train station?" as *Please fondle my buttocks.*

At the same time, there is *something* that is objectively true about usage. We can all agree that George W. Bush spoke incorrectly when he asked, "Is our children learning?"—and when he used *inebriating* to mean "exhilarating," referred to the citizens of Greece as "Grecians," and lamented policies that "vulcanize" (rather than *Balkanize*) society. Even Bush, in a self-deprecating speech, agreed that these were errors.[2]

So how can we reconcile the conviction that certain usages are wrong with the absence of any authority that ever decided what was right? The key is to recognize that the rules of usage are *tacit conventions*. A convention is an agreement among the members of a community to abide by a single way of doing things. There need not be any inherent advantage to which choice is made, but there *is* an advantage to everyone making the *same* choice. Familiar examples include standardized weights and measures, electrical voltages and cables, computer file formats, and paper currency.

The conventions of written prose represent a similar standardization. Countless idioms, word senses, and grammatical constructions have been coined and circulated by the universe of English speakers. Linguists capture their regularities in "descriptive rules"—that is, rules that describe how people speak and understand. Here are a few of them:

- The subject of a tensed verb must be in nominative case, such as *I, he, she,* and *they.*
- The first-person singular form of the verb *be* is *am.*
- The verb *vulcanize* means "to strengthen a material such as rubber by combining it with sulfur and then applying heat and pressure."

Many of these rules have become entrenched in a vast community of English speakers, who respect the rules without ever having to think about them. That's why we laugh at Cookie Monster, LOLcats, and George W. Bush.

A subset of these conventions are less widespread and natural, but they have become accepted by a smaller virtual community of literate speakers for use in public forums such as government, journalism, literature, business, and academia. These conventions are "prescriptive rules"—rules that prescribe how one *ought* to speak and write in these forums. Unlike the descriptive rules, many of the prescriptive rules have to be stated explicitly, because they are not second nature to most writers: the rules may not apply in the spoken vernacular, or they may be difficult to implement in complicated sentences which tax the writer's memory (chapter 4). Examples include the rules that govern punctuation, complex forms of agreement, and fine semantic distinctions between uncommon words like *militate* and *mitigate* and *credible* and *credulous.*

What this means is that there is no such thing as a "language war" between Prescriptivists and Descriptivists. The alleged controversy is as bogus as other catchy dichotomies such as *nature versus nurture* and *America: Love It or Leave It.* It is true that descriptive and prescriptive rules are different kinds of things and that descriptive and prescriptive grammarians are engaged in different kinds of activities. But it's not true that if one kind of grammarian is right then the other kind of grammarian is wrong.

Once again I can write from authority. I am, among other things, a descriptive linguist: a card-carrying member of the Linguistic Society of America who has written many articles and books on how people use their mother tongue, including words and constructions that are frowned upon by the purists. But the book you are holding is avowedly prescriptivist: it consists of several hundred pages in which I am bossing you around. While I am fascinated by the linguistic exuberance of the vox populi, I'd be the first to argue that having prescriptive rules is desirable, indeed indispensable, in many arenas of writing. They can lubricate comprehension, reduce misunderstanding, provide a stable platform for the development of style and grace, and signal that a writer has exercised care in crafting a passage.

Once you understand that prescriptive rules are the conventions of a specialized form of the language, most of the iptivist controversies evaporate. One of them surrounds the linguist's defense of nonstandard forms like *ain't, brang,* and *can't get no* (the so-called double negative) against the common accusation that they are products of laziness or illogic (an accusation that easily mixes with racism or class prejudice). History tells us that the reason that standard English prefers the alternatives *isn't, brought,* and *can't get any* is not that the two versions were ever weighed on their merits and the standard forms discovered to be superior. No, they are just frozen historical accidents: the "correct" forms are those that happened to be used in the dialect spoken in the region around London when written English first became standardized several centuries ago. If history had unfolded differently, today's correct forms could have been incorrect, and vice versa. The London dialect became the standard of education, government, and business, and it was also the dialect of better-educated and more affluent speakers throughout the Anglosphere. Double negatives, *ain't,* and other nonstandard forms soon became stigmatized by their association with the less prestigious dialects of English used by its poorer and less educated speakers.

But the claim that there is nothing inherently wrong with *ain't* (which is true) should not be confused with the claim that *ain't* is one of the conventions of standard written English (which is obviously false). This distinction is lost on the purists, who worry that if we point out that people who say *ain't* or *He be working* or *ax a question* are not lazy or careless, then we have no grounds for advising students and writers to avoid them in their prose. So here is an analogy. In the United Kingdom, everyone drives on the left, and there is nothing inherently wrong with that convention; it is in no way sinister, gauche, or socialist. Nonetheless, we have an excellent reason to encourage a person in the United States to drive on the right. There is a joke about a commuter who's on his way to work when he gets a call on his mobile phone from his wife. "Be careful, honey," she says. "They just said on the radio that there's a maniac driving on the wrong side of the freeway." "One maniac?" he replies; "There are thousands of them!"

And not even the supposedly descriptivist dictionaries leave their users in doubt as to what the standard forms are. The endlessly repeated claim that *Webster's Third* treated *ain't* as correct English is a myth.[3] It originated in a press release from the publisher's marketing department which announced "*Ain't* gets official recognition at last." The dictionary, quite reasonably, contained an entry in which people could learn about the word, including, of course, the fact that many speakers disapprove of it. Journalists misinterpreted the press release as saying that the dictionary listed *ain't* without comment.

Another firestorm can be extinguished by recalling that the conventions of usage are *tacit*. The rules of standard English are not legislated by a tribunal of lexicographers but emerge as an implicit consensus within a virtual community of writers, readers, and editors. That consensus can change over the years in a process as unplanned and uncontrollable as the vagaries of fashion. No official ever decided that respectable men and women were permitted to doff their hats and gloves in the 1960s or to get pierced and tattooed in the 1990s. Nor could any authority with powers short of Mao Zedong have stopped them. In a similar manner, centuries of respectable writers have gradually shifted the collective consensus of what is right and wrong while shrugging off now-forgotten edicts by self-appointed guardians of the language. The nineteenth-century prescriptivist Richard White had no luck banning *standpoint* and *washtub*, nor did his contemporary William Cullen Bryant succeed in outlawing *commence, compete, lengthy,* and *leniency*. And we all know how successful Strunk and White were in forbidding *to personalize, to contact*, and *six people*. Lexicographers have always understood this. In resigning themselves to the role of chronicling ever-changing usage, they are acknowledging the wisdom of Thomas Carlyle's famous reply to Margaret Fuller's statement "I accept the universe": "Gad! She'd better."

Although lexicographers have neither the desire nor the power to prevent linguistic conventions from changing, this does not mean, as purists fear, that they cannot state the conventions in force at a given time. That is the rationale behind the *American Heritage Dictionary*'s Usage Panel: two hundred authors, journalists, editors, scholars, and other public figures whose writing shows that they choose their words with care. Every year they fill out questionnaires on pronunciation, meaning, and usage, and the dictionary reports the results in usage notes attached to entries for problematic words. The Usage Panel is intended to be a sample of the virtual community for whom careful writers write. When it comes to best practices in usage, there is no higher authority.

The powerlessness of dictionaries to enforce the prescriptivists' dream of preventing linguistic change does not mean that the dictionaries are doomed to preside over a race to the bottom. Macdonald titled his 1962 review of *Webster's Third* "The String Untuned," an allusion to the calamitous violation of the natural order that Ulysses foresaw in Shakespeare's *Troilus and Cressida*: "The bounded waters should lift their bosoms higher than the shores and make a sop of all this solid globe. Strength should be lord of imbecility and the rude son should strike his father dead." As an example of the cataclysm that would result from *Webster's* untuning of the string, Macdonald worried that the dictionaries of 1988 would list without comment the solecisms *mischievious, inviduous*, and *nuclear* pronounced as "nucular." Here we are more than a quarter-century after the prophesied date and more than a half-century after the prediction, and we can check to see what happened. A peek at the entries for these words in any dictionary will show that Macdonald was wrong about the inevitable degeneration of a language that is not policed by lexicographers. And though I can't prove it, I suspect that even if the dictionaries *had* approved *mischievious, inviduous,* and "nucular," the bounded waters would not have lifted their bosoms higher than the shores, nor would rude sons have struck their fathers dead.

And now we come to the most bogus controversy of all. The fact that many prescriptive rules are worth keeping does not mean that every pet peeve, bit of grammatical folklore, or dimly remembered lesson from Miss Thistlebottom's classroom is worth keeping. As we shall see, many prescriptive rules originated for screwball reasons, impede clear and graceful prose, and have been flouted by the best writers for centuries. Phony rules, which proliferate like urban legends and are just as hard to eradicate, are responsible for vast amounts of ham-fisted copyediting and smarty-pants one-upmanship. Yet when language scholars try to debunk the spurious rules, the dichotomizing mindset imagines that they are trying to abolish all standards of good writing. It is as if anyone who proposed repealing a stupid law, like the one forbidding interracial marriage, must be a black-cloaked, bomb-clutching anarchist.

Experts on usage (not to be confused with the purists, who are often ignoramuses) call these phony rules fetishes, folklore, hobgoblins, superstitions, shibboleths, or (my favorite) bubbe meises, Yiddish for "grandmothers' tales." (Each word has two syllables; the *u* is pronounced like the vowel sound in "book," the *ei* like that of "mice.")

Linguistic bubbe meises arise from a number of sources. Some of them originated in the first English writing guides published in the seventeenth and eighteenth centuries, and have been handed down in an oral tradition ever since.[4] In those days Latin was considered the ideal language for the expression of thought. Guides to English grammar were written as pedagogical steppingstones to mastery of Latin grammar, and they tried to shoehorn English constructions into the

categories designed for Latin. Many perfectly good English constructions were stigmatized because they had no counterparts in the language of Lucretius and Cicero.

Other hobgoblins were the brainchildren of self-proclaimed experts
who cooked up idiosyncratic theories of how language ought to behave,
usually with a puritanical undercurrent in which people's natural
inclinations must be a form of dissoluteness. According to one of these
theories, Greek and Latin forms must never be combined, so *automo-
bile* should have been either *autokinetikon* or *ipsomobile*, and *bigamy,
electrocution, homosexual,* and *sociology* were abominations (the words,
that is). According to another theory, words may never be derived by
back-formation, that is, by extracting a piece of a complex word and
using it on its own, as in the recent verbs *commentate, coronate, incent,*
and *surveil,* and the slightly older ones *intuit* and *enthuse.* Unfortunately, this theory would also retroactively outlaw *choreograph, diagnose, resurrect, edit, sculpt, sleepwalk,* and hundreds of other verbs that
have become completely unexceptionable.

Many purists maintain that the only correct sense of a word is the
original one. That's why they insist, for example, that *transpire* can only
mean "become known," not "take place" (since it initially meant "release
vapor," from the Latin *spirare,* "breathe"), and that *decimate* can only
mean "killing one in ten" (since it originally described the execution of
every tenth soldier in a mutinous Roman legion). The misconception is
so common that it has been given a name: the etymological fallacy. It
can be debunked with a glance at any page of a historical reference
book, such as the *Oxford English Dictionary,* which will show that very
few words retain their original senses. *Deprecate* used to mean "ward
off by prayer," *meticulous* once meant "timid," and *silly* went from
"blessed" to "pious" to "innocent" to "pitiable" to "feeble" to today's
"foolish." And as Kory Stamper, an editor at Merriam-Webster, has
pointed out, if you insist that *decimate* be used only with its original
meaning, "kill one in ten," shouldn't you also insist that *December* be
used with *its* original meaning, "the tenth month in the calendar"?

The last refuge of the stickler is the claim that proper usages are more logical than the alternatives. As we shall see, the claim gets it backwards. Many of the commonest usage errors are the result of writers thinking logically when they should be mindlessly conforming to convention. Writers who spell *lose* as *loose* (which would make it follow the pattern in *choose*), who punctuate the possessive of *it* as *it's* (just as we punctuate the possessive of *Pat* as *Pat's*), or who use *enormity* to mean "the quality of being enormous" (just as we use *hilarity* to mean the quality of being hilarious) are not being illogical. They are being *too* logical, while betraying their lack of familiarity with the conventions of the printed page. This may be grounds for suspicion by the reader and a prod to self-improvement for the writer, but it is not a failure of consistency or logic.

And this brings us to the reasons to obey some prescriptive rules (the ones accepted by good writers, as opposed to the phony ones that good writers have always ignored). One is to provide grounds for confidence that the writer has a history of reading edited English and has given it his full attention. Another is to enforce grammatical consistency: to implement rules, such as agreement, that everyone respects but that may be hard to keep track of when the sentence gets complicated (see chapter 4). The use of consistent grammar reassures a reader that the writer has exercised care in constructing his prose, which in turn increases her confidence that he has exercised care in the research and thinking behind the prose. It is also an act of courtesy, because consistent trees are easier to parse and harder to misunderstand.

Still another reason to care about usage is to ratify a certain attitude to language. Careful writers and discerning readers delight in the profusion of words in the English lexicon, no two of which are exact synonyms. Many words convey subtle shades of meaning, provide glimpses into the history of the language, conform to elegant principles of assembly, or enliven prose with distinctive imagery, sound, and rhythm. Careful writers pick up the nuances of words by focusing on their makeup and their contexts over the course of tens of thousands of hours of reading. Their readers' reward consists of partaking in—and, if they themselves write, helping to preserve—this rich patrimony.

When a not-so-careful writer tries to gussy up his prose with an upmarket word that he mistakenly thinks is a synonym of a common one, like *simplistic* for *simple* or *fulsome* for *full,* his readers are likely to conclude the worst: that he has paid little attention to what he has read, is affecting an air of sophistication on the cheap, and is polluting a common resource.

To be sure, the language, to say nothing of all this solid globe, will survive such lapses. Many preferred senses stand their ground over long stretches of time despite constant battering by careless writers. There is no lexicographical version of Gresham's Law in which the bad meaning of a word always drives out the good one. The preferred sense of *disinterested* as "impartial," for example, has coexisted for centuries with its frowned-upon sense as "bored." This should not be all that surprising, because many words embrace happily coexisting senses, such as *literate,* which means both "able to read" and "familiar with literature," and *religious,* which means both "pertaining to religion" and "obsessively thorough." The senses are usually sorted out by the context, so both survive. A language has plenty of room for multiple meanings, including the ones that good writers hope to preserve.

Still, writers will do themselves a favor, and increase the amount of pleasure in the world, if they use a word in the senses that are accepted by literate readers. This raises the question of how a careful writer can distinguish a legitimate rule of usage from a grandmother's tale. The answer is unbelievably simple: look it up. Consult a modern usage guide or a dictionary with usage notes, such as *Merriam-Webster Unabridged, American Heritage Dictionary, Encarta World English Dictionary,* or *Random House Dictionary* (the one behind www.dictionary.com). Many people, particularly sticklers, are under the impression that every bubbe meise ever loosed on the world by a self-proclaimed purist will be backed up by the major dictionaries and manuals. In fact, these reference works, with their careful attention to history, literature, and actual usage, are the most adamant debunkers of grammatical nonsense. (This is less true of style sheets drawn up by newspapers and professional societies, and of manuals written by amateurs such as critics and journalists, which tend to mindlessly reproduce the folklore of previous guides.)[5]

Take the quintessential bogus rule, the prohibition of split infinitives, according to which Captain Kirk should not have said *to boldly go where no man has gone before,* but rather *to go boldly* or *boldly to go.* Here's what you will find if you look up "split infinitive" in the major guides:

American Heritage Dictionary: "The only rationale for condemning the construction is based on a false analogy with Latin. . . . In general, the Usage Panel accepts the split infinitive."

Merriam-Webster Unabridged online dictionary: "Even though there has never been a rational basis for objecting to the split infinitive, the subject has become a fixture of folk belief about grammar. . . . Modern commentators . . . usually say it's all right to split an infinitive in the interest of clarity. Since clarity is the usual reason for splitting, this advice means merely that you can split them whenever you need to."

Encarta World English Dictionary: "There is no grammatical basis for rejecting split infinitives."

Random House Dictionary: "Nothing in the history of the infinitive in English . . . supports the so-called rule, and in many sentences . . . the only natural place for the modifying adverb is between *to* and the verb."

Theodore Bernstein, *The Careful Writer:* "There is nothing wrong with splitting an infinitive . . . except that eighteenth- and nineteenth-century grammarians, for one reason or another, frowned on it."

Joseph Williams, *Style: Toward Clarity and Grace:* "The split infinitive is now so common among the very best writers that when we make an effort to avoid splitting it, we invite notice, whether we intend to or not."

Roy Copperud, *American Usage and Style: The Consensus:* "Many writers believe they will not go to heaven if they split the infinitive. . . .

After the folly of [the Latin-based] system of grammar was noted, English was analyzed on its own terms, and the rule against splitting infinitives went out the window. . . . The consensus of seven critics is that infinitives may be split when splitting makes the sentence read more smoothly and does not cause awkwardness."

So split if you need to (as I did in the first line on the preceding page); the experts have your back.

What follows is a judicious guide to a hundred of the most common issues of grammar, diction (word choice), and punctuation. These are the ones that repeatedly turn up in style guides, pet-peeve lists, newspaper language columns, irate letters to the editor, and inventories of common errors in student papers. I will use the following criteria to distinguish the legitimate concerns of a careful writer from the folklore and superstitions: Does the prescriptive rule merely extend the logic of an intuitive grammatical phenomenon to more complicated cases, like enforcing agreement in a sentence with a bushy tree? Do careful writers who inadvertently flout the rule agree, when the breach is pointed out, that something has gone wrong? Has the rule been respected by the best writers in the past? Is it respected by careful writers in the present? Is there a consensus among discerning writers that it conveys an interesting semantic distinction? And are violations of the rule obvious products of mishearing, careless reading, or a chintzy attempt to sound highfalutin?

A rule should be blown off, in contrast, if the answer to any of the following questions is yes. Is the rule based on some crackpot theory, such as that English should emulate Latin, or that the original meaning of a word is the only correct one? Is it instantly refuted by the facts of English, such as the decree that nouns may not be converted into verbs? Did it originate with the pet peeve of a self-anointed maven? Was it routinely flouted by the great writers of the past? Is it rejected by the careful writers of the present? Is it based on a misdiagnosis of a legitimate problem, such as declaring that a construction which is sometimes ambiguous is always ungrammatical? Do attempts to fix a sentence so that it obeys the rule only make it clumsier and less clear?

Finally, does the putative rule confuse grammar with *formality*? Every writer commands a range of styles that are appropriate to different times and places. A formal style that is appropriate for the inscription on a genocide memorial will differ from a casual style that is appropriate for an email to a close friend. Using an informal style when a formal style is called for results in prose that seems breezy, chatty, casual, flippant. Using a formal style when an informal style is called for results in prose that seems stuffy, pompous, affected, haughty. Both kinds of mismatch are errors. Many prescriptive guides are oblivious to this distinction, and mistake informal style for incorrect grammar.

My advice will often shock purists and occasionally puzzle readers who have always been under the impression that this word meaning or that grammatical usage is an error. But the advice is thoroughly conventional. It combines data from the ballots given to the Usage Panel of the *American Heritage Dictionary*, the usage notes of several dictionaries and style guides, the erudite historical analyses in *Merriam-Webster's Dictionary of English Usage*, the meta-analysis in Roy Copperud's *American Usage and Style: The Consensus,* and the view from modern linguistics represented in *The Cambridge Grammar of the English Language* and the blog *Language Log*.[6] When the experts disagree, or when the examples are all over the map, I will offer my own best judgment.

I divide the hundred usage issues into points of grammar, the expression of quantity and quality, word choice, and punctuation.

GRAMMAR

adjectives and adverbs. Every now and again a language grump complains that the distinction between adverbs and adjectives is disappearing from English. In fact, the distinction is alive and well, but it is governed by two subtleties that go beyond the vague memory that adverbs are words that modify verbs and end in –*ly*.[7]

The first subtlety is a fact about adverbs: many of them (the ones called flat adverbs) are identical to their related adjectives. You can *drive fast* (adverb) or *drive a fast car* (adjective); *hit the ball hard* or *hit a hard ball*. The list of flat adverbs differs across dialects: *real pretty* (as opposed to *really pretty*) and *The house was shaken up bad* (as opposed to *badly*) are common in nonstandard dialects of English and have made inroads into casual and folksy speech in the standard dialect. This crossover is what gave rise to the vague impression that adverbs are endangered. But the historical trend is in the opposite direction: adverbs and adjectives are *more* often distinguished today than they were in the past. Standard English used to have many flat adverbs that have since been separated from their adjectival twins, such as *monstrous fine* (Jonathan Swift), *violent hot* (Daniel Defoe), and *exceeding good memory* (Benjamin Franklin). When today's purists reflect on the ones that remain, like those in *Drive safe, Go slow, She sure fooled me, He spelled my name wrong,* and *The moon is shining bright,* they may hallucinate a grammatical error and promulgate prissy alternatives such as *She surely fooled me* and the one in this *Bizarro* cartoon:

The second subtlety is a fact about adjectives: they don't just modify nouns, but can appear as complements to verbs, as in *This seems excellent, We found it boring,* and *I feel tired.* They can also show up as an adjunct to a verb phrase or clause, as in *She died young* and *They showed up drunk.* Recall from chapter 4 that grammatical categories like adjective are not the same thing as grammatical functions like modifier and complement. People who confuse the two may think that the adjectives in these sentences "modify the verb" and hence ought to be replaced by adverbs. The result is a hypercorrection like *I feel terribly* (which really should be *I feel terrible*). The related expression *I feel badly* may have started out in previous generations as a hypercorrected version of *I feel bad. Badly* has now become an adjective in its own right, meaning "sorrowful" or "regretful." Thankfully, James Brown was never tempted to hypercorrect "I Got You (I Feel Good)" to "I Got You (I Feel Well)."

A failure to appreciate the multiple functions of adjectives also gave rise to the false accusation that Apple made a grammatical error in its slogan *Think Different.* The company was right not to revise it to *Think Differently:* the verb *think* can take an adjectival complement which refers to the nature of the thoughts being entertained. That is why Texans *think big* (not *largely*) and why in the musical *Funny Face* the advertising slogan that set off a lavish production number was *Think Pink,* not *Think Pinkly.*[8]

To be sure, surveys of typical errors in student papers show that inexperienced writers really do mix up adjectives and adverbs. The phrase *The kids he careless fathered* is just careless, and in *The doctor's wife acts irresponsible and selfish* the writer stretched the ability of *act* to take an adjectival complement (as in *act calm*) further than most readers are willing to go.[9]

ain't. No one needs to be reminded that *ain't* is frowned upon. The prohibition has been drilled into children for so long that they have made it into a jump-rope rhyme:

Don't say ain't *or your mother will faint.*
Your father will fall in a bucket of paint.

> *Your sister will cry; your brother will die.*
> *Your dog will call the FBI.*

I like this poetic warning of what will happen if you violate a pre-scriptive rule better than Dwight Macdonald's prophecy that the bounded waters will lift their bosoms higher than the shores and make a sop of all this solid globe. But both warnings are overstatements. Despite the taint of *ain't* from its origin in regional and lower-class English, and more than a century of vilification by schoolteachers, today the word is going strong. It's not that *ain't* is used as a standard contraction for negated forms of *be, have,* and *do;* no writer is that oblivious. But it does have some widely established places. One is in the lyrics of popular songs, where it is a crisp and euphonious substitute for the strident and bisyllabic *isn't, hasn't,* and *doesn't,* as in "It Ain't Necessarily So," "Ain't She Sweet," and "It Don't Mean a Thing (If It Ain't Got That Swing)." Another is in expressions that are meant to capture homespun truths, like *If it ain't broke don't fix it, That ain't chopped liver,* and *It ain't over till it's over.* This use of *ain't* may be found even in relatively formal settings to emphasize that some fact is so obvious as to be beyond further debate—as if to say, "Anyone with a lick of sense can see that." Hilary Putnam, perhaps the most influential analytic philosopher of the second half of the twentieth century, pub-lished a famous article called "The Meaning of Meaning" in a learned academic volume. At one point he summed up his argument with "Cut the pie any way you like, 'meanings' just ain't in the head!" As far as I know, his mother did not lose consciousness.

and, because, but, or, so, also. Many children are taught that it is ungrammatical to begin a sentence with a conjunction (what I have been calling a coordinator). Because they sometimes write in fragments. And are shaky about when to use periods. And when to capitalize. Teachers need a simple way to teach them how to break sentences, so they tell them that sentences beginning with *and* and other conjunc-tions are ungrammatical.

Whatever the pedagogical merits may be of feeding children misinformation, it is inappropriate for adults. There is nothing wrong with beginning a sentence with a coordinator. As we saw in chapter 5, *and, but,* and *so* are among the commonest coherence markers, and they may be used to begin a sentence whenever the clauses being connected are too long or complicated to fit comfortably into a single megasentence. I've begun about a hundred sentences with *and* or *but* in the book so far, such as "And we all know how successful Strunk and White were in forbidding *to personalize, to contact,* and *six people,*" which capped off a series of sentences about purists who failed to change the language.

The preposition *because* (commonly misidentified as a conjunction) can also happily sit at the beginning of a sentence. Most commonly it ends up there when it introduces an explanation that has been preposed in front of a main clause, as in *Because you're mine, I walk the line.* But it can also kick off a single clause when the clause serves as the answer to a *why*-question. The question can be explicit, as in *Why can't I have a pony? Because I said so.* It can also be implicit in a series of related assertions that calls for a single explanation, which the author then provides, as in Aleksandr Solzhenitsyn's reflection on the twentieth-century's genocidal tyrants:

> Macbeth's self-justifications were feeble—and his conscience devoured him. Yes, even Iago was a little lamb too. The imagination and the spiritual strength of Shakespeare's evildoers stopped short at a dozen corpses. Because they had no *ideology.*

between you and I. This commonly heard phrase is often held out as an excruciating grammatical blunder. I spelled out the reason in chapter 4 when discussing the example *Give Al Gore and I a chance to bring America back.* Rigorous tree-thinking demands that a complicated phrase behave in the same way as a simpler phrase in the same position. The object of a preposition like *between* must be in the accusative case: we say *between us* or *between them,* not *between we* or *between they.* Therefore, according to this way of thinking, the pronouns in a coordination must also be accusative: *between you and me.* The phrase *between you and I* appears to be a hypercorrection, which arose when speakers who were corrected for *Me and Amanda are going to the mall* took away the crude moral that you should always say *X and I,* never *me and X* or *X and me.*

But the conviction that *between you and I* is an error needs a second look, together with the explanation that the phrase is a hypercorrection. When enough careful writers and speakers fail to do something that a theory of syntax says they should, it could mean that it's the theory that's wrong, not the writers.

A coordination phrase is a strange entity, and the logic of trees that applies elsewhere in English syntax does not apply to it. Most phrases have a head: a single word inside the phrase that determines its properties. The phrase *the bridge to the islands* has the head *bridge,* which is a singular noun, so we call the phrase a noun phrase, interpret it as referring to a kind of bridge, and treat the phrase as singular—that's why everyone agrees that one should say The bridge to the islands is crowded, not are crowded. Not so for a coordination, which is headless: it cannot be equated with any of its components. In the coordination the bridge and the causeway, the first noun phrase, the bridge, is singular, and the second noun phrase, the causeway, is also singular, but the coordination as a whole is plural: The bridge and the causeway are crowded, not is crowded.

Perhaps the same is true of case: the case that applies to a whole coordination phrase is not necessarily the same as the case that applies to its parts. When we strive to apply tree-thinking as we write, we may furrow our brows and consciously force the parts to harmonize with the whole. But because coordination phrases are headless, the harmony is not a requirement of our intuitive grammar, and few of us can consistently pull it off. Thus even an assiduous speaker might say *Give Al Gore and I a chance* or *between you and I.* The *Cambridge Grammar* suggests that in contemporary English many speakers have settled on a rule that allows a nominative pronoun like *I* or *he* after the coordinator *and.* And even more of them—the ones who say *Me and Amanda are going to the mall*—allow an accusative pronoun before *and.* It is a natural preference, because the accusative is the default case in English, occurring in a motley range of contexts (such as the bare exclamation *Me!?*), pretty much anywhere it is not preempted by the more selective nominative or genitive.

You might think that the standard prescriptive recommendation, with its ironclad application of tree analysis, is more logical and elegant, and that we should all just try harder to implement it and thereby make our language more consistent. But when it comes to coordination, this is an unrealizable dream. Not only does the grammatical number of a coordination systematically differ from the number of the nouns inside it, but sometimes the number and person of a coordination cannot be determined from the tree at all. Which alternative in each of these pairs of sentences is correct?[10]

Either Elissa or the twins are sure to be there.	Either Elissa or the twins is sure to be there.
Either the twins or Elissa is sure to be there.	Either the twins or Elissa are sure to be there.
You mustn't go unless either I or your father comes home with you.	You mustn't go unless either I or your father come home with you.
Either your father or I am going to have to come with you.	Either your father or I is going to have to come with you.

No amount of tree-thinking will help you here. Even the style manuals throw up their hands and suggest that writers just look at the linear order of words in the string and make the verb agree with the noun phrase closest to it, like the versions in the left column. Coordination phrases simply don't follow the logic of ordinary headed phrases. Writers are well advised to avoid *between you and I,* since it makes many readers bristle, but it is not a heinous error.

***can* versus *may*.** This cartoon explains a traditional rule about two common modal auxiliaries:

At least Mrs. O'Malley didn't give the standard grown-up's answer to a child's request with *can:* "You can, but the question is, may you?" A colleague of mine recalls that whenever she said, "Daddy, can I ask you a question?" the response was "You just did, but you may ask me another."

As the puzzlement of the young man in the cartoon suggests, the traditional distinction between the meaning of *can* (capability or possibility) and the meaning of *may* (permissibility) is tenuous at best. Even many sticklers don't have the courage of their convictions, such as the maven who insisted on the distinction in one entry in his usage guide but slipped up in another entry and ruled that a certain verb "can only be followed by *for.*"[11] (Gotcha! He should have written *may.*) Conversely, *may* is commonly and innocuously used for possibility rather than permission, as in *It may rain this afternoon.*

In formal style we see a slight preference for using *may* for permission. But as Mrs. O'Malley suggested, it is only when one is asking (or granting) permission that *may* is preferable, not when one is merely talking about it. The sentence *Students can submit their papers anytime Friday* might be said by one student to another, but *Students may submit their papers anytime Friday* is more likely to be an announcement of the policy by the professor. Since most prose neither grants nor requests permission, the distinction is usually moot, and the two words may (or can) be used more or less interchangeably.

dangling modifiers. Do you see a problem with the sentences that follow?

Checking into the hotel, it was nice to see a few of my old classmates in the lobby.

Turning the corner, the view was quite different.

Born and raised in city apartments, it was always a marvel to me.

In order to contain the epidemic, the area was sealed off.

Considering the hour, it is surprising that he arrived at all.

Looking at the subject dispassionately, what evidence is there for this theory?

In order to start the motor, it is essential that the retroflex cam connecting rod be disengaged.

To summarize, unemployment remains the state's major economic and social problem.

According to an old rule about "dangling modifiers," these sentences are ungrammatical. (Sometimes the rule is stated as applying to "dangling participles," namely the gerund form of a verb ending with –*ing* or the passive form typically ending in –*ed* or –*en,* but the examples include infinitival modifiers as well.) The rule decrees that the implied subject of the modifier (the one doing the checking, turning, and so on) must be identical to the overt subject of the main clause (*it, the view,* and so on). Most copy editors would recast the main clause, supplying it with a subject (underlined) to which the modifier can be properly fastened:

Checking into the hotel, I was pleased to see a few of my old classmates in the lobby.

Turning the corner, I saw that the view was quite different.

Born and raised in city apartments, I always found it a marvel.

In order to contain the epidemic, authorities sealed off the area.

Considering the hour, we should be surprised that he arrived at all.

Looking at the subject dispassionately, what evidence do we find for this theory?

In order to start the motor, <u>one</u> should ensure that the retroflex cam connecting rod is disengaged.

To summarize, <u>we</u> see that unemployment remains the state's major economic and social problem.

Newspaper columns on usage are filled with apologies for "errors" like these, spotted by ombudsmen or managing editors who have trained themselves to flag them. Danglers are extremely common, not just in deadline-pressured journalism but in the works of distinguished authors. Considering how often these forms turn up in edited prose and how readily they are accepted even by careful readers, two conclusions are possible: either dangling modifiers are a particularly insidious grammatical error for which writers must develop sensitive radar, or they are not grammatical errors at all. (Did you notice the dangler in the sentence before last?)

The second conclusion is the right one: some dangling modifiers should be avoided, but they are not grammatical errors. The problem with dangling modifiers is that their subjects are inherently ambiguous and sometimes a sentence will inadvertently attract a reader to the wrong choice. Many style guides reproduce (or contrive) dangling modifiers with unintentionally comical interpretations, such as these ones from Richard Lederer's *Anguished English:*

Having killed a man and served four years in prison, I feel that Tom Joad is ripe to get into trouble.

Plunging 1,000 feet into the gorge, we saw Yosemite Falls.

As a baboon who grew up wild in the jungle, I realized that Wiki had special nutritional needs.

Locked in a vault for 50 years, the owner of the jewels has decided to sell them.

When a small boy, a girl is of little interest.

It's easy—and wrong—to diagnose the problem as a violation of a grammatical rule called subject control. Most verbs that take subjectless complements, such as *try* in *Alice tried to calm down,* are governed by an ironclad rule that forces the overt subject to be identical to the missing subject. That is, we have to interpret *Alice tried to calm down* as "Alice tried to get Alice to calm down," rather than "Alice tried to get someone to calm down" or "Alice tried to get everyone to calm down." But with modifiers there is no such rule. The missing subject of a modifier is identified with the protagonist whose point of view we are assuming as we read the sentence, which is often, but need not always be, the grammatical subject of the main clause. The problem is not one of ungrammaticality but of ambiguity, as in the examples we saw in chapter 4. The jewelry owner who was locked in a vault for fifty years is like the panel on sex with four professors and the recommendation of the candidate with no qualifications.

Some so-called danglers are perfectly acceptable. Many participles have turned into prepositions, such as *according, allowing, barring, concerning, considering, excepting, excluding, failing, following, given, granted, including, owing, regarding,* and *respecting,* and they don't need subjects at all. Inserting *we find* or *we see* into the main clause to avoid a dangler can make the sentence stuffy and self-conscious. More generally, a modifier can dangle when its implied subject is the writer and the reader, as in *To summarize* and *In order to start the motor* in the examples above. And when the subject of the main clause is the dummy element *it* or *there,* the reader glides right over it, and it poses no danger of attracting a dangler.

The decision of whether to recast a sentence to align its subject with the subject of a modifier is a matter of judgment, not grammar. A thoughtlessly placed dangler can confuse the reader or slow her down, and occasionally it can lure her into a ludicrous interpretation. Also, even if a dangler is in no danger of being misinterpreted, enough readers have trained themselves to spot danglers that a writer who leaves it incurs the risk of being judged as slovenly. So in formal styles it's not a bad idea to keep an eye open for them and to correct the obtrusive ones.

fused participles (possessives with gerunds). Do you have a problem with the sentence *She approved of Sheila taking the job*? Do you insist that it should be *She approved of Sheila's taking the job,* in which the gerund (*taking*) has a subject (*Sheila's*) that is marked with genitive case? Perhaps you think that the first version, the one with the unmarked subject, is an increasingly common symptom of grammatical laziness. If so, you are a victim of the spurious rule about so-called fused participles. (The term was coined by Fowler to suggest that the participle *taking* has been illicitly fused with the noun *Sheila* into the mongrel *Sheila-taking:* the theory made little sense, but the term stuck.) In fact, gerunds with unmarked subjects were the historically earlier form, have long been used by the language's best writers, and are perfectly idiomatic. Unfusing a participle can make a sentence clumsy or pretentious:[12]

> Any alleged evils of capitalism are simply the result of people's being free to choose.
> The police had no record of my car's having been towed.
> I don't like the delays caused by my computer's being underpowered.
> The ladies will pardon my mouth's being full.

And often it cannot be done at all:

> I was annoyed by the people behind me in line's being served first.
> You can't visit them without Ethel's pulling out pictures of her grand-children.
> What she objects to is men's making more money than women for the same work.
> Imagine a child with an ear infection who cannot get penicillin's los-ing his hearing.

In these cases, dropping the *'s* results in a perfectly acceptable sentence: *I was annoyed by the people behind me in line being served first.* A substantial majority of the *AHD* Usage Panel accept the so-called fused participle, not just in these complicated sentences but in simple ones like *I can understand him not wanting to go*. For sentences that have been repeated verbatim in questionnaires over the decades, the rate of acceptance has increased over time.

How should a writer choose? Any semantic difference between the alternatives is elusive, and the choice mainly hinges on style: the genitive subject (*I approve of Sheila's taking the job*) is appropriate in more formal writing, the unmarked subject (*I approve of Sheila taking the job*) in informal writing and speech. The nature of the grammatical subject matters, too. The clumsy examples above show that long and complicated subjects are best left unmarked, whereas simpler ones like pronouns work well in the genitive, as in *I appreciate your coming over to help*. Some writers sense a subtle distinction in the focus of attention. When the focus is on the entire event, packaged into a conceptual whole, the genitive subject seems better: if the fact that Sheila is taking the job had been mentioned previously, and we were all discussing whether this was a good thing or a bad thing (not just for Sheila but for the company, her friends, and her family), I might say *I approve of Sheila's taking the job*. But if the focus is on the subject and her possible courses of action, say, if I was a friend of Sheila's and had been advising her whether to stay in school or accept the offer, I might say *I approve of Sheila taking the job*.

if-then. Something is slightly off in these sentences, but what?

> If I didn't have my seat belt on, I'd be dead.
> If he didn't come to America, our team never would have won the championship.
> If only she would have listened to me, this would never have happened.

Many conditional constructions (those with an *if* and a *then*) seem bewilderingly picky about which tenses, moods, and auxiliaries may go into them, particularly *had* and *would*. Fortunately, there is a formula for writing graceful conditionals, and it becomes clear once you recognize two distinctions.

The first is that English has *two* kinds of conditional constructions:[13]

> If you leave now, you will get there on time. [an open conditional]
> If you left now, you would get there on time. [a remote conditional]

The first is called an open conditional, from the expression "an open possibility." It refers to a situation that the writer is uncertain about, and it invites the reader to draw inferences or make predictions about that situation. Here are a couple of other examples:

> If he is here, he'll be in the kitchen.
> If it rains tomorrow, the picnic will be canceled.

With these conditionals, anything goes: you can use pretty much any tense in the *if* and *then* clauses, depending only on when the relevant events take place or are discovered.

The second kind is called a remote conditional, from the expression "a remote possibility." It refers to a counterfactual, highly improbable, blue-sky, or make-believe world, one that the writer thinks is unlikely to be true but whose implications are worth exploring:

> If I were a rich man, I wouldn't have to work hard.
> If pigs had wings, they would fly.

Remote conditionals are the finicky ones, though their demands, as we shall see, are not as arbitrary as they at first seem. The formula is that the *if*-clause must have a past-tense verb, and the *then*-clause must contain *would* or a similar auxiliary such as *could, should,* or *might*. If we take a typical double-*would* conditional (left side) and put the *if*-clause into the past tense, it instantly sounds classier:

If only she would have listened to me, this would never have happened.	If only she had listened to me, this would never have happened.

The problem with the left-hand version is that *would have* does not belong in the *if*-clause, only in the *then*-clause. The job of the conditional *would* is to explain what ought to happen in the make-believe world; it does not set up that world, a task that is reserved for the *if*-clause and its past-tense verb. By the way, this is true for counterfactuals in general, not just for ones that are found in *if-then* constructions. Doesn't the right-hand version in this pair sound better?

I wish you would have told me about this sooner.

I wish you had told me about this sooner.

Now here's the rationale behind the formula. When I said that the *if*-clause must be in the past tense, I did not mean that it refers to a past *time*. "Past tense" is a grammatical term referring to one of the forms an English verb can take, namely the verb plus *–ed*, or, in the case of irregular verbs, some variant such as *make-made, sell-sold,* or *bring-brought*. "Past time," in contrast, is a semantic concept referring to an event that took place before the moment of speaking or writing. In English, a past-tense form is typically used to refer to past time, but it can also be used with a second meaning, *factual remoteness*. That's the meaning it's expressing in the *if*-clause. Consider the sentence *If you left tomorrow, you'd save a lot of money*. The verb *left* couldn't possibly refer to an event in the past: the sentence says "tomorrow." But the past-tense form is fine, because it refers to a hypothetical (factually remote) event.

(By the way, with 99.98 percent of the common verbs in English, the same verb form, past tense, is used to convey both past time and factual remoteness. But one verb has a special form to express remoteness: *be*, which distinguishes *If I was* from *If I were*. We'll deal with it in the discussion of the subjunctive.)

What about the second half of the conditional, the *then*-clause, which calls for the auxiliaries *would, could, should,* or *might*? It turns out they are just like the verbs in the *if*-clause: they are in the past tense, with a factual-remoteness meaning. The *d*'s and the *t* at the ends of these auxiliaries are a giveaway: *would* is just the irregular past-tense form of *will, could* the past-tense form of *can, should* the past-tense form of *shall,* and *might* the past-tense form of *may.* We can see this in the contrast between open conditionals in the present tense and their remote conditionals in the past tense:

If you leave now, you <u>can</u> get there on time.	If you left now, you <u>could</u> get there on time.
If you leave now, you <u>will</u> get there on time.	If you left now, you <u>would</u> get there on time.
If you leave now, you <u>may</u> get there on time.	If you left now, you <u>might</u> get there on time.
If you leave now, you <u>shall</u> get there on time.	If you left now, you <u>should</u> get there on time.

So the rule for remote conditionals turns out to be simpler than it looks: the *if*-clause contains a verb which sets up a hypothetical world; the *then*-clause explores what will happen in that world, using a modal auxiliary. Both clauses use the past tense to express the meaning "factual remoteness."

There is one more piece to the puzzle of how to write classy conditionals. Why do they so often contain the verb form *had,* as in *If I hadn't had my seat belt on, I'd be dead,* which sounds better than *If I didn't have my seat belt on, I'd be dead*? The key is that *had* turns up when the *if*-clause refers to an event whose time of occurrence really *is* the past. Recall that the *if*-clause in a remote conditional demands the past tense but has nothing to do with past time. Now when a writer really does want to refer to a past-time event in a remote conditional, he needs the past tense of a past-tense form. The past-of-the-past is called the pluperfect, and it is formed with the auxiliary *had,* as in *I had already eaten.* So whenever the time of the make-believe world of the *if*-clause is prior to the time of writing, the clause needs to be in the pluperfect: *If you had left earlier, you would have been on time.*

Though the rules are perfectly logical, the conditions are hard to keep track of. Together with forgetting to use *had* in a past-time *if*-clause, writers sometimes overcompensate by using too many of them, as in *If that hadn't have happened, he would not be the musician he is today*—a hypercorrection sometimes called the plupluperfect. One instance of *have* is enough: it should be *If that hadn't happened.*

like, as, such as. Long ago, in the *Mad Men* era when cigarettes were advertised on radio and television, every brand had a slogan. "I'd walk a mile for a Camel." "Lucky Strike means fine tobacco." "Come to where the flavor is. Come to Marlboro Country." And most infamously, "Winston tastes good, like a cigarette should."

The infamy did not come from the fact that the company was using a catchy jingle to get people addicted to carcinogens. It came from the fact that the jingle allegedly contained a grammatical error. *Like* is a preposition, said the accusers, and may take only a noun phrase object, as in *crazy like a fox* or *like a bat out of hell.* It is not a conjunction (what I have been calling a coordinator) and so may not be followed by a clause. *The New Yorker* sneered at the error, Ogden Nash wrote a poem about it, Walter Cronkite refused to say it on the air, and Strunk and White declared it illiterate. The slogan, they agreed, should have been "Winston tastes good, *as* a cigarette should." The advertising agency and the tobacco company were delighted by the unpaid publicity and were only too happy to confess to the error in the coda, "What do you want, good grammar or good taste?"

Like many usage controversies, the brouhaha over *like a cigarette should* is a product of grammatical ineptitude and historical ignorance. To start with, the fact that *like* is a preposition, which typically takes a noun phrase complement, does not mean that it may not take a clausal complement as well. As we saw in chapter 4, many prepositions, such as *after* and *before,* take either one, so the question of whether *like* is a conjunction is a red herring. Even if it *is* a preposition, it could very well precede a clause.

More important, the ad's use of *like* with a clause was not a recent corruption. The combination has been in use for six hundred years throughout the English-speaking world, though with greater frequency in the nineteenth century and in the United States. It has been used in literary works by dozens of great writers (including Shakespeare, Dickens, Twain, Wells, and Faulkner) and has flown beneath the radar of the purists themselves, who have inadvertently used it in their own style guides. This does not show that purists are only human and sometimes make errors; it shows that the alleged error is not an error. The R. J. Reynolds Tobacco Company was confessing to the wrong crime; its slogan was perfectly grammatical. Writers are free to use either *like* or *as*, mindful only that *as* is a bit more formal, and that the Winston-tastes-good controversy became such a bloody shirt in the grammar wars that readers may mistakenly think the writer has made an error.

A related superstition, ruthlessly enforced by many copy editors, is that *like* may not be used to introduce examples, as in *Many technical terms have become familiar to laypeople, like "cloning" and "DNA."* They would correct it to *such as "cloning" and "DNA."* According to this guideline, *like* may be used only for resemblance to an exemplar, as in *I'll find someone like you* and *Poems are made by fools like me.* Few writers consistently follow this bogus rule, including the mavens who insist on it (one of whom, for example, wrote, "Avoid clipped forms like *bike, prof, doc*"). *Such as* is more formal than *like*, but both are legitimate.

possessive antecedents. Ready for another example of pointless purist dudgeon? Then consider this question from a 2002 College Board exam, which asked students to identify the grammatical error, if there was one, in the following sentence:

Toni Morrison's genius enables her to create novels that arise
from and express the injustices African Americans have endured.

The official answer was that the sentence did not contain an error. A high school teacher complained that it did, because the possessive phrase *Toni Morrison's* cannot serve as the antecedent of the pronoun *her.* The College Board caved in to his pressure and retroactively gave credit to all the students who had identified *her* as incorrect. On cue, pundits moaned about declining standards.[14]

But the rule against possessive (more accurately, genitive) antecedents is a figment of the purists' misunderstanding. Far from being an established principle of grammar, the rule seems to have been conjured out of thin air by a usage maven in the 1960s and has been uncomprehendingly copied by others ever since. Genitive antecedents have been considered unexceptionable throughout the history of English, and may be found in Shakespeare, the King James Bible ("And Joseph's master took him, and put him into the prison"), Dickens, and Thackeray, together with Strunk and White ("The writer's colleagues . . . have greatly helped him in the preparation of his manuscript") and one of the irate pundits himself ("It may be Bush's utter lack of self-doubt that his detractors hate most about him").

Why would anyone think that this perfectly natural construction is ungrammatical? The rationale stated by one rule-giver was that "there is in fact no person named for the *him* to refer to." Say what? Is there a neurologically intact reader anywhere who can't figure out whom the pronoun refers to in *Bob's mother loved him* or *Stacy's dog bit her*?

The other rationale is that *Toni Morrison's* is an adjective, and pronouns must refer back to nouns. But *Toni Morrison's* is not an adjective, like *red* or *beautiful*; it's a noun phrase in genitive case. (How do we know? Because you can't use genitives in clear adjectival contexts like *That child seems Lisa's* or *Hand me the red and John's sweater*.) The confusion comes from the vague impression that the phrase is a "modifier." But the impression not only confuses a grammatical category (adjective) with a grammatical function (modifier) but also gets the function wrong. *Toni Morrison's* isn't functioning as a modifier, which shades the meaning of *genius,* but as a determiner, which pins down its referent, in the same way that an article like *the* or *this* would do. (How do we know? Because a count noun cannot stand on its own—you can't say *Daughter cooked dinner*—and a modifier doesn't help; *Beautiful daughter cooked dinner* is still bad. But add either an article, as in *A daughter cooked dinner,* or a genitive, as in *Jenny's daughter cooked dinner,* and the sentence is complete. This shows that genitives have the same function as articles, namely determiner.)

As with any pronoun, a writer can confuse his readers if he fails to make the antecedent clear, such as in *Sophie's mother thinks she's fat,* where we don't know whether it's Sophie or her mother who is thought to be fat. But that has nothing to do with the antecedent being in the genitive case; it's just as much of a problem in *Sophie and her mother think she's fat.*

Though it's only fair that the students who thought they spotted an error got credit for their answer (since they may have been miseducated by purists), the ire of language lovers ought to be directed at the stylistic clumsiness of the godawful sentence about Toni Morrison, not at a fictitious error in it.

preposition at the end of a sentence. Winston Churchill did not, as legend has it, reply to an editor who had corrected his prose with "This is pedantry up with which I will not put."[15] Nor is that witticism (originally from a 1942 *Wall Street Journal* article) a particularly good example of the construction that linguists call preposition stranding, as in *Who did you talk to?* or *That's the bridge I walked across.* The particle *up* is an intransitive preposition and does not require an object, so even the most pedantic of pedants would have no objection to a phrase like *This is pedantry with which I will not put up.*

Though the attribution and the example are spurious, the mockery is appropriate. As with split infinitives, the prohibition against clause-final prepositions is considered a superstition even by the language mavens, and it persists only among know-it-alls who have never opened a dictionary or style manual to check. There is nothing, repeat nothing, wrong with *Who are you looking at?* or *The better to see you with* or *We are such stuff as dreams are made on* or *It's you she's thinking of.* The pseudo-rule was invented by John Dryden based on a silly analogy with Latin (where the equivalent to a preposition is attached to the noun and cannot be separated from it) in an effort to show that Ben Jonson was an inferior poet. As the linguist Mark Liberman remarked, "It's a shame that Jonson had been dead for 35 years at the time, since he would otherwise have challenged Dryden to a duel, and saved subsequent generations a lot of grief."[16]

The alternative to stranding a preposition at the end of a clause is allowing it to accompany a *wh*-word to the front, a rule that the linguist J. R. (Haj) Ross dubbed pied-piping, because it reminded him of the way that the Pied Piper lured the rats out of the village of Hamelin. The standard question rule in English converts *You are seeing what?* into *What are you seeing?* and hence *You are looking at what?* into *What are you looking at?* The pied-piping rule allows the *what* to pull the *at* with it to the front of the sentence, yielding *At what are you looking?* The same rule creates relative clauses that begin with a preposition and a *wh*-word such as *the better with which to see you* or *It's you of whom she's thinking.*

Sometimes it really is better to pied-pipe a preposition to the beginning of a clause than to strand it at the end. Most obviously, pied-piping sounds better in a formal style. Abraham Lincoln knew what he was doing at the graves of the fallen soldiers at Gettysburg when he vowed "increased devotion to that cause for which they gave the last full measure of devotion," rather than "increased devotion to that cause which they gave the last full measure of devotion for." Pied-piping is also a good choice when a stranded preposition would get lost in a hubbub of little grammatical words, such as *One of the beliefs which we can be highly confident in is that other people are conscious.* The sentence is easier to parse when the role of the preposition is settled before we get to that busy crossroads: *One of the beliefs in which we can be highly confident is that other people are conscious.*

A good piece of advice on when to pied-pipe and when to strand comes from Theodore Bernstein, who invokes the principle emphasized in chapter 4: select the construction that allows you to end a sentence with a phrase that is heavy or informative or both. The problem with stranding a preposition is that it can end the sentence with a word that is too lightweight to serve as its focal point, making the sentence sound like "the last sputter of an engine going dead." As an example

Bernstein cites *He felt it offered the best opportunity to do fundamental research in chemistry, which was what he had taken his Doctor of Philosophy degree in.* By the same principle, a preposition *should* be stranded at the end of a sentence when it contributes a crucial bit of information, as in *music to read by, something to guard against,* and *that's what this tool is for,* or when it pins down the meaning of an idiom, as in *It's nothing to sneeze at, He doesn't know what he's talking about,* or *She's a woman who can be counted on.*

predicative nominative. When you come home after a day at the office, do you call out to your spouse, "Hi, honey, it's I"? If you do, you are the victim of a schoolmarm rule that insists that a pronoun serving as the complement of *be* must be in nominative case (*I, he, she, we, they*) rather than accusative case (*me, him, her, us, them*). According to this rule, Psalms (120:5), Isaiah (6:5), Jeremiah (4:31), and Ophelia should have cried out, "Woe is I," and the cartoon possum Pogo should have reworded his famous declaration as "We have met the enemy, and he is we."

The rule is a product of the usual three confusions: English with Latin, informal style with incorrect grammar, and syntax with semantics. Though the *referent* of the noun phrase after *be* is the same as that of the subject (enemy = we), the *case* of the noun phrase is determined by its position after the verb, which can always be accusative. (The accusative case is the default in English, and it can be used anywhere except in the subject of a tensed verb; thus we have *hit me, give me a hand, with me, Who, me?, What, me get a tattoo?,* and *Molly will be giving the first lecture, me the second.*) Accusative predicates have been used for centuries by many respected writers (including Pepys, Steele, Hemingway, and Woolf), and the choice between *It is he* and *It is him* is strictly one of formal versus informal style.

sequence of tenses and other perspective shifts. A common error in student writing is to shift the tense from a main clause to a subordinate one even when they refer to the same time period.[17]

She <u>started</u> panicking and got stressed out because she <u>doesn't</u> have enough money.	She <u>started</u> panicking and got stressed out because she <u>didn't</u> have enough money.
The new law <u>requires</u> the public school system to abandon any programs that <u>involved</u> bilingual students.	The new law <u>requires</u> the public school system to abandon any programs that <u>involve</u> bilingual students.

The incorrect versions on the left make the reader feel like she is being yanked back and forth along the time line between the moment at which the sentence was written (present) and the time of the situation being described (past). They belong to a family of "inappropriate shifts" in which the writer fails to stay put at a single vantage point but vanishes from one and pops up at another. The reader can get vertigo when the writer flip-flops within a sentence between persons (first, second, and third), voices (active and passive), or types of discourse (a direct quotation of the speaker's exact words, usually set off with quotation marks, versus an indirect report of the gist, usually set off with *that*):

Love brings out the joy in <u>people's</u> hearts and puts a glow in <u>your</u> eyes.	Love brings out the joy in <u>people's</u> hearts and puts a glow in <u>their</u> eyes.
People <u>express themselves</u> more offensively when their comments <u>are delivered</u> through the Internet rather than personally.	People <u>express themselves</u> more offensively when they <u>deliver</u> their comments through the Internet rather than personally.
The instructor told us<u>, "</u>Please read the next two stories before the next class<u>"</u> and <u>that</u> she might give us a quiz on them.	The instructor told us <u>that</u> we should read the next two stories before the next class and <u>that</u> she might give us a quiz on them.

Sticking to a consistent vantage point is the first step in getting the tenses in a complex story to come out right, but there's more to it than that. A writer also has to harmonize the tenses according to a scheme called sequence of tenses, tense agreement, or backshift. Most readers sense that there is something askew in the sentences on the left:

But at some point following the shootout and car chase, the younger brother fled on foot, according to State Police, who <u>said</u> Friday night they <u>don't</u> believe he <u>has</u> access to a car.

But at some point following the shootout and car chase, the younger brother fled on foot, according to State Police, who <u>said</u> Friday night they <u>didn't</u> believe he <u>had</u> access to a car.

Mark Williams-Thomas, a former detective who amassed much of the evidence against Mr. Savile last year, <u>said</u> that he <u>is</u> continuing to help the police in coaxing people who might have been victimized years ago to come forward.[18]

Mark Williams-Thomas, a former detective who amassed much of the evidence against Mr. Savile last year, <u>said</u> that he <u>was</u> continuing to help the police in coaxing people who might have been victimized years ago to come forward.

Security officials <u>said</u> that only some of the gunmen <u>are</u> from the Muslim Brotherhood.

Security officials <u>said</u> that only some of the gunmen <u>were</u> from the Muslim Brotherhood.

In indirect discourse in the past tense (a staple of news reporting), the tense of a verb often sounds better when it, too, is in the past tense, even though the event was in the present from the vantage point of the person speaking.[19] This is clear enough in simple sentences. One would say *I* <u>*mentioned*</u> *that I* <u>*was*</u> *thirsty,* not *I* <u>*mentioned*</u> *that I* <u>*am*</u> *thirsty,* even though what I actually mentioned at the time was "I am thirsty." Though backshifting usually occurs when someone said something in the past, it also occurs when a proposition was generally *believed* in the past, as in *This* <u>*meant*</u> *that Amy* <u>*was*</u> *taking on too many responsibilities.*

At first glance, the conditions that govern sequences of tenses seem daunting. Bernstein's *The Careful Writer,* an informal style manual, takes five pages to explain fourteen rules, exceptions, and exceptions to the exceptions. Surely not even the most careful writer has learned them one by one. It's better to understand a few principles that govern time, tense, and discourse than to try to memorize a list of regulations that are tailored to the sequence-of-tense phenomenon itself.

The first is to remember that past tense is not the same thing as past time. Recall from the discussion of *if-then* constructions that the past tense is used not just for events that took place in the past but for events that are remote possibilities (as in *If you left tomorrow, you'd save a lot of money*). We now see that the past tense has a third meaning in English: a backshifted event in a sequence of tenses. (Though the meaning of backshifting may seem to be just past time, there are subtle semantic differences between the two.)[20]

The second principle is that backshifting is not mandatory, which means that violating the sequence-of-tense rules and keeping the reported content in the present tense is not always an error. Grammarians distinguish the "attracted" or backshifted sequence, in which the tense of the embedded verb is metaphorically attracted to the tense of the verb of saying, from the "vivid," "natural," or "breakthrough" sequence, in which the embedded verb metaphorically breaks out of the story line of its clause and is located in the real time of the writer and reader. The vivid, nonbackshifted sequence feels more natural when the state being spoken about is not just true at the time that the speaker was speaking but true for all time, or at least indubitably true at the time that the writer is writing and the reader is reading. It would be odd to say *The teacher told the class that water froze at 32 degrees Fahrenheit,* which seems to suggest that perhaps it no longer does; one should violate the backshifting rule here and say *The teacher told the class that water freezes at 32 degrees Fahrenheit.* This leaves plenty of leeway for judgment, depending on whether the writer wishes to emphasize the continuing truth of some idea that was bruited in the past. The backshifted *Simone de Beauvoir noted that women faced discrimination* is neutral as to whether such discrimination is a persistent feature of our society. *Simone de Beauvoir noted that women face discrimination* takes the more feminist position that it is.

A third principle is that indirect discourse is not always introduced with an expression like *he said that* or *she thought that;* sometimes it is implicit in the context. Journalists get tired of repeating *he said,* and novelists sometimes skip it by using a technique called free indirect style, in which the narration of the author incorporates the interior monologue of a protagonist:

According to the Prime Minister, there <u>was</u> no cause for alarm.
As long as the country <u>kept</u> its defense up and its alliances intact,
all <u>would</u> be well.

Renee was getting more and more anxious. What <u>could</u> have
happened to him? <u>Had</u> he leapt from the tower of Fine Hall? <u>Was</u>
his body being pulled out of Lake Carnegie?

A writer can do the opposite, too, and interrupt his narration of an
indirect discourse with an aside directed to the reader, which breaks
out of the backshifted tense and into the present:

Mayor Menino <u>said</u> the Turnpike Authority, which <u>is</u> responsible
for the maintenance of the tunnel, had set up a committee to
investigate the accident.

The final key to using sequences of tenses should be familiar from
our discussion of *if* and *then*. The past-tense forms of *can, will,* and *may*
are *could, would,* and *might,* and these are the forms to use in backshifting:

Amy can play the bassoon.	Amy <u>said</u> that she <u>could</u> play the bassoon.
Paul will leave on Tuesday.	Paul <u>said</u> that he <u>would</u> leave on Tuesday.
The Liberals may try to form a coalition government.	Sonia <u>said</u> that the Liberals <u>might</u> try to form a coalition government.

And the past tense of a past tense (the pluperfect) uses the auxiliary
had, so when the backshifted verb refers to a past time, *had* is sum-
moned into action:

He wrote it himself.	He <u>said</u> that he <u>had</u> written it himself.

It's not obligatory, though; writers often simplify things by using the simple past tense in both places (*He said that he wrote it himself*), which (for complicated reasons) is technically consistent with the semantics of backshifting.

shall and *will*. According to another old rule, when speaking about an event in the future one must use *shall* in the first person (*I shall, we shall*) but *will* in the second and third person (*you will, he will, she will, they will*). But when expressing determination or permission, it's the other way around. Thus Lillian Hellman, when she defied the House Un-American Activities Committee in 1952, properly declared *I will not cut my conscience to fit this year's fashions.* Had her comrades been speaking on her behalf, they would have said *She shall not cut her conscience to fit this year's fashions.*

The rule is suspiciously complicated for something as basic to everyday expression as future time, and it turns out not to be a rule at all. The authors of *Merriam-Webster's Dictionary of English Usage,* having surveyed the uses of the two forms over six hundred years, conclude, "The traditional rules about *shall* and *will* do not appear to have described real usage of these words precisely at any time, although there is no question that they do describe the usage of some people some of the time and that they are more applicable in England than elsewhere."

Even with some Englishmen some of the time, it can be hard to distinguish future time in the first person from determination in the first person because of the metaphysical peculiarity of future time: no one knows what the future will bring, but we can choose to try to affect it.[21] When Churchill said, "We shall fight on the beaches, we shall fight on the landing grounds, . . . we shall never surrender," was he fiercely proclaiming the determination of the British people, or was he calmly prophesying a future that was certain because of the determination of the British people?

With everyone else—the Scots, Irish, Americans, and Canadians (other than those with traditional English schooling)—the rule about *shall* and *will* never applied. In his manual *Plain Words,* Ernest Gowers wrote, "The story is a very old one of the drowning Scot who was mis-understood by English onlookers and left to his fate because he cried, 'I will drown and nobody shall save me!'" Outside England (and for a growing number of speakers there as well), *shall* sounds prissy as an expression of future tense: no one says *I shall pick up the toilet paper at Walmart this afternoon*. And when *shall* is used at all, particularly in the first person, it tends to defy the rule and convey *non*-future senses such as permission (*Shall we dance?*) and determination (as in General Douglas MacArthur's famous declaration "I shall return" and the civil rights anthem "We Shall Overcome"). As Copperud wrote, "*Shall*, then, seems well on the way to extinction, much like the hapless Scot."

split infinitives. Most mythical usage rules are merely harmless. The prohibition of split infinitives (as in *Are you sure you want to perma-nently delete all the items and subfolders in the "Deleted Items" folder?*) and the even more sweeping prohibition of "split verbs" (as in *I will always love you* and *I would never have guessed*) is downright perni-cious. Good writers who have been brainwashed into unsplitting their infinitives can come out with monstrosities such as these:

> Hobbes concluded that the only way out of the mess is for everyone <u>permanently to surrender</u> to an authoritarian ruler.

> David Rockefeller, a member of the Harvard College Class of 1936 and longtime University benefactor, has pledged $100 million <u>to increase dramatically</u> learning opportunities for Harvard undergraduates through international experiences and participation in the arts.[22]

The split-verb superstition can even lead to a crisis of governance. During the 2009 presidential inauguration, Chief Justice John Roberts, a famous stickler for grammar, could not bring himself to have Barack Obama "solemnly swear that I will faithfully execute the office of president of the United States." Abandoning his strict constructionism, Roberts unilaterally amended the Constitution and had Obama "solemnly swear that I will execute the office of president to the United States faithfully." The garbled oath raised fears about whether the transfer of power had been legitimate, and so they repeated the oath verbatim, split verb and all, in a private meeting later that afternoon.

The very terms "split infinitive" and "split verb" are based on a thick-witted analogy to Latin, in which it is impossible to split a verb because it consists of a single word, such as *amare,* "to love." But in English, the so-called infinitive *to write* consists of two words, not one: the subordinator *to* and the plain form of the verb *write,* which can also appear without *to* in constructions such as *She helped him pack* and *You must be brave.*[23] Similarly, the allegedly unsplittable verb *will execute* is not a verb at all but two verbs, the auxiliary verb *will* and the main verb *execute.*

There is not the slightest reason to interdict an adverb from the position before the main verb, and great writers in English have placed it there for centuries.[24] Indeed, the spot in front of the main verb is often the most natural resting place for an adverb. Sometimes it is the *only* resting place, particularly when the modifier is a negation or quantifier such as *not* or *more than.* (Recall from chapter 5 that the placement of *not* affects its logical scope and thus the meaning of the sentence.) In each of the examples below, unsplitting the infinitive either changes the sense or leads to garble:

The policy of the Army at that time was to not send women into combat roles.[25]	The policy of the Army at that time was not to send women into combat roles.
I'm moving to France to not get fat [caption of a *New Yorker* cartoon].[26]	I'm moving to France not to get fat.
Profits are expected to more than double next year.[27]	Profits are expected more than to double next year.

More generally, the preverbal position is the only one in which the adverb unambiguously modifies the verb. In a sentence in which the author may have taken pains to unsplit an infinitive, such as *The board voted immediately to approve the casino,* the reader has to wonder whether it was the vote that was immediate, or the approval. With the infinitive left split—*The board voted to immediately approve the casino*—it can only be the approval.

This does not mean that infinitives should always be split. When the adverbial modifier is long and heavy, or when it contains the most important information in a sentence, it should be moved to the end, just like any other heavy or newsworthy phrase:

Flynn wanted to <u>more definitively</u> identify the source of the rising IQ scores.	Flynn wanted to identify the source of the rising IQ scores <u>more definitively</u>.
Scholars today are confronted with the problem of how to <u>non-arbitrarily</u> interpret the Qur'an.	Scholars today are confronted with the problem of how to interpret the Qur'an <u>non-arbitrarily</u>.

Indeed, it's a good habit to at least consider moving an adverb to the end of the verb phrase. If the adverb conveys important information, it belongs there; if it doesn't (such as *really, just, actually,* and other hedges), it might be a verbal fluffball that is best omitted altogether. And since there are benighted sticklers out there who will mistakenly accuse you of making an error when you split an infinitive, you might as well not ask for trouble if it makes no difference to the sentence anyway.

Finally, in many cases a quantifier naturally floats leftward away from the verb, unsplitting the infinitive, as in the examples on the right:

It seems monstrous <u>to even suggest</u> the possibility.	It seems monstrous <u>even to suggest</u> the possibility.
Is it better <u>to never have</u> been born?	Is it better <u>never to have</u> been born?
Statesmen are not called upon <u>to only settle</u> easy questions.	Statesmen are not called upon <u>only to settle</u> easy questions.[28]
I find it hard to specify when <u>to not split</u> an infinitive.	I find it hard to specify when <u>not to split</u> an infinitive.

The unsplit versions sound more elegant to me, though I can't be sure that my ears haven't been contaminated by a habit of cravenly unsplitting infinitives to avoid spitballs from the Gotcha! Gang.

subjunctive mood and irrealis *were*. For several hundred years commentators on the English language have been predicting, lamenting, or celebrating the imminent extinction of the subjunctive mood. But here we are in the twenty-first century and it refuses to die, at least in writing. To appreciate this, one has to get straight what the subjunctive is, because most people, including traditional grammarians, are confused about it.

There is no distinctive subjunctive form in English; the construction just uses the unmarked form of the verb, such as *live, come,* and *be.* This makes subjunctives hard to spot: they are noticeable only when the verb has a third-person singular subject (in which case it ordinarily takes the suffix *–s,* as in *lives* and *comes*) or when the verb is *to be* (which ordinarily shape-shifts to *am, is,* or *are*). Subjunctives can be sighted in a few clichés that have come down to us from a time in which the form was more common in English:

> So <u>be</u> it; <u>Be</u> that as it may; Far <u>be</u> it from me; If need <u>be</u>.
> Long <u>live</u> our noble queen.
> Heaven <u>forbid</u>.
> <u>Suffice</u> it to say.
> <u>Come</u> what may.

But otherwise the subjunctive is found only in subordinate clauses, generally with mandative verbs and adjectives, which indicate that something is demanded or required:[29]

> I insist that she <u>be</u> kept in the loop.
> It's essential that he <u>see</u> a draft of the speech before it is given.
> We must cooperate in order that the system <u>operate</u> efficiently.

Subjunctives also turn up with certain prepositions and subordinators that specify hypothetical situations:

Bridget was racked with anxiety lest her plagiarism <u>become</u> known.

He dared not light a candle for fear that it <u>be</u> spotted by some prowling savage.

Dwight decided he would post every review on his Web site, whether it <u>be</u> good or bad.

Some of the examples are a bit formal and can be replaced by the indicative, such as *It's essential that he sees a draft* and *whether it is good or bad*. But many subjunctives can be found in everyday writing and speech, such as *I would stress that people just be aware of the danger*, showing that reports of the death of the subjunctive are greatly exaggerated.

Traditional grammarians get tripped up by the verb *be* because they have to squeeze two different forms, *be* and *were* (as in *If I were free*), into a single slot called "subjunctive." Sometimes they call *be* the "present subjunctive" and *were* the "past subjunctive," but in reality there's no difference in tense between them. Rather, the two belong to different moods: *whether he be rich or poor* is subjunctive; *If I were a rich man* is irrealis ("not real"). The irrealis mood is found in many languages, where it expresses situations that are not known to have happened, including hypotheticals, imperatives, and questions. In English it exists only in the form *were*, where it conveys factual remoteness: an irrealis proposition is not just hypothetical (the speaker does not know whether it is true or false) but counterfactual (the speaker believes it's false). Tevye the Milkman was emphatically not a rich man, nor were Tim Hardin, Bobby Darin, Johnny Cash, or Robert Plant (all of whom sang "If I Were a Carpenter") in any doubt as to whether they were carpenters. Counterfactual, by the way, need not mean outlandish— one can say *If she were half an inch taller, that dress would be perfect*—it just means "known to be not the case."

So what's the difference between the past-tense *was*, in those contexts in which it has the meaning of factual remoteness, and the irrealis *were*, which also has the meaning of factual remoteness? The obvious difference is the level of formality: irrealis *I wish I were younger* is fancier than past-tense *I wish I was younger.* Also, in careful writing, *were* conveys a somewhat stronger sense of remoteness than *was* does, implying that the scenario is contrary to fact: *If he were in love with her, he'd propose* accuses him of not being in love; *If he was in love with her, he'd propose* leaves the door open a crack, and the present-tense open conditional *If he is in love with her, he'll propose* doesn't commit the writer either way.

Some writers, dimly sensing that *were* is posher, hypercorrect themselves and use it with open possibilities, such as *He looked at me as if he suspected I were cheating on him* and *If he were surprised, he didn't show it.*[30] In both cases, *was* is appropriate.

***than* and *as*.** Is anything wrong with the sentences on the left?

Rose is smarter than him.	Rose is smarter than he.
George went to the same school as me.	George went to the same school as I.

Many students are taught that they are ungrammatical, because *than* and *as* are conjunctions (which precede clauses), not prepositions (which precede noun phrases). The material that follows them must be a clause, albeit an elliptical clause, from which the predicate has been amputated: the full versions are *Rose is smarter than he is* and *George went to the same school as I did.* Since the noun phrases coming after *than* and *as* are the subjects of the truncated clauses, they must be in nominative case: *he* and *I.*

But if you squirm at the thought of using the "correct" versions on the right because they sound insufferably fussy, you have grammar and history on your side. Like the words *before* and *like,* which we examined earlier, the words *than* and *as* are not conjunctions in the first place but prepositions that take a clause as a complement.[31] The only question is whether they may also take a noun phrase as a complement. Several centuries of great writers—Milton, Shakespeare, Pope, Swift, Johnson, Austen, Thurber, Faulkner, Baldwin—have voted with their pens, and the answer is yes. The difference is just one of style: *than I* is more suited to formal writing, *than me* to writing that is closer to speech.

Though the pedants are mistaken in insisting that *than* and *as* may only be conjunctions, the tree-thinking that motivates their judgment is sound. First, if you do opt for a formal style, don't go overboard and write things like *It affected them more than I.* The chopped-off material after *than* is *it affected me,* not *it affected I,* so even the snootiest of the snoots would call for *me* in this sentence. Second, the two elements being compared should be grammatically and semantically parallel, a requirement that's easy to flub when the first is complex. *The condition of the first house we visited was better than the second* can pass unnoticed in speech but can be grating on the page, because it compares apples (the condition) with oranges (the house). A careful reader will be happier with *was better than that of the second;* the cost of the additional empty words is outweighed by the pleasure of parallel syntax and semantics (a condition in each case). Finally, the casual version (*than me, as her,* and so on) can be ambiguous: *Biff likes the professor more than me* can mean that he likes the professor more than he likes me or that he likes the professor more than I do. In these cases, using a nominative subject is technically clear but a bit stuffy—*Biff likes the professor more than I*—and the best solution is to saw off less of the sentence, leaving *Biff likes the professor more than I do.*

The debate on the correct syntactic category of *than* also feeds the tempest over whether you can say *different than the rest,* where *than,* once again, is a preposition with a noun phrase object, or you must say *different from the rest,* using the uncontroversial preposition *from.* Though *different than NP* is disliked by a slim majority of the *AHD* Usage Panel, it has long been common in carefully written prose. H. L. Mencken reported that a futile attempt to ban it in the 1920s elicited the following comment from the editors of the *New York Sun:* "The excellent tribe of grammarians, the precisians who strive to be correct and correctors, have as much power to prohibit a single word or phrase as a gray squirrel has to put out Orion with a flicker of its tail."[32]

that and *which*. Many spurious rules start out as helpful hints intended to rescue indecisive writers from paralysis when faced with a choice provided by the richness of English. These guides for the perplexed also make the lives of copy editors easier, so they may get incorporated into style sheets. Before you know it, a rule of thumb morphs into a rule of grammar, and a perfectly innocuous (albeit second-choice) construction is demonized as incorrect. Nowhere is this transition better documented than with the phony but ubiquitous rule on when to use *which* and when to use *that*.[33]

According to the traditional rule, the choice depends on which of two kinds of relative clause the word is introducing. A nonrestrictive relative clause is set off by commas, dashes, or parentheses, and expresses a comment from the peanut gallery, as in *The pair of shoes, which cost five thousand dollars, was hideous*. A restrictive relative clause is essential to the meaning of the sentence, often because it pinpoints the referent of the noun from among a set of alternatives. If we were narrating a documentary about Imelda Marcos's vast shoe collection and wanted to single out one of the pairs by how much she paid for it and then say something about that pair alone, we would write *The pair of shoes that cost five thousand dollars was hideous*. The choice between *that* and *which*, according to the rule, is simple: nonrestrictive relative clauses take *which*; restrictive relative clauses take *that*.

One part of the rule is correct: it's odd to use *that* with a nonrestrictive relative clause, as in *The pair of shoes, that cost a thousand dollars, was hideous*. So odd, in fact, that few people write that way, rule or no rule.

The other part of the rule is utterly incorrect. There is nothing wrong with using *which* to introduce a restrictive relative clause, as in *The pair of shoes which cost five thousand dollars was hideous*. Indeed, with some restrictive relatives, *which* is the only option, such as *That which doesn't kill you makes you stronger* and *The book in which I scribbled my notes is worthless*. Even when *which* isn't mandatory, great writers have been using it for centuries, as in the King James Bible's "Render therefore unto Caesar the things which are Caesar's" and Franklin Roosevelt's "a day which will live in infamy." The linguist Geoffrey Pullum searched through a sample of classic novels by authors such as Dickens, Conrad, Melville, and Brontë and found that on average readers will bump into a restrictive relative clause with *which* by the time they are 3 percent of the way into it.[34] Turning to edited prose in twenty-first-century English, he found that *which* was used in about a fifth of the restrictive relative clauses in American newspapers and in more than half of those in British newspapers. Even the grammar nannies can't help themselves. In *The Elements of Style* E. B. White recommended "*which*-hunting," but in his classic essay "Death of a Pig" he wrote, "The premature expiration of a pig is, I soon discovered, a departure which the community marks solemnly on its calendar."

The spurious rule against restrictive *which* sprang from a daydream by Henry Fowler in *Modern English Usage* in 1926: "If writers would agree to regard *that* as the defining relative pronoun, & *which* as the non-defining, there would be much gain both in lucidity & in ease. Some there are who follow this principle now; but it would be idle to pretend that it is the practice either of most or of the best writers." The lexicographer Bergen Evans punctured the reverie with an observation that should be embossed on little cards and handed out to language pedants: "What is not the practice of most, or of the best, is not part of our common language."[35]

So what's a writer to do? The real decision is not whether to use *that* or *which* but whether to use a restrictive or a nonrestrictive relative clause. If a phrase which expresses a comment about a noun can be omitted without substantially changing the meaning, and if it would be pronounced after a slight pause and with its own intonation contour, then be sure to set it off with commas (or dashes or parentheses): *The Cambridge restaurant, which had failed to clean its grease trap, was infested with roaches.* Having done so, you don't have to worry about whether to use *that* or *which,* because if you're tempted to use *that* it means either that you are more than two hundred years old or that your ear for the English language is so mistuned that the choice of *that* and *which* is the least of your worries.

If, on the other hand, a phrase provides information about a noun that is crucial to the point of the sentence (as in *Every Cambridge restaurant <u>which failed to clean its grease trap</u> was infested with roaches,* where omitting the underlined phrase would radically alter the meaning), and if it is pronounced within the same intonation contour as the noun, then don't set it off with punctuation. As for the choice you now face between *which* and *that:* if you hate making decisions, you generally won't go wrong if you use *that.* You'll be a good boy or girl in the eyes of copy editors, and will have avoided a sibilant, which many readers find ugly. Some guidelines recommend a switch to *which* when the relative clause is separated from the noun it modifies, as in *An application to renew a license <u>which had previously been rejected</u> must be resubmitted within thirty days,* where the underlined clause modifies the faraway noun *application,* not the next-door noun *license.* Otherwise you could tilt toward *that* depending on the degree of restrictiveness, that is, the degree to which the meaning of the sentence critically depends on the relative clause. When the modified noun is quantified with *every, only, all, some,* or *few,* the relative changes everything: *Every iPad that has been dropped in the bathtub stops working* is very different from *Every iPad stops working,* and with those noun phrases *that* tends to sound a bit better. Or you could trust your ear, or flip a coin. Level of style won't help you here: unlike the alternatives set apart by other pseudo-rules in the oral tradition, neither *which* nor *that* is more formal than the other.

verbing and other neologisms. Many language lovers recoil from neologisms in which a noun is repurposed as a verb:

Dilbert © 2001 Scott Adams. Used By permission of Universal Uclick. All rights reserved.

Other denominal verbs which have shattered the worlds of anal-retentives include *author, conference, contact, critique, demagogue, dialogue, funnel, gift, guilt, impact, input, journal, leverage, mentor, message, parent, premiere,* and *process* (in the sense of "think over").

But the retentives are misdiagnosing their anomie if they blame it on the English rule that converts nouns into verbs without an identifying affix such as *–ize, –ify, en–,* or *be–*. (Come to think of it, they hate many of those, too, like *incentivize, finalize, personalize, prioritize,* and *empower*.) Probably a fifth of English verbs started out life as nouns or adjectives, and you can find them in pretty much any paragraph of English prose.[36] A glance at the most emailed stories in today's *New York Times* turns up arriviste verbs such as *biopsy, channel, freebase, gear, headline, home, level, mask, moonlight, outfit, panic, post, ramp, scapegoat, screen, sequence, showroom, sight, skyrocket, stack up,* and *tan,* together with verbs derived from nouns or adjectives by affixation such as *cannibalize, dramatize, ensnarl, envision, finalize, generalize, jeopardize, maximize,* and *upend.*

The English language welcomes converts to the verb category and has done so for a thousand years. Many novel verbs that set purists' teeth on edge become unexceptionable to their grown children. It's hard to get worked up, for example, over the now-indispensable verbs *contact, finalize, funnel, host, personalize,* and *prioritize.* Even many of the denominal verbs that gained traction in the past couple of decades have earned a permanent place in the lexicon because they convey a meaning more transparently and succinctly than any alternative, including *incentivize, leverage, mentor, monetize, guilt* (as in *She guilted me into buying a bridesmaid's dress*), and *demagogue* (as in *Weiner tried to demagogue the mainly African-American crowd by playing the victim*).

What really gets on the nerves of Ms. Retentive and her ilk is not verbing per se but neologisms from certain walks of life. Many people are irritated by buzzwords from the cubicle farm, such as *drill down, grow the company, new paradigm, proactive,* and *synergies.* They also bristle at psychobabble from the encounter group and therapy couch, such as *conflicted, dysfunctional, empower, facilitate, quality time, recover, role model, survivor, journal* as a verb, *issues* in the sense of "concerns," *process* in the sense of "think over," and *share* in the sense of "speak."

Recently converted verbs and other neologisms should be treated as matters of taste, not grammatical correctness. You don't have to accept all of them, particularly instant clichés like *no-brainer, game-changer,* and *think outside the box,* or trendy terms which tart up a banal meaning with an aura of technical sophistication, like *interface, synergy, paradigm, parameter,* and *metrics*.

But many neologisms earn a place in the language by making it easy to express concepts that would otherwise require tedious circumlocutions. The fifth edition of the *American Heritage Dictionary,* published in 2011, added ten thousand words and senses to the edition published a decade before. Many of them express invaluable new concepts, including *adverse selection, chaos* (in the sense of the theory of nonlinear dynamics), *comorbid, drama queen, false memory, parallel universe, perfect storm, probability cloud, reverse-engineering, short-sell, sock puppet,* and *swiftboating*. In a very real sense such neologisms make it easier to think. The philosopher James Flynn, who discovered that IQ scores rose by three points a decade throughout the twentieth century, attributes part of the rise to the trickling down of technical ideas from academia and technology into the everyday thinking of laypeople.[37] The transfer was expedited by the dissemination of shorthand terms for abstract concepts such as *causation, circular argument, control group, cost-benefit analysis, correlation, empirical, false positive, percentage, placebo, post hoc, proportional, statistical, tradeoff,* and *variability*. It is foolish, and fortunately impossible, to choke off the influx of new words and freeze English vocabulary in its current state, thereby preventing its speakers from acquiring the tools to share new ideas efficiently.

Neologisms also replenish the lexical richness of a language, compensating for the unavoidable loss of words and erosion of senses. Much of the joy of writing comes from shopping from the hundreds of thousands of words that English makes available, and it's good to remember that each of them was a neologism in its day. The new entries in *AHD* 5 are a showcase for the linguistic exuberance and recent cultural history of the Anglosphere:

> Abrahamic, air rage, amuse-bouche, backward-compatible, brain freeze, butterfly effect, carbon footprint, camel toe, community policing, crowdsourcing, Disneyfication, dispensationalism, dream catcher, earbud, emo, encephalization, farklempt, fashionista, fast-twitch, Goldilocks zone, grayscale, Grinch, hall of mirrors, hat hair, heterochrony, infographics, interoperable, Islamofascism, jelly sandal, jiggy, judicial activism, ka-ching, kegger, kerfuffle, leet, liminal, lipstick lesbian, manboob, McMansion, metabolic syndrome, nanobot, neuroethics, nonperforming, off the grid, Onesie, overdiagnosis, parkour, patriline, phish, quantum entanglement, queer theory, quilling, race-bait, recursive, rope-a-dope, scattergram, semifreddo, sexting, tag-team, time-suck, tranche, ubuntu, unfunny, universal Turing machine, vacuum energy, velociraptor, vocal percussion, waterboard, webmistress, wetware, Xanax, xenoestrogen, x-ray fish, yadda yadda yadda, yellow dog, yutz, Zelig, zettabyte, zipline

If I were allowed to take just one book to the proverbial desert island, it might be a dictionary.

***who* and *whom*.** When Groucho Marx was once asked a long and orotund question, he replied, "Whom knows?" A 1928 short story by George Ade contains the line "'Whom are you?' he said, for he had been to night school." In 2000 the comic strip *Mother Goose and Grimm* showed an owl in a tree calling "Whom" and a raccoon on the ground replying "Show-off!" A cartoon entitled "Grammar Dalek" shows one of the robots shouting, "I think you mean Doctor Whom!" And an old *Rocky and Bullwinkle* cartoon contains the following dialogue between the Pottsylvanian spies Boris Badenov and Natasha Fatale:

> NATASHA: Ve need a safecracker!
> BORIS: Ve already got a safecracker!
> NATASHA: Ve do? Whom?
> BORIS: Meem, dat's whom!

The popularity of *whom* humor tells us two things about the distinction between *who* and *whom*.[38] First, *whom* has long been perceived as formal verging on pompous. Second, the rules for its proper use are obscure to many speakers, tempting them to drop *whom* into their speech whenever they want to sound posh.

As we saw in chapter 4, the distinction between *who* and *whom* ought to be straightforward. If you mentally rewind the transformational rule that moves the *wh*-word to the front of a sentence, the distinction between *who* and *whom* is identical to the distinction between *he* and *him* or between *she* and *her,* which no one finds difficult. The declarative sentence *She tickled him* can be turned into the question *Who tickled him?* in which the *wh*-word replaces the subject and appears in nominative case, *who.* Or it can be turned into the question *Whom did she tickle?* in which the *wh*-word replaces the object and hence appears in accusative case, *whom.*

But the cognitive difficulty of mentally undoing the movement rule, combined with the historical disappearance of case-marking from English (except for the personal pronouns and the genitive *'s*), has long made it hard for English speakers to keep track of the distinction. Shakespeare and his contemporaries frequently used *who* where the rules would call for *whom* and vice versa, and even after a century of nagging by prescriptive grammarians the *who-whom* distinction remains tenuous in speech and informal writing. Only the stuffiest prig would use *whom* to begin a short question or relative clause:

> Whom are you going to believe, me or your own eyes?
> It's not what you know; it's whom you know.
> Do you know whom you're talking to?

And when people do try to write with *whom,* they often get it wrong:

> In 1983, Auerbach named former Celtics player K.C. Jones coach of the Celtics, whom starting in 1984 coached the Celtics to four straight appearances in the NBA Finals.

Whomever installed the shutters originally did not consider proper build out, and the curtains were too close to your window and door frames.

The exploration of syntactic trees in chapter 4 turned up an especially common fumble of *whom*. When the deep-structure position of the *wh*-word is the subject of a clause (demanding *who*), but it occurs adjacent to a verb which takes the clause as its complement (whispering *whom*), writers lose sight of the tree and allow their eyes to be caught by the adjacent verb, resulting in *The French actor plays a man whom she suspects __ is her husband* (pages 101 and 102). These sequences have been so common for so long, and arouse so little reaction even in many careful writers, that some linguists have argued that they are no longer errors at all. In the dialect of these writers, they argue, the rules for *whom* call for it to be used when it links to the position following a verb, even if it is the subject of a clause.[39]

Like the subjunctive mood, the pronoun *whom* is widely thought to be circling the drain. Indeed, tabulations of its frequency in printed text confirm that it has been sinking for almost two centuries. The declining fortunes of *whom* may represent not a grammatical change in English but a cultural change in Anglophones, namely the informalization of writing, which makes it increasingly resemble speech. But it's always risky to extrapolate a downward slope all the way to zero, and since the 1980s the curve seems to be leveling off.[40] Though *whom* is pompous in short questions and relative clauses, it is a natural choice in certain other circumstances, even in informal speech and writing. We still use *whom* in double questions like *Who's dating whom?*, in fixed expressions like *To whom it may concern* and *With whom do you wish to speak?*, and in sentences in which a writer has decided not to strand a preposition at the end of a clause but to pied-pipe it to the front. A scan of my email turns up hundreds of hits for *whom* (even after I discarded the ones with the boilerplate "The information in this email is intended only for the person to whom it is addressed"). Here are a few unmistakably informal sentences in which *whom* is so natural as to be unnoticeable:

> I realize it's short notice, but are you around on Monday? Al Kim from Boulder (grad student friend of Jesse's and someone with whom I've worked a lot as well) will be in town.
>
> Not sure if you remember me; I'm the fellow from Casasanto's lab with whom you had a hair showdown while at Hunter.
>
> Hi Steven. We have some master's degree applicants for whom I need to know whether they passed prosem with a B+ or better. Are those grades available?
>
> Reminder: I am the guy who sent you the Amy Winehouse CD. And the one for whom you wrote "kiss the cunt of a cow" at your book signing.[41]

The best advice to writers is to calibrate their use of *whom* to the complexity of the construction and the degree of formality they desire. In casual prose, *whom* can be reserved for the object of a preposition and other positions in which *who* would be conspicuously wrong; all other uses will sound pompous. In formal prose, a writer should mentally move the *wh*-word back to its original position in the tree and choose *who* or *whom* accordingly. But even in formal prose, an author may want a voice that is lean and direct rather than ornate and flowery, and in that case *who* has a place in simple constructions. If William Safire, who wrote the *New York Times*' "On Language" column and coined the term *language maven* in reference to himself, could write, "Let tomorrow's people decide who they want to be president," so can you.[42]

QUANTITY, QUALITY, AND DEGREE

The rules of usage we just examined were centered on grammatical form, such as distinctions among grammatical categories and the marking of tense and mood. But other prescriptive rules—those that govern the expression of quality, quantity, and degree—are alleged to be closer to the truths of logic and mathematics than to the conventions of grammar. To flout these rules, the purists claim, is no mere peccadillo but an assault on reason itself.

Claims of this kind are always fishy. Though language certainly provides writers with the means to express fine logical distinctions, none of the distinctions is mechanically conveyed by a single word or construction. All words have multiple meanings which must be sorted out by the context, and each of those meanings is far subtler than the ones invoked by purists. Let's examine some of the sophistry behind claims that issues of usage can be settled by logical or mathematical consistency.

absolute and graded qualities (*very unique*). They say you can't be a little bit married or a little bit pregnant, and purists believe that the same is true for certain other adjectives. One of the commonest insults to the sensibility of the purist is the expression *very unique* and other phrases in which an "absolute" or "incomparable" adjective is modified by an adverb of degree such as *more, less, somewhat, quite, relatively,* or *almost.* Uniqueness, the purists say, is like marriage and pregnancy: something is either unique (one of a kind) or not unique, so referring to degrees of uniqueness is meaningless. Nor can one sensibly modify *absolute, certain, complete, equal, eternal, perfect,* or *the same.* One may not write, for instance, that one statement is *more certain* than another, or that an inventory is now *more complete,* or that an apartment is *relatively perfect.*

A glance at the facts of usage immediately sets off Klaxon horns. Great writers have been modifying absolute adjectives for centuries, including the framers of the American Constitution, who sought *a more perfect union.* Many of the examples pass unnoticed by careful writers and are approved by large majorities of the *AHD* Usage Panel, including *nothing could be more certain, there could be no more perfect spot,* and *a more equal allocation of resources.* Though the phrase *very unique* is universally despised, other modifications of *unique* are unobjectionable. Martin Luther King wrote, "I am in the rather unique position of being the son, the grandson, and the great grandson of preachers." The *New York Times* science section recently had an article which said, "The creature is so unique in its style and appearance that the biologists who discovered it have given it not just its own species name . . . but have declared that it is an entirely new phylum."

Even *very unique* might have a place. Last night while I was walking by a cabaret in Provincetown, I was handed a glossy postcard inviting passersby to the show. The card showed a well-toned man wearing a silver lamé dinner jacket with matching bow tie, pasties, codpiece, and nothing else, surrounded by a bevy of voluptuous big-haired showgirls of both genders, and at his feet an androgynous waif with a pencil mustache in a turquoise sequined sailor suit. The copy read: "The *Atomic* BOMBSHELLS. A Drag-tastic BURLESQUE Extravaganza! Featuring Boyleseque superstar JETT ADORE! Hosted by Seattle's Premiere Fancy Lady BEN DELACREME." The hostess who handed me the card promised that it would be a "very unique show." Who would argue?

Here is the flaw in the purists' logic. Uniqueness is *not* like pregnancy and marriage; it must be defined relative to some scale of measurement. I am told that all snowflakes are unique, and so they may be under a microscope, but frankly, they all look the same to me. Conversely, each of the proverbial two peas in a pod is unique if you squint hard enough through a magnifying glass. Does this mean that nothing is unique, or does it mean that everything is unique? The answer is neither: the concept "unique" is meaningful only after you specify which qualities are of interest to you and which degree of resolution or grain size you're applying.

Occasionally we can state the quality explicitly and the scale is discrete, as in *Hawaii is unique among states in being surrounded by water,* or *The number 30 may be factored into the unique set of primes 2, 3, and 5.* Purists would like to reserve the word *unique* for those circumstances, in which adverbs of comparison are indeed incongruous. But often our eye is caught by many qualities, some of them continuous, and the item we are considering may either be close to others on the scale or be miles away. Calling something *quite unique* or *very unique* implies that the item differs from the others in an unusual number of qualities, that it differs from them to an unusual degree, or both. In other words, pick any scale or cutoff you want, and the item will still be unique. This "distinctive" sense has coexisted with the "having no like or equal" sense for as long as the word *unique* has been in common use. The other supposedly absolute adjectives also depend on the granularity of the comparison scale, and thus may be qualified by how coarse or fine a scale is being used in that comparison.

This doesn't mean that you should go ahead and use *very unique*, even if you are handing out postcards for The Atomic Bombshells. As we saw in chapter 2, *very* is a soggy modifier in the best of circumstances, and the combination with *unique* grates on enough readers that it's wise to avoid it. (If you must qualify the word, *really unique* and *truly unique*, which convey degree of confidence rather than degree of distinctness, will meet with fewer objections.) But comparisons of supposedly absolute adjectives are not illogical, and often they are unavoidable.

singulars and plurals (*none is* versus *none are*). The neat dichotomy in English grammar between singular and plural leaves many situations out in the cold. The problem is that there is a mismatch between the simplistic theory of number baked into our grammar and the true nature of number in all its mathematical and logical glory. Suppose I name a bunch of things and ask you to sort them into two piles, one pile for quantities equal to 1 and the other pile for quantities greater than 1. Here's how our dialogue might go. Ready?

"A cup."	Easy! 1.
"The potted plants."	Easy! More than 1.
"A cup and a spoon."	Still easy! 1 + 1 = 2, which is more than 1.

"A pair of gloves."	Well, that depends . . . I see two objects, but they count as one item on my sales receipt, and when I decide whether I can use the express checkout lane.
"The dining room set."	Gee, that also depends. It's one set, but four chairs and a table.
"The gravel under the flowerpot."	Hey, am I supposed to count every pebble, or can I consider it just a saucerful of gravel?
"Nothing."	Hmmm . . . Neither, I guess. What am I supposed to do now?
"The desk or the chair."	Huh?
"Each object in the room."	Wait—do you want me to stand back and consider all those things at once (that would be greater than 1) or zoom in and examine them one at a time (that would be 1 each time)?

These are the brainteasers that English writers must solve when they shoehorn expressions with *none, every,* and other quantifiers into the singular-plural dichotomy.

Purists insist that *none* means "no one" and therefore must be singular: *None of them was home,* not *None of them were home.* This is false; you can look it up. *None* has always been either singular or plural, depending on whether the writer is pondering the entire group at once or each member individually. The singular (*None of the students was doing well*) feels a bit more specific and emphatic than the plural (*None of the students were doing well*), and is often stylistically preferable for that reason. But when an additional quantifier forces us to carve out a subset of the group and say something about that subset, the plural is irresistible: *Almost none of them are honest* (not *is*); *None but his closest friends believe his alibi* (not *believes*). *Any* can also swing both ways: *Are any of the children coming? Any of the tools is fine.* And so it is with *no,* depending on the number of the noun it quantifies: *No man is an island; No men are islands.*

In contrast to these three terms, which specify pure not-ness and lack an inherent number, some quantifiers do single out one individual at a time. *Neither* means "not one of the two," and it is singular: *Neither book was any good,* not *Neither book were any good.* The same is true of *either,* even when it picks one item from a pair: *Either of the candidates is experienced enough to run the country,* not *are.* Likewise, the *one* in *anyone* and *everyone,* the *body* in *somebody* and *everybody,* and the *thing* in *nothing* shout that they are referring to one thing at a time (even though the words rope in the entire universe of individuals), and that makes each of them singular: *Anyone is welcome to try; Everyone eats at my house; Everybody is a star; Nothing is easy.*

When two singular nouns are coordinated with *and,* the phrase is usually plural, as if the language is acknowledging that one plus one equals two: *A fool and his money are soon parted; Frankie and Johnny were lovers.* But when the duo is mentally packaged as a single entity, it can be singular: *One and one and one is three; Macaroni and cheese is a good dinner for kids.* This is part of a larger phenomenon called notional agreement, in which the grammatical number of a noun phrase can depend on whether the writer *conceives of* its referent as singular or plural, rather than on whether it is *grammatically marked* as singular or plural. A writer can mentally package a conjoined phrase into a single unit (*Bobbing and weaving is an effective tactic*). Or he can do the opposite: peer into a singular collective noun and see the plurality of individual members composing it (as in *The panel were informed of the new rules*). This is far more common in British English; Americans do a double take when they read *The government are listening at last, The* Guardian *are giving you the chance to win books,* and *Microsoft are considering the offer.*

What happens with other words that join nouns together, like *with, plus,* and *or*? *With* is a preposition, so the phrase *a man with his son* is not a coordination at all but an ordinary phrase with the head *a man,* modified by *with his son.* It inherits the singular number of its head, so we say *A man with his son is coming up the walk.* The word *plus* began as a preposition, and again we say *All that food plus the weight of the backpack is a lot to carry.* But *plus* is increasingly being used as a coordinator as well, and it's natural to say *The hotel room charge plus the surcharge add up to a lot of money.*

And then we have to figure out what to do with *or* (an issue we met on page 207). A disjunction of two singular nouns is singular: *Either beer or wine is served.* A disjunction of two plurals is plural: *Either nuts or pretzels are served.* With a disjunction of a singular and a plural, traditional grammar books say that number agreement goes with the noun closest to the verb: *Either a burrito or nachos are served; Either nachos or a burrito is served.* But that policy leaves many writers queasy (the Usage Panel divides up the middle on it), and it may be best to spare readers from stretching their grammatical intuitions and recast the sentence, such as *They serve either nachos or a burrito.*

Certain nouns specify a measure and then indicate what they're measuring using an *of*-phrase, such as *a lot of peanuts, a pair of socks,* and *a majority of the voters.* These Zelig-like nouns can be singular or plural depending on the number of the *of*-phrase: *A lot of work was done; A lot of errors were made.* (It's possible that their trees differ, with *a lot* being the head of the phrase in the first version but a determiner of the head *errors* in the second.) When the *of*-phrase is absent, the writer mentally supplies it, and the phantom phrase determines the number: *A lot [of people] were coming; A lot [of money] was spent.* Other chameleonic quantifiers include *couple, majority, more than one, pair, percentage, plenty, remainder, rest,* and *subset.*

And then there is the puzzling construction *one of those who.* Recently I endorsed a book by Douglas Hofstadter and Emmanuel Sander with a blurb that began, "I am one of those cognitive scientists who believes that analogy is a key to explaining human intelligence." Hofstadter thanked me but sheepishly asked if I would mind correcting *who believes* to *who believe.* I even more sheepishly agreed, because Hofstadter (as his readers might expect) was engaging in impeccable tree-thinking. The relative clause beginning with *who* is attached to the plural *cognitive scientists,* not the singular *one:* there is a set of cognitive scientists (plural) who value analogy, and I belong to that set. So it must take the plural verb *believe.*

Though I couldn't defend my original wording, it still sounded fine to my ears, so I did a bit of research on the construction. It turns out I am not alone. For more than a thousand years the siren song of singular *one* has overridden the syntactic demand of the plural *those,* and writer after writer has gone with the singular. This includes the über-purist James Kilpatrick, who to his chagrin repeatedly found himself using it even after having been corrected by the UofAllPeople Club. (He wrote, for example, "In Washington, we encounter 'to prioritize' all the time; it is one of those things that makes Washington unbearable.") Often the technically correct version sounds off-kilter. More than 40 percent of the Usage Panel rejected *The sports car turned out to be one of the most successful products that were ever manufactured in this country.* Sometimes the dilemma can be sidestepped by artful rewording (in this example, deleting *that were*), but not always. In *Tina is one of the few students who turns to the jittery guidance counselor, Emma, for help with her feelings,* a switch to *turn* would require a parallel switch of *her feelings* to *their feelings,* which makes it seem as if each girl sought counseling for all the girls' feelings, not her own.

The *Cambridge Grammar* suggests that the construction is a hybrid of two trees that mingle in the reader's mind: one in which the relative clause is attached to the downstairs noun (*cognitive scientists who believe*), and it determines the meaning, and one in which it is attached to the upstairs noun (*one . . . who believes*), and it determines the number agreement. Usage guides today suggest that either the singular or plural is acceptable in this construction, depending on whether *one* or *those* looms larger in the writer's mind.[43]

duals and plurals (*between/among* and other distinctions between two and more than two). Many languages distinguish three quantities in their number system: singular (one), dual (two), and plural (many). Hebrew, for example, distinguishes *yom,* "day," *yomayim,* "two days," and *yamim,* "days." English doesn't have dual number marking, but it does recognize twoness in words like *pair* and *couple,* and, with varying degrees of controversy, in other quantifying words.

between and *among*. Many students are taught that *between* must be used with just two items (since *tween* is related to *two* and *twain*) and *among* with more than two: *between you and me* but *among the three of us*. This is only half right. It's certainly true that *among* may not be used with a twosome: *among you and me* is impossible. But it's not true that *between* is reserved for two: no one would say *I've got sand among my toes, I never snack among meals,* or *Let's keep this among you, me, and the lamppost.* Nonetheless some writers have dutifully followed this pseudo-rule to the bitter end and have concocted fussy expressions like *sexual intercourse among two men and a woman, a book that falls among many stools,* and *The author alternates among mod slang, clichés, and quotes from literary giants.* The real principle is that *between* is used for a relationship of an individual to any number of other individuals, as long as they are being considered two at a time, whereas *among* is used for a relationship of an individual to an amorphous mass or collectivity. *Thistles grew between the roses* suggests an orderly row in a formal garden, and *Thistles grew among the roses* more of an entwined profusion.

each other and *one another*. A traditional rule of the same ilk assigns *each other* to twosomes and *one another* to groups larger than two. If you don't trust your ear you will never get into trouble if you follow the rule, and that's what a majority of the Usage Panel claims to do. But the common practice is to use them interchangeably—*the teammates hugged each other, the teammates hugged one another*—and the major dictionaries and usage guides say that's fine.

alternatives. There is a claim in Prescriptistan that *alternative* refers only to two possibilities, never more than two. It's a bubbe meise; forget it.

either and *any*. The twosome restriction is on firmer ground with *either,* at least when it is used as a noun or a determiner. The phrases *Either of the three movies* and *Either boy of the three* are decidedly odd, and *either* should be replaced with *any*. But when *either* is used in an *either-or* construction, threesomes are more acceptable, if not always graceful: *Either Tom, Dick, or Harry can do the job; Either lead, follow, or get out of the way.*

–er and *–est; more* and *most.* Adjectives can be inflected for degree, giving us comparatives (*harder, better, faster, stronger*) and superlatives (*hardest, best, fastest, strongest*). Tradition says that you should reserve the comparative for two things and use the superlative for more than two: you should refer to *the faster of the two runners,* rather than *the fastest,* but it's all right to refer to *the fastest of three runners.* The same is true for polysyllabic adjectives that shun *–er* and *–est* in favor of *more* and *most: the more intelligent of the two; the most intelligent of the three.* But it's not a hard-and-fast rule: we say *May the best team win,* not *the better team,* and *Put your best foot forward,* not *your better foot.* Once again the traditional rule is stated too crudely. It's not the sheer number of items that determines the choice but the manner in which they are being compared. A comparative adjective is appropriate when the two items are being directly contrasted, one against the other; a superlative can work when an item is superior not just to the alternative in view at the time but to a larger implicit comparison group. If Usain Bolt and I happened to be competing for a spot on an Olympic Dream Team, it would be misleading to say that they picked the faster of the two men for the team; they picked the fastest man.

things and stuff (count nouns, mass nouns and *ten items or less*). Finally, let's turn to the pebbles and gravel, which represent the two ways that English speakers can conceptualize aggregates: as discrete things, which are expressed as plural count nouns, and as continuous substances, which are expressed as mass nouns. Some quantifiers are choosy as to which they apply to. We can talk about *many pebbles* but not *much pebbles, much gravel* but not *many gravel.* Some quantifiers are not choosy: We can talk about *more pebbles* or *more gravel.*[44]

Now, you might think that if *more* can be used with both count and mass nouns, so can *less.* But it doesn't work that way: you may have *less gravel,* but most writers agree that you can only have *fewer pebbles,* not *less pebbles.* This is a reasonable distinction, but purists have extended it with a vengeance. The sign over supermarket express checkout lanes,

TEN ITEMS OR LESS, is a grammatical error, they say, and as a result of their carping whole-food and other upscale supermarkets have replaced the signs with TEN ITEMS OR FEWER. The director of the Bicycle Transportation Alliance has apologized for his organization's popular T-shirt that reads ONE LESS CAR, conceding that it should read ONE FEWER CAR. By this logic, liquor stores should refuse to sell beer to customers who are fewer than twenty-one years old, law-abiding motorists should drive at fewer than seventy miles an hour, and the poverty line should be defined by those who make fewer than eleven thousand five hundred dollars a year. And once you master this distinction, well, that's one fewer thing for you to worry about.[45]

If this is all starting to sound weird to you, you're not alone. The caption of this cartoon reminds us that while sloppy grammar can be a turnoff, so can the kind of pedantry that takes a grammatical distinction too far:

Looking for: ...

Describe yourself in 50 words or (less) ✗
It's 50 words or FEWER actually. Less is used for non-countable quantities, collective amounts or degrees. Fewer means 'not as many'. The terms are NOT interchangable.

The dating agency found no matches.

© Luke Surl 2008

What's going on? As many linguists have pointed out, the purists have botched the *less-fewer* distinction. It is certainly true that *less* is clumsy when applied to the plurals of count nouns for discrete items: *fewer pebbles* really does sound better than *less pebbles*. But it's not true that *less* is forbidden to apply to count nouns across the board. *Less* is perfectly natural with a *singular* count noun, as in *one less car* and *one less thing to worry about.* It's also natural when the entity being quantified is a continuous extent and the count noun refers to units of measurement. After all, *six inches, six months, six miles,* and a bill for *six dollars* don't actually correspond to six hunks of matter; the units, like the 1–11 scale on Nigel Tufnel's favorite amplifier in *This Is Spinal Tap,* are arbitrary. In these cases *less* is natural and *fewer* is a hypercorrection. And *less* is idiomatic in certain expressions in which a quantity is being compared to a standard, including *He made no less than fifteen mistakes* and *Describe yourself in fifty words or less.* Nor are these idioms recent corruptions: for much of the history of the English language, *less* could be used with both count and mass nouns, just as *more* is today.

Like many dubious rules of usage, the *less-fewer* distinction has a smidgen of validity as a pointer of style. In cases where *less* and *fewer* are both available to a writer, such as *Less/fewer than twenty of the students voted,* the word *fewer* is the better choice in classic style because it enhances vividness and concreteness. But that does not mean that *less* is a grammatical error.

The same kind of judgment applies to the choice between *over* and *more than.* When the plural refers to countable objects, it's a good idea to use *more than. He owns more than a hundred pairs of boots* is more classic-stylish than *He owns over a hundred pairs of boots,* because it encourages us to imagine the pairs individually rather than lumping them together as an amorphous collection. But when the plural defines a point on a scale of measurement, as in *These rocks are over five million years old,* it's perverse to insist that it can only be *more than five million years old,* because no one is counting the years one by one. In neither of these cases, usage guides agree, is *over* a grammatical error.

I can't resist the temptation to sum up this review with a short story by the writer Lawrence Bush (reproduced with his kind permission), which alludes to many of the points of usage we have examined (see how many you can spot) while speaking to the claim that the traditional rules reduce misunderstanding:[46]

I had only just arrived at the club when I bumped into Roger. After we had exchanged a few pleasantries, he lowered his voice and asked, "What do you think of Martha and I as a potential twosome?"

"That," I replied, "would be a mistake. Martha and me is more like it."

"You're interested in Martha?"

"I'm interested in clear communication."

"Fair enough," he agreed. "May the best man win." Then he sighed. "Here I thought we had a clear path to becoming a very unique couple."

"You couldn't be a very unique couple, Roger."

"Oh? And why is that?"

"Martha couldn't be a little pregnant, could she?"

"Say what? You think that Martha and me . . ."

"Martha and I."

"Oh." Roger blushed and set down his drink. "Gee, I didn't know."

"Of course you didn't," I assured him. "Most people don't."

"I feel very badly about this."

"You shouldn't say that: I feel bad . . ."

"Please, don't," Roger said. "If anyone's at fault here, it's me."

masculine and feminine (nonsexist language and singular *they*). In a 2013 press release President Barack Obama praised a Supreme Court decision striking down a discriminatory law with the sentence "No American should ever live under a cloud of suspicion just because of what they look like."[47] In doing so he touched one of the hottest usage buttons of the past forty years: the use of the plural pronouns *they, them, their,* and *themselves* with a grammatically singular antecedent like *no American.* Why didn't the president write *because of what he looks like,* or *because of what he or she looks like*?

Many purists claim that singular *they* is a LOLcat-worthy grammatical howler which is tolerated only as a sop to the women's movement.

According to this theory, the pronoun *he* is a perfectly serviceable gender-neutral pronoun; as grammar students used to be taught, "The masculine embraces the feminine, even in grammar." But feminist sensibilities could not abide even the illusory sexism of using a masculine form to represent both genders, and so they engaged in a campaign of linguistic engineering that started with a mandate to use the clumsy *he or she* and slipped down a slope that ended in singular *they*. The computer scientist David Gelernter explains: "Unsatisfied with having rammed their 80-ton 16-wheeler into the nimble sports-car of English style, [feminist authorities] proceeded to shoot the legs out from under grammar—which collapsed in a heap after agreement between subject and pronoun was declared to be optional."[48] (He should have written "antecedent and pronoun"—the issue has nothing to do with subjects.)

The webcomic artist Ryan North addresses the same usage problem with a lighter touch and no hostility toward feminism. One of his creations, T-Rex, is more skeptical than Gelernter about how nimble English really is, and confronts the language in the second person, asking it to admit one of the gender-neutral pronouns that have been proposed over the years, such as *hir, zhe,* or *thon:*

But in a subsequent panel in this strip, the talking dinosaur equivocates, first worrying that "invented pronouns always sound strange," and then reversing himself and wondering whether he should learn to like *There comes a time when thon must look thonself in the mirror.*

Let's try to sort this out. To begin with, T-Rex is right and the purists are wrong: English has no gender-neutral pronoun. At least in grammar, the masculine does not embrace the feminine. Experiments have shown that when people read the word *he* they are likely to assume that the writer intended to refer to a male.[49] But the experiments hardly needed to be run, because it's a brute fact of English grammar that *he* is a masculine and not a common-gender pronoun. If you don't believe it, just read these sentences:[50]

> Is it your brother or your sister who can hold his breath for four
> minutes?
> The average American needs the small routines of getting ready for
> work. As he shaves or pulls on his pantyhose, he is easing himself
> by small stages into the demands of the day.
> She and Louis had a game—who could find the ugliest photograph of
> himself.
> I support the liberty of every father or mother to educate his children
> as he desires.

Do you still think that *he* is gender-neutral? It's hard to disagree with T-Rex's accusation that there is a bug in the English language. It would seem that a writer who wants to embrace both sexes in a quantified sentence must either make an error in number by writing *No American should be under a cloud of suspicion because of what they look like* or make an error in gender by writing *No American should be under a cloud of suspicion because of what he looks like.* And as the dinosaur explained, other solutions—*it, one, he or she, s/he, his/her,* novel pronouns like *thon*—have problems as well.

One theoretical possibility is no longer an actual possibility: blow off concerns with gender inclusiveness, use masculine terms, and let the reader read between the lines and infer that women are included, too. No major publication today will allow this "sexist usage," nor should they. Quite aside from the moral principle that half of humanity should not be excluded from generic statements about the species, we now know that the major objections to nonsexist language that were first voiced forty years ago have been refuted. Not only have the grace and expressiveness of the English language survived the substitution of gender-neutral terms for masculine ones (*humanity* for *man*, *firefighter* for *fireman*, *chair* for *chairman*, and so on), but the generation of readers that has grown up with the new norms has turned the traditionalists' startle reaction on its head. Today it is sexist usage that stops readers in their tracks and distracts them from the writer's message.[51] It's hard, for example, not to cringe when reading this sentence from a famous 1967 article by a Nobel laureate: "In the good society a man should be free . . . of other men's limitations on his beliefs and actions."[52]

This brings us back to the solution of singular *they*. The first thing to realize about the usage is that it is not a recent contrivance forced on writers by militant 1970s feminists. Gelernter pines for "Shakespeare's most perfect phrases" and Jane Austen's "pure simple English," but this turns out to be a pratfall of slapstick proportions, because both writers were exuberant users of—you guessed it—singular *they*. Shakespeare used it at least four times, and in a paper entitled "Everyone Loves Their Jane Austen," the scholar Henry Churchyard counts eighty-seven instances in her works, of which thirty-seven were in her own voice rather than her characters' (for example, "Every body began to have their vexation," from *Mansfield Park*).[53] Chaucer, the King James Bible, Swift, Byron, Thackeray, Wharton, Shaw, and Auden also used the form, as did Robert Burchfield, editor of the *Supplement to the Oxford English Dictionary* and the most recent edition of *Fowler's Modern English Usage*.

A second thing to understand about singular *they* is that even though it offers a handy solution to the need for a gender-free pronoun, that is not its only or even its primary appeal. Many writers use it even when the gender is unambiguously male or female. George Bernard Shaw, for example, wrote the lines "*No man goes to battle to be killed.*" "*But they do get killed.*" Since the dialogue was about men, Shaw had no need to pander to feminism, but he used singular *they* anyway, because the supposedly correct form with *he* would have turned the exchange into hash: "*No man goes to battle to be killed.*" "*But he does get killed.*" (The same is true for a sentence I used two paragraphs ago: *No major publication today will allow this "sexist usage," nor should they.* The alternative *nor should it* would make it sound as if I had a particular publication in mind and raise the question "Nor should which?") A contemporary example with an unambiguous female referent comes from a spoken interview with Sean Ono Lennon in which he specified the kind of person he was seeking as a romantic partner: "Any girl who is interested must simply be born female and between the ages of 18 and 45. They must have an IQ above 130 and they must be honest."[54] Once again he did not need *they* as a gender-neutral pronoun; he had already stipulated the congenital and current sex of his desired mate (nowadays perhaps you have to specify both). But since he was speaking not of an individual female but of the entire pool, *they* felt right to him. In each of these cases *they* takes part in a kind of notional agreement. *No man* and *any girl* are grammatically singular but psychologically plural: they pertain to classes with many individuals. The mismatch is similar to the one we saw in examples like *None are coming* and *Are any of them coming?*

Indeed, "singular *they*" is a misnomer. In these constructions, *they* is not being used as a singular pronoun being wrenched into agreement with a singular antecedent like *each dinosaur, everyone, no American, the average American,* or *any girl.* Remember when we tried to sort descriptions of objects into piles for "one" and "more than one"? We discovered that the very idea of the numerosity of a quantified expression like *nothing* or *each object* is obscure. Does *no American* refer to one American or to many Americans? Whom knows? $0 \neq 1$, but then $0 \not> 1$ either. This indeterminism forces us to realize that the word *they* in the sentences we have been considering does not have the usual semantics of a pronoun and an antecedent, as it does in *The musicians are here and they expect to be fed.* Rather, the pronoun *they* is functioning as a bound variable: a symbol that keeps track of an individual across multiple descriptions of that individual. So-called singular *they* really means "x" in an expression like "For all x, if x is an American, then x should not be under a cloud of suspicion because of x's appearance," or "For all *x,* if Sean Ono Lennon considers marrying *x,* then *x* is born female & *x* has an IQ above 130 & *x* is honest."[55]

So singular *they* has history and logic behind it. Experiments that measure readers' comprehension times to the thousandth of a second have shown that singular *they* causes little or no delay, but generic *he* slows them down a lot.[56] Even T-Rex, in a subsequent *Dinosaur Comics* strip, conceded that his purism was mistaken:

Assuming you aren't willing to start a campaign for *thon,* does that mean you should go ahead and use singular *they*? It depends on the level of formality, the nature of the antecedent, and the available alternatives. Obviously singular *they* is less acceptable in formal than in informal writing. It is also more conspicuous when the antecedent is an indefinite noun phrase like *a man,* whose singular aroma makes the apparent plurality of *they* stand out. It's not as problematic with a universally quantified antecedent like *everyone,* and barely noticeable with a negative quantifier like *no* or *any.*

The judgments of the Usage Panel are sensitive to this difference. Only a minority accepts *A person at that level should not have to keep track of the hours they put in*—though the size of that minority has doubled in the past decade, from 20 percent to almost 40 percent, one of many signs that we are in the midst of a historical change that's returning singular *they* to the acceptability it enjoyed before a purist crackdown in the nineteenth century. A slim majority of the panel accepts *If anyone calls, tell them I can't come to the phone* and *Everyone returned to their seats.* The main danger in using these forms is that a more-grammatical-than-thou reader may falsely accuse you of making an error. If they do, tell them that Jane Austen and I think it's fine.

For many decades usage manuals have recommended two escape hatches for the singular pronoun trap. The easiest is to express the quantified description as a plural, which makes *they* a grammatically honest pronoun. If you think that you can improve on Jane Austen's prose, for example, you could change *Every body began to have their vexation* to *They all began to have their vexations.* This is the solution that experienced writers use most often, and you would be surprised how many generic or universal sentences can be recast with plural subjects without anyone noticing: *Every writer should shorten their sentences* is easily transformed into *All writers should shorten their sentences* or just *Writers should shorten their sentences.*

The other escape hatch is to replace the pronoun with an indefinite or generic alternative and count on the reader's common sense to fill in the referent: *Every body began to have their vexation* becomes *Every body began to have a vexation,* and *Every dinosaur should look in his or her mirror* becomes *Every dinosaur should look in the mirror.*

Neither solution is perfect. Sometimes a writer really does need to focus on a single individual, which makes a plural inappropriate. In *Americans must never live under a cloud of suspicion just because of what they look like,* the generic plural *Americans* can be interpreted to mean "the typical American" or "most Americans," which undermines Obama's declaration that freedom from discrimination must apply to each and every one without exception. With Shaw's dialogue, plural subjects in *Men never go to battle to be killed. But many of them do get killed* would have undercut the point of the exchange, in which the listener is asked to ponder the foolhardiness of an individual enlistee, and the replacements would also have sabotaged Shaw's juxtaposition of the low probability that any given individual will be killed with the high probability that some of them will be killed. Nor can a pronoun always be replaced by an indefinite or generic noun:

| During an emergency, every parent must pick up their child. | During an emergency, every parent must pick up a child. |

The replacement makes it seem as if a parent could choose a child at random to pick up, rather than being responsible for picking up his or her own child.

Because of these complexities, writers always have to consider the full inventory of devices that the English language makes available to convey generic information, each imperfect for a different reason: *he, she, he or she, they,* a plural antecedent, replacing the pronoun, and who knows, perhaps someday even using *thon*.

For some purists, these complexities provide an excuse to dismiss all concerns with gender inclusiveness and stick with the flawed option of *he*. Gelernter complains, "Why should I worry about feminist ideology while I write? . . . Writing is a tricky business that requires one's whole concentration." But the reaction is disingenuous. Every sentence requires a writer to grapple with tradeoffs between clarity, concision, tone, cadence, accuracy, and other values. Why should the value of not excluding women be the only one whose weight is set to zero?

DICTION

Even writers who are skeptical of traditional prescriptions on grammar tend to give more weight to prescriptions on word choice. Fewer superstitions have grown up around word meaning than around grammar, because lexicographers are pack rats who accumulate vast collections of examples and compose their definitions empirically rather than kibitzing in an armchair with half-baked theories about how English ought to work. As a result, the definitions in contemporary dictionaries are usually faithful to the consensus of literate readers. A writer who is unsure of the consensus for a word is well advised to look it up rather than embarrass himself and annoy his readers with a malaprop. (The word *malaprop,* short for *malapropism,* comes from Mrs. Malaprop, a character in Richard Sheridan's 1775 play *The Rivals,* who misused words to comic effect, such as *reprehend* for *apprehend* and *epitaph* for *epithet*.)

Though less nonsense is disseminated about word meanings than about grammar, the nonsense factor is far from zero. With the backing of data from the *AHD* Usage Panel, historical analyses from several dictionaries, and a pinch of my own judgment, I will review a few fuss-budget decrees you can safely ignore before turning to living distinctions you'd be wise to respect.

Word	Only Sense Allowed by Purists	Sense Commonly Used	Comment
aggravate	make worse (*aggravate the crisis*)	annoy (*aggravate the teacher*)	The "annoy" sense has been in use since the 17th century and is accepted by 83% of the Usage Panel.
anticipate	deal with in advance (*We anticipated the shortage by stocking up on toilet paper.*)	expect (*We anticipated a pleasant sabbatical year.*)	The "expect" sense is accepted by 87% of the Usage Panel.
anxious	worried (*Flying makes me anxious.*)	eager (*I'm anxious to leave.*)	The Usage Panel splits 50-50, but the "eager" sense has long been in use and is included without comment in most dictionaries.
comprise	contain (*The US comprises 50 states.*)	compose, make up (*The US is comprised of 50 states.*)	The "compose" sense is often used and increasingly accepted, particularly in the passive.

Word	Only Sense Allowed by Purists	Sense Commonly Used	Comment
convince	cause to believe (*She convinced him that vaccines are harmless.*)	cause to act (*She convinced him to have his child vaccinated.*)	*Convince* supposedly contrasts with *persuade,* which means "cause to act," but few writers care.
crescendo	gradual increase (*a long crescendo*)	climax, peak (*reach a crescendo*)	The insistence on the "increase" sense is an etymological fallacy, based on the Italian source and the technical term in music. The "climax" sense is entrenched, and accepted by a slim majority of the Usage Panel.
critique	noun (*a critique*)	verb (*to critique*)	The verb is widely disliked but venerable, and usefully different from *criticize* in implying analysis rather than censure.
decimate	destroy a tenth	destroy most	An etymological fallacy, based on the Roman punishment of mutinous legions.
due to	adjective (*The plane crash was due to a storm.*)	preposition (*The plane crashed due to a storm.*)	Actually, both are prepositions, and both are fine.[57]

Word	Only Sense Allowed by Purists	Sense Commonly Used	Comment
Frankenstein	the fictional scientist	a monster	If you insist on *We've created a Frankenstein's monster!* you probably also popped champagne on Jan. 1, 2001, wondering where all the other revelers were. ("You see, there was no Year 0, so the third millennium really begins in 2001 . . .") Give it up.
graduate	transitive and usually passive (*She was graduated from Harvard.*)	intransitive (*She graduated from Harvard.*)	The "correct" sense in the passive is increasingly obscure, though it persists in the active *Harvard graduated more lawyers this year.* The Usage Panel embraces the intransitive, though it hates the flipped transitive *She graduated Harvard.*
healthy	possessing good health (*Mabel is healthy.*)	healthful, conducive to good health (*Carrot juice is a healthy drink.*)	*Healthy* meaning "conducive to health" has been more common than *healthful* for 500 years.

Word	Only Sense Allowed by Purists	Sense Commonly Used	Comment
hopefully	verb phrase adverb: in a hopeful manner (*Hopefully, he invited her upstairs to see his etchings.*)	sentence adverb: it is to be hoped that (*Hopefully, it will stop hailing.*)	Many adverbs, such as *candidly, frankly,* and *mercifully,* modify both verb phrases and sentences. *Hopefully* is just newer, and became a purist cause célèbre in the 1960s. Irrational resistance lingers, but dictionaries and newspapers increasingly accept it.
intrigue	noun: a plot (*She got involved in another intrigue.*)	verb: to interest (*This really intrigues me.*)	This innocent verb is a target of two quack theories: verbs from nouns are bad; loan words from French are bad.
livid	black and blue, the color of a bruise	angry	Look it up.
loan	noun (*a loan*)	verb (*to loan*)	The verb goes back to 1200 CE, but after the 17th century was lost in England and preserved in the US; that was enough to taint it.
masterful	domineering (*a masterful personality*)	expert, masterly (*a masterful performance*)	One of Fowler's harebrained schemes to tidy up the language. A few purists slavishly copied his rule into their stylebooks, but writers ignore him.

Word	Only Sense Allowed by Purists	Sense Commonly Used	Comment
momentarily	for a moment (*It rained momentarily.*)	in a moment (*I'll be with you momentarily.*)	The "in a moment" sense is more recent, and less common in Britain than in the US, but completely acceptable. The two meanings can be distinguished by the context.
nauseous	nauseating (*a nauseous smell*)	nauseated (*The smell made me nauseous.*)	Despite furious opposition, the "nauseated" sense has taken over.
presently	soon	now	The more transparent "now" sense has been in continuous use for 500 years, particularly in speech, and the word is rarely ambiguous in context. About half the Usage Panel reject it, but for no good reason.
quote	verb (*to quote*)	noun, a truncation of *quotation* (*a quote*)	A matter of style: the noun is acceptable in speech and informal writing, a bit less so in formal writing.
raise	nurture a farm animal or grow a crop (*raise a lamb, raise corn*)	rear a child, nurture a child (*raise a child*)	The childrearing sense dropped out of British English but remained in American, and is accepted by a resounding 93% of the Usage Panel.

Word	Only Sense Allowed by Purists	Sense Commonly Used	Comment
transpire	become known (*It transpired that he had been sleeping with his campaign manager.*)	happen (*A lot has transpired since we last spoke.*)	The "become known" sense is fading; the "happen" sense has taken over, though it is perceived by many as pretentious.
while	at the same time (*While Rome burned, Nero fiddled.*)	whereas (*While some rules make sense, others don't.*)	The "whereas" sense has been standard since 1749 and is as common as the "same time" sense. Usually it creates no ambiguity; if it does, rewrite the sentence.
whose	of a person (*a man whose heart is in the right place*)	of an entity (*an idea whose time has come; trees whose trunks were coated with ice*)	This handy pronoun can rescue many a phrase from awkwardness, e.g., *trees the trunks of which were coated with ice*. There's no good reason to avoid it with nonhuman antecedents.

And now the moment I've been waiting for: I get to be a purist! Here is a list of words which I am prepared to try to dissuade you from using in their nonstandard senses. (I'll use the linguist's convention of marking them with an asterisk.) Most of the nonstandard usages are malaprops traceable to a mishearing, a misunderstanding, or a kitschy attempt to sound sophisticated. A general rule for avoiding malaprops is to assume that the English language never tolerates two words with the same root and different affixes but the same meaning, like *amused* and *bemused*, *fortunate* and *fortuitous*, *full* and *fulsome*, *simple* and *simplistic.* If you know a word and then come across a similar one with a fancy prefix or suffix, resist the temptation to use it as a hoity-toity synonym. Your readers are likely to react as Inigo Montoya did in *The Princess Bride* to Vizzini's repeated use of *inconceivable* to refer to events that just happened: "You keep using that word. I do not think it means what you think it means."

Word	Preferred Usage	Problematic Usage	Comment
adverse	detrimental (*adverse effects*)	averse, disinclined (**I'm not adverse to doing that.*)	It should be *I'm not averse to doing that.*
appraise	ascertain the value (*I appraised the jewels.*)	apprise, inform (**I appraised him of the situation.*)	It should be *I apprised him of the situation.*
as far as	*As far as the money is concerned, we should apply for new funding.*	**As far as the money, we should apply for new funding.*	The *is concerned* (or *goes*) is redundant and wordy, but without it readers wait for the other shoe to drop. The error is encouraged by the lure of the similar *As for,* which needs no such continuation.

Word	Preferred Usage	Problematic Usage	Comment
beg the question	assumes what it should be proving (*When I asked the dealer why I should pay more for a German car, he said I would be getting "German quality," but that just begs the question.*)	raises the question (**The store has cut its hours and laid off staff, which begs the question of whether it will soon be closing.*)	The "raise the question" sense is more transparent (particularly when the question is urgent, as if it were begging to be raised), and it is common enough that many dictionaries list it. But the "circular reasoning" sense is standard in the scholarly communities that originated the expression and has no good substitute, so using *beg* to mean "raise" will irritate such readers.
bemused	bewildered	amused	Dictionaries and the Usage Panel are clear on this.
cliché	noun (*Shakespeare used a lot of clichés.*)	adjective (**"To be or not to be" is so cliché.*)	Don't be fooled by the French *-é*, which often creates adjectives like *passé* and *risqué*; the adjective is *clichéd*, "being a cliché," analogous to *talented*, "having talent."
credible	believable (*His sales pitch was not credible.*)	credulous, gullible (**He was too credible when the salesman delivered his pitch.*)	*-ible* and *-able* mean "able," in this case "able to be believed, able to be credited."

Word	Preferred Usage	Problematic Usage	Comment
criteria	plural of *criterion* (*These are important criteria.*)	singular of *criterion* (**This is an important criteria.*)	Nails on a chalkboard.
data	plural count noun (*This datum supports the theory, but many of the other data refute it.*)	mass noun (**This piece of data supports the theory, but much of the other data refutes it*).	I like to use *data* as a plural of *datum*, but I'm in a fussy minority even among scientists. *Data* is rarely used as a plural today, just as *candelabra* and *agenda* long ago ceased to be plurals. But I still like it.
depreciate	decrease in value (*My Volvo has depreciated a lot since I bought it*).	deprecate, disparage (**She depreciated his efforts.*)	The "disparage" sense is not a malaprop, and it's accepted in dictionaries, but many writers like to reserve that sense for *deprecate*.
dichotomy	two mutually exclusive alternatives (*the dichotomy between even and odd numbers*)	difference, discrepancy (**There is a dichotomy between what we see and what is really there.*)	A tacky attempt to sound fancy-shmancy. The *tom* means "cut," as in *atomic* (originally "unsplittable"), *anatomy*, and *tomography* (x-ray cross sections).

Word	Preferred Usage	Problematic Usage	Comment
disinterested	unbiased; without a vested interest (*The dispute should be resolved by a disinterested judge.*)	uninterested (**Why are you so disinterested when I tell you about my day?*)	The "uninterested" sense is older, and has a continuous and respectable history. But since we have the word *uninterested* and lack an exact synonym for *disinterested*, readers will appreciate your maintaining the distinction.
enervate	sap, weaken (*an enervating commute*)	energize (**an enervating double espresso*)	Literally "to remove the nerves" (originally "to remove the sinews").
enormity	extreme evil	enormousness	The allegedly incorrect usage is both old and common, but many careful writers reserve *enormity* for evil. Some use *enormity* in the hybrid sense "deplorable enormousness," writing of the *enormity* of population pressure in India, the task faced by teachers in slums, or the stockpile of nuclear weapons.

Word	Preferred Usage	Problematic Usage	Comment
flaunt	show off (*She flaunted her abs.*)	flout (**She flaunted the rules.*)	A malaprop based on the similar sound and spelling, together with the shared meaning "brazenly."
flounder	flop around ineffectually (*The indecisive chairman floundered.*)	founder, sink to the bottom (**The headstrong chairman floundered.*)	In practice *flounder* and *founder* are often interchangeable, being two ways of slowly failing. To keep them straight, remember that *to flounder* is what flounders do; *to founder* is related to other bottom-words like *foundation* and *fundamental*.
fortuitous	coincidental, unplanned (*Running into my ex-husband at the party was purely fortuitous.*)	fortunate (**It was fortuitous that I worked overtime because I ended up needing the money.*)	Many writers, including a majority of the Usage Panel, approve the "fortunate" sense (particularly in the hybrid sense of good luck), and it is recognized in most dictionaries. But some readers still bristle.
fulsome	unctuous; excessively and insincerely complimentary (*She didn't believe his fulsome valentine for a second.*)	full, copious (**a fulsome sound; *The contrite mayor offered a fulsome apology.*)	The "copious" sense is historically respectable, but the Usage Panel hates it, and it could get you into trouble, because readers may assume you're impugning something when you don't mean to.

Word	Preferred Usage	Problematic Usage	Comment
homogeneous	with the suffix *-eous*, pronounced "homo-genius"	with the suffix *-ous*, pronounced like "homogenized"	*homogenous* is listed in dictionaries, but it's a corruption which crept in after homogenized milk became popular. Similarly, *heterogeneous* is preferable to *heterogenous*.
hone	sharpen (*hone the knife, hone her writing skills*)	home in on, converge upon (**I think we're honing in on a solution.*)	*AHD* accepts *to hone in on*, but it is a malaprop of *to home*, "return home" (what homing pigeons do). The overlap in meaning ("gradually converge on a precise point or edge") conspires with the similar sounds to encourage the malaprop.
hot button	an emotional, divisive controversy (*She tried to stay away from the hot button of abortion.*)	hot topic (**The hot button in the robotics industry is to get people and robots to work together.*)	Slang and vogue words give rise to malaprops, too (see also *New Age, politically correct, urban legend*). The *button* metaphor pertains to eliciting an instant, reflexive response, as in *He tried to press my buttons.*

Word	Preferred Usage	Problematic Usage	Comment
hung	suspended (*hung the picture*)	suspended from the neck until dead (**hung the prisoner*)	*Hung the prisoner* is not incorrect, but the Usage Panel and other careful writers prefer *hanged*.
intern (verb)	detain, imprison (*The rebels were interned in the palace basement for three weeks.*)	inter, bury (**The good men do is oft interned with their bones.*)	It's *interred with their bones.* The meanings overlap, but listen for the *terr* (earth, as in "terrestrial") in *inter*, and for the *internal* related to *intern*.
ironic	uncannily incongruent; seemingly designed to violate expectations (*It was ironic that I forgot my textbook on human memory.*)	inconvenient, unfortunate (**It was ironic that I forgot my textbook on organic chemistry.*)	You keep using that word. I do not think it means what you think it means.
irregardless	There isn't one.	regardless, irrespective	Purists have been ranting about this misnegated portmanteau for decades, but it's not particularly common, and virtually all the Web hits are to claims that "*irregardless* is not a word." The purists should declare victory and move on.

Word	Preferred Usage	Problematic Usage	Comment
literally	in actual fact (*I literally blushed.*)	figuratively (**I literally exploded.*)	The "figuratively" sense is a common hyperbole, and it is rarely confusing in context. But it drives careful readers crazy. Like other intensifiers it is usually superfluous, whereas the "actual fact" sense is indispensable and has no equivalent. And since the figurative use can evoke ludicrous imagery (e.g., *The press has literally emasculated the president*), it screams, "I don't think about what my words mean."
luxuriant	abundant, florid (*luxuriant hair, a luxuriant imagination*)	luxurious (*a luxuriant car)	The "luxurious" sense is not incorrect (all dictionaries list it), but as a showy synonym for a perfectly good word it's in bad taste.
meretricious	tawdry; offensively insincere (*a meretricious hotel lobby; a meretricious speech*)	meritorious (**a meretricious public servant, *a meretricious benefactor*)	The word originally referred to prostitutes. My advice: Never try to compliment something by calling it meretricious. See also *fulsome, opportunism, simplistic.*

Word	Preferred Usage	Problematic Usage	Comment
mitigate	alleviate (*Setting out traps will mitigate the ant problem.*)	militate, provide reasons for (**The profusion of ants mitigated toward setting out traps.*)	Some good writers have been caught using *mitigate* for *militate*, but it's widely considered a malaprop.
New Age	spiritualistic, holistic (*He treated his lumbago with New Age remedies, like chanting and burning incense.*)	modern, futuristic (**This countertop is made from a New Age plastic.*)	Just because the expression contains the word *new*, that does not mean it can refer to any new thing.
noisome	smelly	noisy	It's from *annoy*, not from *noise*.
nonplussed	stunned, bewildered (*The market crash left the experts nonplussed.*)	bored, unimpressed (**His market pitch left the investors nonplussed.*)	From the Latin *non plus*, "no more." It means "nothing more can be done."
opportunism	seizing or exploiting opportunities (*His opportunism helped him get to the top, but it makes me sick.*)	creating or promoting opportunities (**The Republicans advocated economic opportunism and fiscal restraint.*)	The correct sense can be a compliment ("resourcefulness") or an insult ("unscrupulousness"), more often the latter. As with *fulsome,* if you use it carelessly you may insult something you meant to praise.

Word	Preferred Usage	Problematic Usage	Comment
parameter	a variable (*Our prediction depends on certain parameters, like inflation and interest rates.*)	a boundary condition, a limit (**We have to work within certain parameters, like our deadline and budget.*)	The pseudo-technical "boundary" sense, a blend with *perimeter*, has become standard, and is accepted by most of the Usage Panel. But as with *beg the question*, the sloppy usage gets on the nerves of technically sophisticated readers who need the original sense.
phenomena	plural of *phenomenon* (*These are interesting phenomena.*)	singular of *phenomenon* (**This is an interesting phenomena.*)	See *criteria*.
politically correct	dogmatically left-liberal (*The theory that little boys fight because of the way they have been socialized is the politically correct one.*)	fashionable, trendy (**The Loft District is the new politically correct place to live.*)	See *hot button, New Age, urban legend.* The *correct* is sarcastic, lampooning the idea that only one kind of political opinion may be expressed.
practicable	easily put into practice (*Learning French would be practical, because he often goes to France on business, but because of his busy schedule it was not practicable.*)	practical (**Learning French would be practicable, because he often goes to France on business.*)	The *–able* means "able," as in *ability*. See also *credible, unexceptionable.*

Word	Preferred Usage	Problematic Usage	Comment
proscribe	condemn, forbid (*The policies proscribe amorous interactions between faculty and students.*)	prescribe, recommend, direct (**The policies proscribe careful citation of all sources.*)	A doctor writes a prescription, not a proscription, when he tells you what you should do.
protagonist	actor, active character (*Vito Corleone was the protagonist in* The Godfather.)	proponent (**Leo was a protagonist of nuclear power.*)	The "proponent" sense is definitely a malaprop.
refute	prove to be false (*She refuted the theory that the earth was flat.*)	allege to be false, try to refute (**She refuted the theory that the earth was round.*)	*Refute* is a factive or success verb, like *know* and *remember*, which presupposes the objective truth or falsity of the proposition. Many writers, including a slim majority of the Usage Panel, accept the non-factive "try to refute" sense, but the distinction is worth respecting.
reticent	shy, restrained (*My son is too reticent to ask a girl out.*)	reluctant (**When rain threatens, fans are reticent to buy tickets to the ballgame.*)	The Usage Panel hates the "reluctant" sense.

Word	Preferred Usage	Problematic Usage	Comment
shrunk, sprung, stunk, sunk	past participle (*Honey, I've shrunk the kids.*)	past tense (**Honey, I shrunk the kids.*)	Admittedly, *Honey, I shrank the kids* might not have worked as the title of the Disney movie, and past-tense *shrunk* and similar forms are venerable and respectable. But it's classier to distinguish pasts from participles (*sank–has sunk, sprang–has sprung, stank–has stunk*) and to avail oneself of other lovely irregular forms like *shone, slew, strode–has stridden, and strove–has striven.*
simplistic	Naïvely or overly simple (*His proposal to end war by having children sing Kumbaya was simplistic.*)	simple, pleasingly simple (**We bought Danish furniture because we liked its simplistic look. *)	Though not uncommon in art and design journalism, using *simplistic* for *simple* sets many readers' teeth on edge, and can insult something it means to praise. See also *fulsome, opportunism.*
staunch	loyal, sturdy (*a staunch supporter*)	stop a flow, stanch a flow (**staunch the bleeding*)	Dictionaries say that both spellings are fine with both meanings, but it's classier to keep them distinct.

Word	Preferred Usage	Problematic Usage	Comment
tortuous	twisting (*a tortuous road, tortuous reasoning*)	torturous (**Watching Porky's Part VII was a tortuous experience.*)	Both come from the Latin word for "twist," as in *torque* and *torsion*, because twisting limbs was a common form of torture.
unexceptionable	not worthy of objection (*No one protested her getting the prize, because she was an unexceptionable choice.*)	unexceptional, ordinary (**They protested her getting the prize, because she was an unexceptionable actress.*)	*Unexceptional* means "not an exception." *Unexceptionable* means "no one is able to take exception to it."
untenable	indefensible, unsustainable (*Flat-Earthism is an untenable theory; Caring for quadruplets while running IBM was an untenable situation.*)	painful, unbearable (**an untenable tragedy; *untenable sadness*)	The hybrid sense "so unbearable as to be unsustainable" is accepted by the Usage Panel, as in Isabel Wilkerson's "when life became untenable."
urban legend	an intriguing and widely circulated but false story (*Alligators in the sewers is an urban legend.*)	someone who is legendary in a city (**Fiorello LaGuardia became an urban legend.*)	See also *hot button, New Age, politically correct.* The *legend* pertains to the original sense "a myth passed down for generations," not the journalistic sense "a celebrity."

Word	Preferred Usage	Problematic Usage	Comment
verbal	in linguistic form (*Verbal memories fade more quickly than visual ones.*)	oral, spoken (**A verbal contract isn't worth the paper it's written on.*)	The "spoken" sense has been standard for centuries and is by no means incorrect (the famous Goldwynism wouldn't work without it), but sometimes it is confusing.

The differences between two other families of similar-sounding words are so tortuous (and torturous) as to need a bit more explanation.

The words *affect* and *effect* come in both noun and verb versions. Though it's easy to confuse them, it's worth mastering the distinction, because the common errors in the third column will make you look like an amateur.

Word	Correct Use and Spelling	Incorrect Use and Spelling
an effect	an influence: *Strunk and White had a big effect on my writing style.*	**Strunk and White had a big affect on my writing style.*
to effect	to put into effect, to implement: *I effected all the changes recommended by Strunk and White.*	**I affected all the changes recommended by Strunk and White.*
to affect (first sense)	to influence: *Strunk and White affected my writing style.*	**Strunk and White effected my writing style.*
to affect (second sense)	to fake: *He used big words to affect an air of sophistication.*	**He used big words to effect an air of sophistication.*

But the most twisted family of look-alike and mean-alike words in the English lexicon is the one with *lie* and *lay*. Here are the gruesome details:

Verb	Meaning and Syntax	Present Tense	Past Tense	Past Participle
to lie	to recline (an intransitive irregular verb)	*He lies on the couch all day.*	*He lay on the couch all day.*	*He has lain on the couch all day.*
to lay	to set down, to cause to lie (a transitive regular verb)	*He lays a book upon the table.*	*He laid a book upon the table.*	*He has laid a book upon the table.*
to lie	to fib (an intransitive regular verb)	*He lies about what he does.*	*He lied about what he did.*	*He has lied about what he has done.*

The imbroglio arises from the fact that we have two distinct verbs fighting over the form *lay*: it's the past tense of *lie,* and it's the plain form of *lay,* whose meaning—just to torment you further—is "cause to lie." It's no wonder that English speakers commonly say *lay down* or *I'm going to lay on the couch,* collapsing the transitive and intransitive versions of *lie.* Or are they collapsing the past and present tenses of *lie*? Both have same result:

*to lay	to recline (an intransitive regular verb)	**He lays on the couch all day.*	**He laid on the couch all day.*	**He has laid on the couch all day.*

Don't blame the usage on Bob Dylan's "Lay, Lady, Lay" or Eric Clapton's "Lay Down, Sally"; careful English writers have been using it since 1300, right up to William Safire's "The dead hand of the present should not lay on the future" (no doubt triggering a flurry of mail for his UofAllPeople file). Intransitive *lay* is by no means incorrect, but to the ears of many, *lie* sounds better:

PUNCTUATION

The main job of punctuation is to eliminate the ambiguities and garden paths that would mislead a reader if print consisted only of vowels, consonants, and spaces.[58] Punctuation restores some of the prosody (melody, pausing, and stress) that is missing from print, and it provides hints about the invisible syntactic tree that determines a sentence's meaning. As the T-shirt observes, punctuation matters: *Let's eat, Grandma* has a different meaning from *Let's eat Grandma*.

The problem for the writer is that punctuation indicates prosody in some places, syntax in others, and neither of them consistently anywhere. After centuries of chaos, the rules of punctuation began to settle down only a bit more than a century ago, and even today the rules differ on the two sides of the Atlantic and from one publication to another. The rules, moreover, are subject to changes in fashion, including an ongoing trend to reduce all punctuation to the bare minimum. They fill scores of pages in reference manuals, and no one but a professional copy editor knows them all. Even the sticklers can't agree on how to stickle. In 2003 the journalist Lynne Truss published the unlikely bestseller *Eats, Shoots & Leaves: The Zero Tolerance Approach to Punctuation* (whose title comes from the punch line of a joke about a panda who shot up a restaurant because he had read a mispunctuated description of his dietary habits). In her book Truss decries the punctuation errors she spotted in ads, signs, and newspapers. In a 2004 *New Yorker* review, the critic Louis Menand decries the punctuation errors he spotted in Truss's book. In a *Guardian* article on the response to Truss, the English scholar John Mullan decries the punctuation flaws he spotted in Menand's review.[59]

Still, a few common errors are so uncontroversial—the run-on sentence, the comma splice, the grocer's apostrophe, the comma between subject and predicate, the possessive *it's*—that they have become tantamount to the confession "I am illiterate," and no writer should be caught making them. As I mentioned, the problem with these errors is not that they betray an absence of logical thinking but that they betray a history of inattention to the printed page. In the hope that an ability to distinguish the logical and illogical features of punctuation may help a reader master both, I'll say a few words about the design of the system, highlighting the major bugs that have been locked into it.

commas and other connectors (colons, semicolons, and dashes). The first of the comma's two major functions is to separate parenthetical comments about an event or a state—the time, place, manner, purpose, result, significance, writer's opinion, and other by-the-way remarks—from the words that are necessary to pin down the event or state itself. We already met this function in the distinction between restrictive and nonrestrictive relative clauses. A restrictive relative clause, such as the one in *Sticklers who don't understand the conventions of punctuation shouldn't criticize errors by others,* is free of commas, and thereby singles out a subset of sticklers, namely those who don't understand the conventions of punctuation. The same phrase set off by commas,

Sticklers, who don't understand the conventions of punctuation, shouldn't criticize errors by others, slips in a snide comment on the competence of a typical stickler, but that jibe is irrelevant to the advice conveyed by the sentence, which is offered to sticklers across the board.

The traditional terms "restrictive" and "nonrestrictive" are misnomers, because the comma-less versions (called "integrated relative clauses" by the *Cambridge Grammar*) don't always restrict the referents of the noun to some subset. What they do is specify information that is necessary to make the sentence true. In the sentence *Barbara has two sons <u>whom she can rely on</u> and hence is not unduly worried,* the underlined relative clause does not pare down the set of Barbara's sons from the full brood to just the two she can rely on; she may only have two. It indicates that *because* those two sons are sons on whom Barbara can rely, *therefore* she has no need to worry.[60]

And that is a key to understanding where to put commas in other constructions. Commas set off a phrase that is not an integral constituent of the sentence, and which as a result is not essential to understanding its meaning. The sentence *Susan visited her friend Teresa* tells us that it's important for us to know that Susan singled out Teresa as the person she intended to visit. In *Susan visited her friend, Teresa,* it's only significant that Susan visited a friend (oh, and by the way, the friend's name is Teresa). In the headline NATIONAL ZOO PANDA GIVES BIRTH TO 2ND, STILLBORN CUB, the comma between the two modifiers indicates that the panda gave birth to a second cub and (here's another fact) the cub was stillborn. Without the comma, the *stillborn* would be embedded beneath the *2nd* in the tree, and the meaning would be that this is the second time she has given birth to a stillborn cub. Strings of modifiers without commas progressively narrow down the referent of a noun, like nested circles in a Venn diagram, whereas strings of modifiers with commas just keep adding interesting facts about it, like overlapping circles. If the phrase had been *2nd, stillborn, male cub* we would now know one more fact about the dead offspring, namely that it was male. If it had been *2nd stillborn male cub* we would know that the previous stillborn cub was male, too.

This doesn't sound all that hard. So why are there so many comma errors out there for the zero-tolerance squad to get incensed about? Why do comma errors account for more than a quarter of all language errors in student papers, occurring at a rate of about four errors per paper?[61] The main reason is that a comma does not *just* signal a syntactic break (marking a phrase that is not integrated into a larger phrase) together with the corresponding semantic break (marking a meaning that is not essential to the meaning of the sentence). It also signals a *prosodic* break: a slight pause in pronunciation. Now, often these breaks line up: a supplementary phrase, the kind that calls for a comma, is typically preceded and followed by a pause. But often they do not line up, and that lays out a minefield for an inexperienced or inattentive writer.

When a supplementary phrase is short a speaker naturally skates right over it to the next phrase in the sentence, and the current rules of punctuation give writers the option of going with the sound and leaving out the commas—as I did just now, omitting the comma after *short*. The rationale is that too many commas too close together can give a sentence a herky-jerky feel. Also, since a sentence may have many levels of branching while English provides only the puny comma to separate them all on the page, a writer may choose to keep the comma in reserve to demarcate the major branches in the tree, rather than dicing the sentence into many small pieces that the reader must then reassemble. The reason I refrained from inserting a comma after *When a supplementary phrase is short* was that I wanted the comma between the end of that clause and the beginning of the next one to neatly cleave the sentence in two. The cleft would have been obscured if the first clause had also been riven by a comma. Here are some other sentences in which the comma may be omitted, at least in a "light" or "open" punctuation style, because the following phrase is short and clear enough not to require a pause before it:

Man plans and God laughs.
If you lived here you'd be home by now.

By the time I get to Phoenix she'll be rising.

Einstein he's not.

But it's all right now; in fact it's a gas!

Frankly my dear, I don't give a damn.

That is the choice that Lynne Truss made in the dedication to *Eats, Shoots & Leaves*:

To the memory of the striking Bolshevik printers of St Petersburg who, in 1905, demanded to be paid the same rate for punctuation marks as for letters, and thereby directly precipitated the first Russian Revolution.

Menand poked fun at her, pointing out that the relative clause beginning with *who* was nonrestrictive (Truss meant to dedicate her book to all the striking printers, not to a subset who demanded payment for punctuation) and thus demanded a comma before it. Truss's defenders pointed out that the alternative (*To the striking Bolshevik printers of St Petersburg, who, in 1905, demanded . . .*) would have been awkwardly thick with commas, forcing the reader to hopscotch through that part of the sentence a word or two at a time. One pointed out that Menand was universalizing the famously eccentric policy of his major outlet, *The New Yorker*, which sets off all supplementary phrases with commas, no matter how gratuitous in context or how juddering the pronunciation. Consider this sentence from a 2012 *New Yorker* article on electoral strategists for the Republican Party:[62]

Before [Lee] Atwater died, of brain cancer, in 1991, he expressed regret over the "naked cruelty" he had shown to [Michael] Dukakis in making "Willie Horton his running mate."

The commas around *of brain cancer* are there to make it clear that the cause of death is mentioned as a mere comment: it isn't the case that

Atwater died multiple times and that he expressed remorse only before his brain-cancer death, not before the other ones. This fussiness is too much even for some of *The New Yorker*'s own copy editors, one of whom kept a "comma-shaker" on her desk to remind her colleagues to sprinkle them more sparingly.[63]

Not only are commas partly regulated by prosody, but until recently that was their principal function. Writers used to place them wherever they thought a pause felt natural, regardless of the sentence's syntax:

> It is a truth universally acknowledged, that a single man in possession of a good fortune, must be in want of a wife.

> A well-regulated militia, being necessary to the security of a free state, the right of the people to keep and bear arms, shall not be infringed.

Jane Austen and the framers of the American Constitution would get poor grades from composition teachers today, because commas are regulated less by prosody and more by syntax (this is the trend that *The New Yorker* has taken to an extreme). Austen's sentence today would be stripped of both commas, and the Second Amendment would get to keep only the one after "free state."

Though the comma which demarcates a supplementary phrase may be omitted when the pronunciation zips right through it, the converse is no longer true: a comma may not separate the elements of an integrated phrase (such as a subject and its predicate), no matter how badly its narrator may want to take a breath at that juncture. With the rules for comma placement being such a mishmash of syntax and prosody, it's no wonder that the complaints of composition instructors about comma placement in their students' writing fall into the same two categories as the complaints of people writing to Ann Landers about sex in their marriages: (1) too much, and (2) too little.[64]

In the "too much" category we have errors in which students place a comma in front of an integrated phrase, usually because they would pause at that point in pronouncing it:

[Between the subject and a predicate:] His brilliant mind and curiosity, have left.

[Between the verb and its complement:] He mentions, that not knowing how to bring someone back can be a deadly problem.

[Between a noun for an idea and a clause spelling out its content:] I believe the theory, that burning fossil fuels has caused global warming.

[Between a noun and an integrated relative clause:] The ethnocentric view, that many Americans have, leads to much conflict in the world.

[Between a subordinator and its clause:] There was a woman taking care of her husband because, an accident left him unable to work.

[Within a coordination of two phrases:] This conclusion also applies to the United States, and the rest of the world.

[Between a definite generic noun and the name identifying its referent (neither comma is correct here):] I went to see the movie, "Midnight in Paris" with my friend, Jessie.

And in the "too little" category, students forget to insert a comma to set off a supplementary word or phrase:

[Surrounding a sentence adverb:] In many ways however life in a small town is much more pleasant.

[Between a preposed adjunct and the main clause:] Using a scooping motion toss it in the air.

[Before a result adjunct:] The molecule has one double bond between carbons generating a monounsaturated fat.

[Before a contrast adjunct:] Their religion is all for equal rights yet they have no freedom.

[Before a supplementary relative clause:] There are monounsaturated fatty acids which lack two hydrogen atoms.

[Before a direct quotation:] She said "I don't want to go." [Compare the complementary error with an indirect quotation: *She said that, she didn't want to go.*]

Sloppy writers also tend to forget that when a supplementary phrase is poked into the middle of a sentence, it needs to be set off with commas at both ends, like matching parentheses, not just at the beginning:

Tsui's poem "A Chinese Banquet," on the other hand partly focuses on Asian culture.
One of the women, Esra Naama stated her case.
Philip Roth, author of "Portnoy's Complaint" and many other books is a perennial contender for the Nobel Prize.
My father, who gave new meaning to the expression "hard working" never took a vacation.

The other comma mistake is so common that composition teachers have invented many terms of abuse for it: the comma splice, comma error, comma fault, and comma blunder. It consists in using a comma to join two complete sentences, each of which could stand on its own:

There isn't much variety, everything looks kind of the same.
I am going to try and outline the logic again briefly here, please let me know if this is still unclear.
Your lecture is scheduled for 5:00 pm on Tuesday, it is preceded by a meeting with our seminar hosts.
There is no trail, visitors must hike up the creek bed.

Unskilled writers are tempted to splice two sentences with a comma when the sentences are conceptually linked by one of the coherence relations discussed in chapter 5 and seem to want to snuggle up together in a single ensemble. But there are two reasons that comma splices drive careful readers crazy. (I won't tolerate them in my students' writing, not even in email.) They always create a garden path, distracting and annoying the reader. And they are easy to avoid, requiring no greater skill than the ability to identify a sentence.

There are several legitimate ways to splice two sentences, depending on the coherence relation that connects them. When two sentences are conceptually pretty much independent, the first should end with a period and the next should begin with a capital, just like they teach you in third grade. When the two are conceptually linked but the writer feels no need to pinpoint the coherence relation that holds between them, they can be joined with a semicolon; the semicolon is the all-purpose way to eliminate a comma splice. When the coherence relation is elaboration or exemplification (when one is tempted to say *that is, in other words, which is to say, for example, here's what I have in mind,* or *Voilà!*), they may be linked with a colon: like this. When the second sentence intentionally interrupts the flow of the discussion, requiring the reader to wake up, think twice, or snap out of it, a writer can use a dash—dashes can enliven writing, as long as they are used sparingly. And when the writer pinpoints the coherence relation he has in mind with an explicit connective such as a coordinator (*and, or, but, yet, so, nor*) or a preposition (*although, except, if, before, after, because, for*), a comma is fine, <u>because the phrase is a mere supplement</u> (like the underlined clause, which I fastened to the preceding one with a comma). Just don't confuse these connectives with sentence adverbs, such as *however, nonetheless, consequently,* or *therefore,* which are *themselves* supplements of the clause they precede. The clause with the adverb is a freestanding sentence; <u>consequently, it cannot be joined to its predecessor with a comma.</u> Here, then, are the possibilities (the asterisk indicates an illicit comma splice):

*Your lecture is scheduled for 5 PM, it is preceded by a meeting.

Your lecture is scheduled for 5 PM; it is preceded by a meeting.

Your lecture is scheduled for 5 PM—it is preceded by a meeting.

Your lecture is scheduled for 5 PM, but it is preceded by a meeting.

Your lecture is scheduled for 5 PM; however, it is preceded by a meeting.

*Your lecture is scheduled for 5 PM, however, it is preceded by a meeting.

The other bit of comma jargon that has spread beyond the world of copyediting is the serial comma or Oxford comma. It pertains to the second major function of the comma, which is to separate the items in a list. Everyone knows that when two items are joined with a conjunction, they cannot have a comma joining them, too: *Simon and Garfunkel*, not *Simon, and Garfunkel*. But when three or more items are joined, a comma must introduce every subsequent item except—and here comes the controversy—the last one: *Crosby, Stills and Nash; Crosby, Stills, Nash and Young*. The controversial question is whether you should also put a comma before the final item, resulting in *Crosby, Stills, and Nash*, or *Crosby, Stills, Nash, and Young*. This is the serial comma. On one side we have most British publishers (other than Oxford University Press), most American newspapers, and the rock group that calls itself *Crosby, Stills and Nash*. They argue that an item in a list should be introduced either with *and* or with a comma, not redundantly with both. On the other side we have Oxford University Press, most American book publishers, and the many wise guys who have discovered that omitting a serial comma can result in ambiguity:[65]

> Among those interviewed were Merle Haggard's two ex-wives, Kris Kristofferson and Robert Duvall.
> This book is dedicated to my parents, Ayn Rand and God.
> Highlights of Peter Ustinov's global tour include encounters with Nelson Mandela, an 800-year-old demigod and a dildo collector.

The absence of a serial comma in a list of phrases can also create garden paths. *He enjoyed his farm, conversations with his wife and his horse* momentarily calls to mind the famous Mister Ed, and a reader who is unfamiliar with the popular music of the 1970s might well be tripped up by the sentence on the left, stumbling over the mythical duo

Nash and Young and the run-on sequence *Lake and Palmer and Seals and Crofts:*

Without the serial comma:

My favorite performers of the 1970s are Simon and Garfunkel, Crosby, Stills, Nash and Young, Emerson, Lake and Palmer and Seals and Crofts.

With the serial comma:

My favorite performers of the 1970s are Simon and Garfunkel, Crosby, Stills, Nash, and Young, Emerson, Lake, and Palmer, and Seals and Crofts.

I say that unless a house style forbids it, you should use the serial comma. And if you're enumerating lists of lists, then you can eliminate all ambiguity by availing yourself of one of the few punctuation tricks in English that explicitly signal tree structure, the use of a semicolon to demarcate lists of phrases containing commas:

> My favorite performers of the 1970s are Simon and Garfunkel; Crosby, Stills, Nash, and Young; Emerson, Lake, and Palmer; and Seals and Crofts.

apostrophes. The serial comma is not the only punctuation sin that will hurt you in life:

"I was willing to overlook his comma abuse, but when he started misplacing his apostrophes I knew it was over."

The disenchanted girlfriend, I surmise, is referring to three common errors with apostrophes. If I were her companion, I would advise her to consider which quality she values more in a soulmate, logic or literacy, because each of the errors is thoroughly systematic, albeit contrary to accepted usage.

The first is the grocer's apostrophe, as in APPLE'S 99¢ EACH. The error is by no means restricted to grocers; the British press had a field day when a protesting student was spotted with the sign DOWN WITH FEE's. The rule is straightforward: the plural *s* may not be connected to a noun using an apostrophe, but must be jammed right up against it without punctuation—*apples, fees.*

The error seduces grocers and students with three lures. One is that it is easy to confuse the plural *s* with the genitive *'s* and the contraction *'s,* both of which require an apostrophe: *the apple's color* is impeccable, as is *This apple's sweet.* Second, the grocers are, if anything, *too* conscious of grammatical structure: they seem to want to signal the difference between the phoneme *s* that is an intrinsic part of a word and the morpheme *–s* that is tacked on to mark the plural, as in the distinction between *lens* and *pens* (*pen + –s*), or *species* and *genies.* Marking a morpheme boundary is particularly tempting with words that end in vowels, because the correct, unpunctuated plural makes the word look like something else entirely, as in *radios* (which looks like *adios*) and *avocados* (which looks like *asbestos*). Perhaps if the grocers had their way and plurals were consistently marked with apostrophes (*radio's, avocado's, potato's,* and so on), no one would ever mistakenly refer to a *kudo* (the word is *kudos,* a singular Greek noun meaning "praise"), and Dan Quayle would have been spared the embarrassment of publicly miscorrecting a schoolchild's *potato* to *potatoe.* Most seductively of all, the rule banning apostrophes in plurals is not as straightforward as I said it was. With some nouns, an apostrophe really is (or at least was) legitimate. The apostrophe is mandatory with a letter of the alphabet (*p's and q's*) and common with words mentioned as words (*There are too many* however's *in this paragraph*), unless they are clichés like *dos and don'ts* or *no ifs, ands, or buts.* Before the recent trend toward light punctuation, apostrophes were often used to pluralize years (*the 1970's*), abbreviations (*CPU's*), and symbols (*@'s*), and in some newspapers (such as the *New York Times*) they still are.[66]

The rules may not be logical, but if you want your literate lover not to leave you, don't pluralize with an apostrophe. It's also a good idea to know when to keep an apostrophe away from a pronoun. Dave Barry's alter ego Mr. Language Person fielded the following question:

> Q: Like millions of Americans, I cannot grasp the extremely subtle difference between the words "your" and "you're."
>
> A: . . . The best way to tell them apart is to remember that "you're" is a contraction, which is a type of word used during childbirth, as in: "Hang on, Marlene, here comes you're baby!" Whereas "your" is, grammatically, a prosthetic infarction, which means a word that is used to score a debating point in an Internet chat room, as in: "Your a looser, you morron!"

The first part of Mr. Language Person's answer is correct: an apostrophe must be used to mark the contraction of an auxiliary with a pronoun, as in *you're* (you are), *he's* (he is), and *we'd* (we would). And his first example (assuming you get the joke that *you're baby* is mispunctuated) is also correct: an apostrophe is *never* used to mark the genitive (possessive) of a pronoun, no matter how logical it may seem to do so. Although we write *the cat's pajamas* and *Dylan's dream,* as soon as you replace the noun with a pronoun the apostrophe goes out the window: one must write *its pajamas,* not *it's pajamas; your baby,* not *you're baby; their car,* not *they're car; Those hats are hers, ours, and theirs,* not *Those hats are her's, our's, and their's.* Deep in the mists of time, someone decided that an apostrophe doesn't belong in a possessive pronoun, and you'll just have to live with it.

The last of the great apostrophe errors is explained in this cartoon, in which the boy shows that an unconventional family does not necessarily lead to unconventional punctuation:

"I have two mommies. I know where the apostrophe goes."

The possessive of a singular is spelled *'s: He is his mother's son.* The possessive of a regular plural is spelled *s': He is his parents' son,* or, with a same-sex couple, *He is his mothers' son.* As for names ending in *s* like *Charles* and *Jones,* go with grammatical logic and treat them as the singulars they are: *Charles's son,* not *Charles' son.* Some manuals stipulate an exception for *Moses* and *Jesus,* but grammarians should make no law respecting an establishment of religion, and the exception in fact applies to other ancient names ending in *s* (*Achilles' heel, Sophocles' play*).[67] It also applies to modern names which already end with a *ses* sound, whose genitives contain the tongue-twister *seses* (*Kansas', Texas'*).

quotation marks. Another insult to punctuational punctiliousness is the use of quotation marks for emphasis, commonly seen in signs like WE SELL "ICE", CELL PHONES MAY "NOT" BE USED IN THIS AREA, and the disconcerting "FRESH" SEAFOOD PLATTER and even more disconcerting EMPLOYEES MUST "WASH HANDS". The error is common enough to have inspired the cartoon on the following page.

Why do so many signmakers commit the error? What they are doing is what we all used to do in the Paleolithic days of word processing, when terminals and printers lacked italics and underlining (and what many of us still do when composing email in plain text format), which is to emphasize a word by bracketing it with symbols, like *this* or _this_ or <this>. But not like "this". As Griffy explains in the cartoon, quotation marks already have a standard function: they signal that the author is not using words to convey their usual meaning but merely mentioning them as words. If you use quotation marks for emphasis, readers will think you're unschooled or worse.

No discussion of the illogic of punctuation would be complete without the infamous case of the ordering of a quotation mark with respect to a comma or period. The rule in American publications (the British are more sensible about this) is that when quoted material appears at the end of a phrase or sentence, the closing quotation mark goes *outside* the comma or period, "like this," rather than inside, "like this". The practice is patently illogical: the quotation marks enclose a *part* of the phrase or sentence, and the comma or period signals the end of that *entire* phrase or sentence, so putting the comma or period inside the quotation marks is like Superman's famous wardrobe malfunction of wearing his underwear outside his pants. But long ago some American printer decided that the page looks prettier without all that unsightly white space above and to the left of a naked period or comma, and we have been living with the consequences ever since.

The American punctuation rule sticks in the craw of every computer scientist, logician, and linguist, because any ordering of typographical delimiters that fails to reflect the logical nesting of the content makes a shambles of their work. On top of its galling irrationality, the American rule prevents a writer from expressing certain thoughts. In his semi-serious 1984 essay "Punctuation and Human Freedom," Geoffrey Pullum discusses the commonly misquoted first two lines of Shakespeare's *King Richard III:* "Now is the winter of our discontent / Made glorious summer by this sun of York."[68] Many people misremember it as "Now is the winter of our discontent", full stop. Now suppose one wanted to comment on the error by writing:

> Shakespeare's *King Richard III* contains the line "Now is the winter of our discontent".

This is a true sentence. But an American copy editor would change it to:

> Shakespeare's *King Richard III* contains the line "Now is the winter of our discontent."

But this is a false sentence, or at least there's no way for the writer to make it unambiguously true or false. Pullum called for a campaign of civil disobedience, and with the subsequent rise of the Internet his wish has come true. Many logic-conscious and computer-savvy writers have taken advantage of the freedom from copy editors they enjoy on the Web and have explicitly disavowed the American system, most notably on Wikipedia, which has endorsed the alternative called Logical Punctuation.[69] Punctuation nerds may have noticed that I myself recently defied the American rule in four places (underlined):

> The final insult to punctuational punctiliousness is the use of quotation marks for emphasis, commonly seen in signs like WE SELL "ICE"_, CELL PHONES MAY "NOT" BE USED IN THIS AREA, and the disconcerting "FRESH" SEAFOOD PLATTER and even more disconcerting EMPLOYEES MUST "WASH HANDS"_.
>
> But not like "this"_.

Many people misremember it as "Now is the winter of our discontent", full stop.

These acts of civil disobedience were necessary to make it clear where the punctuation marks went in the examples I was citing. You should do the same if you ever need to discuss quotations or punctuation, if you write for Wikipedia or another tech-friendly platform, or if you have a temperament that is both logical and rebellious. The movement may someday change typographical practice in the same way that the feminist movement in the 1970s replaced *Miss* and *Mrs.* with *Ms.* But until that day comes, if you write for an edited American publication, be prepared to live with the illogic of putting a period or comma inside quotation marks.

I hope to have convinced you that dealing with matters of usage is not like playing chess, proving theorems, or solving textbook problems in physics, where the rules are clear and flouting them is an error. It is more like research, journalism, criticism, and other exercises of discernment. In considering questions of usage, a writer must critically evaluate claims of correctness, discount the dubious ones, and make choices which inevitably trade off conflicting values.

Anyone who reviews the history of prescriptive grammar can't help but be struck by the misplaced emotion the topic evokes. At least since Henry Higgins decried "the cold-blooded murder of the English tongue," the self-proclaimed defenders of high standards have been outdoing each other with tasteless invective.[70] David Foster Wallace expressed "despair" at the "Evil" inherent in "voguish linguistic methane." David Gelernter refers to advocates of singular *they* as "language rapists," while John Simon has likened the people who use words in ways he disapproves of to slave traders, child molesters, and the guards at Nazi death camps. The hyperbole often shades into misanthropy, as when Lynne Truss suggests that people who misuse apostrophes "deserve to be struck by lightning, hacked up on the spot and buried in an unmarked grave." Robert Hartwell Fiske, after calling *humongous* a "hideous, ugly word," adds, "Though it's not fair to say that people who use the word are hideous and ugly as well, at some point we come to be—or at the least are known by—what we say, what we write."

The irony, of course, is that all too often it is the targets of the vituperation who have history and usage on their side, and the vilifiers who are full of baloney. Geoffrey Pullum, whose *Language Log* analyzes claims about the use and misuse of language, has noted the tendency among faultfinders "to move straight to high dudgeon, skipping right over the stage where you check the reference books to make sure you have something to be in high dudgeon about. . . . People just don't look in reference books when it comes to language; they seem to think their status as writers combined with their emotion of anger gives them all the standing they need."[71]

Though correct usage is well worth pursuing, we have to keep it in perspective. Not even the most irksome errors are portents of the death of the language, to say nothing of civilization, as the webcomic *XKCD* reminds us:

Yes, writers today sometimes make unfortunate choices. But so did the writers of yesterday and the day before, while many of the kids today, the target of so much purist bile, write gorgeous prose, comment incisively on usage, and even develop their own forms of purism (such as the Typo Eradication Advancement League, which stealthily corrects grocers' signs with correction fluid and felt markers).[72]

And for all the vitriol brought out by matters of correct usage, they are the smallest part of good writing. They pale in importance behind coherence, classic style, and overcoming the curse of knowledge, to say nothing of standards of intellectual conscientiousness. If you really want to improve the quality of your writing, or if you want to thunder about sins in the writing of others, the principles you should worry about the most are not the ones that govern fused participles and possessive antecedents but the ones that govern critical thinking and factual diligence. Here are a few which are commonly flouted—not least in purist rants—and which are worth bearing in mind every time you put pen to paper or fingers to keyboard.

First, look things up. Humans are cursed with the deadly combination of a highly fallible memory and an overconfidence in how much they know.[73] Our social networks, traditional and electronic, multiply the errors, so that much of our conventional wisdom consists of friend-of-a-friend legends and factoids that are too good to be true. As Mark Twain said, "The trouble with the world is not that people know too little, but that they know so many things that aren't so." Actually, he didn't say that—I looked it up.[74] But whoever said it (probably Josh Billings) made an important point. We are blessed to live in an age in which no subject has gone unresearched by scholars, scientists, and journalists. The fruits of their research are available within seconds to anyone with a laptop or smartphone, and within minutes to anyone who can get to a library. Why not take advantage of these blessings and try to restrict the things you know (or at least the things you write) to things that are true?

Second, be sure your arguments are sound. If you are making a factual claim, it should be verifiable in an edited source—one that has been vetted by disinterested gatekeepers such as editors, fact-checkers, or peer reviewers. If you're making an argument, it should proceed from premises that reasonable people already agree upon to your newer or more contentious assertion using valid *if-then* steps. If you're making a moral argument—a claim about what people ought to do—you should show how doing it would satisfy a principle or increase a good that reasonable people already accept.

Third, don't confuse an anecdote or a personal experience with the state of the world. Just because something happened to you, or you read about it in the paper or on the Internet this morning, it doesn't mean it is a trend. In a world of seven billion people, just about anything will happen to someone somewhere, and it's the highly unusual events that will be selected for the news or passed along to friends. An event is a significant phenomenon only if it happens some appreciable number of times relative to the opportunities for it to occur, and it is a trend only if that proportion has been shown to change over time.

Fourth, beware of false dichotomies. Though it's fun to reduce a complex issue to a war between two slogans, two camps, or two schools of thought, it is rarely a path to understanding. Few good ideas can be insightfully captured in a single word ending with *-ism,* and most of our ideas are so crude that we can make more progress by analyzing and refining them than by pitting them against each other in a winner-take-all contest.

Finally, arguments should be based on reasons, not people. Saying that someone you disagree with is motivated by money, fame, politics, or laziness, or slinging around insults like *simplistic, naïve,* or *vulgar,* does not prove that the things the person is saying are false. Nor is the point of disagreement or criticism to show that you are smarter or nobler than your target. Psychologists have shown that in any dispute both sides are convinced that they themselves are reasonable and upright and that their opposite numbers are mulish and dishonest.[75] They can't all be right, at least not all the time. Keep in mind a bit of wisdom from the linguist Ann Farmer: "It isn't about being right. It's about getting it right."

All of these principles lead us back to why we should care about style in the first place. There is no dichotomy between describing how people use language and prescribing how they might use it more effectively. We can share our advice on how to write well without treating the people in need of it with contempt. We can try to remedy shortcomings in writing without bemoaning the degeneration of the language. And we can remind ourselves of the reasons to strive for good style: to enhance the spread of ideas, to exemplify attention to detail, and to add to the beauty of the world.

Acknowledgments

I'm grateful to many people for improving my sense of style and *The Sense of Style*.

For three decades Katya Rice taught me much of what I know about style by copyediting six of my books with precision, thoughtfulness, and taste. Before editing this one, Katya read it as an expert, spotting problems and offering wise advice.

I have the good fortune of being married to my favorite writer. In addition to inspiring me with her own style, Rebecca Newberger Goldstein encouraged this project, expertly commented on the manuscript, and thought up the title.

Many academics have the lamentable habit of using "my mother" as shorthand for an unsophisticated reader. My mother, Roslyn Pinker, is a sophisticated reader, and I've benefited from her acute observations on usage, the many articles on language she's sent me over the decades, and her incisive comments on the manuscript.

Les Perelman was the director of Writing Across the Curriculum at MIT during the two decades I taught there, and offered me invaluable support and advice on the teaching of writing to university students. Jane Rosenzweig, director of the Writing Center of Harvard College, has been similarly encouraging, and both commented helpfully on the manuscript. Thanks go as well to Erin Driver-Linn and Samuel Moulton of the Harvard Initiative for Learning & Teaching.

The Cambridge Grammar of the English Language and *The American Heritage Dictionary,* Fifth Edition, are two great accomplishments of twenty-first-century scholarship, and I have been blessed with advice and comments from their overseers: Rodney Huddleston and Geoffrey Pullum, coauthors of the *Cambridge Grammar,* and Steven Kleinedler, executive editor of *AHD.* Thanks go as well to Joseph Pickett, former executive editor of *AHD,* who invited me to chair the Usage Panel and gave me an insider's look at how a dictionary is made, and to the current editors Peter Chipman and Louise Robbins.

As if this expertise weren't enough, I have benefited from the comments of other wise and knowledgeable colleagues. Ernest Davis, James Donaldson, Edward Gibson, Jane Grimshaw, John R. Hayes, Oliver Kamm, Gary Marcus, and Jeffrey Watumull offered penetrating comments on the first draft. Paul Adams, Christopher Chabris, Philip Corbett, James Engell, Nicholas Epley, Peter C. Gordon, Michael Hallsworth, David Halpern, Joshua Hartshorne, Samuel Jay Keyser, Stephen Kosslyn, Andrea Lunsford, Liz Lutgendorff, John Maguire, Jean-Baptiste Michel, Debra Poole, Jesse Snedeker, and Daniel Wegner answered questions and directed me to relevant research. Various examples in the book were suggested by Ben Backus, Lila Gleitman, Katherine Hobbs, Yael Goldstein Love, Ilavenil Subbiah, and emailers too numerous to list. Special thanks go to Ilavenil for the many subtle variations and shadings of usage she has called to my attention over the years, and for designing the diagrams and trees in this book.

My editors at Penguin, Wendy Wolf in the United States and Thomas Penn and Stefan McGrath in the United Kingdom, and my literary agent, John Brockman, supported this project at every stage, and Wendy provided detailed criticism and advice on the first draft.

I'm grateful, too, for the love and support of the other members of my family: my father, Harry Pinker; my stepdaughters, Yael Goldstein Love and Danielle Blau; my niece and nephews; my in-laws, Martin and Kris; and my sister, Susan Pinker, and brother, Robert Pinker, to whom this book is dedicated.

Parts of chapter 6 have been adapted from my essay on usage in *The American Heritage Dictionary,* Fifth Edition, and from my article "False Fronts in the Language Wars," published in *Slate* in 2012.

Glossary

active voice. The standard form of a clause, in which the actor or cause (if there is one) is the grammatical subject: *A rabbit bit him* (as opposed to the **passive voice:** *He was bitten by a rabbit*).

adjective. The **grammatical category** of words that typically refer to a property or state: *big, round, green, afraid, gratuitous, hesitant.*

adjunct. A **modifier** which adds information about the time, place, manner, purpose, result, or other feature of the event or state: *She opened the bottle <u>with her teeth</u>; He teased the starving wolves, <u>which was foolish</u>; Hank slept <u>in the doghouse</u>.*

adverb. The **grammatical category** of words that modify verbs, adjectives, prepositions, and other adverbs: *tenderly, cleverly, hopefully, very, almost.*

affix. A prefix or suffix: *<u>en</u>rich, <u>re</u>state, black<u>en</u>, slipp<u>ed</u>, squirrel<u>s</u>, cancel<u>lation</u>, Dave'<u>s</u>.*

agreement. Alterations of the form of a word to match some other word or phrase. In English a present-tense verb must agree with the person and number of the subject: *I snicker; He snickers; They snicker.*

AHD. *The American Heritage Dictionary of the English Language.*

anapest. A **foot** with a weak-weak-STRONG **meter:** _Anna LEE_ should _get a LIFE_; _badda-BING!_; _to the DOOR_.

antecedent. The noun phrase that specifies what a pronoun refers to: _Biff forgot his hat; Before Ian left, she sharpened her pencils._

article. A small category of words which mark the definiteness of a noun phrase, including the definite article _the_ and the indefinite articles _a, an,_ and _some._ The _Cambridge Grammar_ subsumes articles in the larger category **determinative**, which also includes **quantifiers** and demonstratives like _this_ and _that._

auxiliary. A special kind of verb which conveys information relevant to the truth of the clause, including **tense, mood,** and negation: _She doesn't love you; I am resting; Bob was criticized; The train has left the station; You should call; I will survive._

backshift. Changing the tense of a verb (usually in indirect or reported speech) to match the tense of the verb of speaking or believing: _Lisa said that she was tired_ (compare with _Lisa said, "I am tired."_) Traditionally called sequence of tenses.

Cambridge Grammar. _The Cambridge Grammar of the English Language,_ a 2002 reference book written by the linguists Rodney Huddleston and Geoffrey Pullum in collaboration with thirteen other linguists. It uses modern linguistics to provide a systematic analysis of virtually every grammatical construction in English. The terminology and analyses in this book are based on the _Cambridge Grammar._

case. The marking of a noun to indicate its **grammatical function,** including nominative case (for subjects), genitive case (for determiners, including possessives), and accusative case (for objects and everything else). In English, case is marked only on pronouns (nominative _I, he, she, we,_ and _they;_ accusative _me, him, her, us,_ and _them;_ and genitive _my, your, his, her, our,_ and _their_), except for genitive case, which can be marked with the suffixes _'s_ on singular noun phrases and _s'_ on plural ones.

classic prose. A term introduced by the literary scholars Francis-Noël Thomas and Mark Turner in their 1994 book, _Clear and Simple as the Truth,_ to refer to a prose style in which the writer appears to direct the reader's attention to an objective, concrete truth about the world by engaging the reader in conversation. It contrasts with practical, self-conscious, contemplative, oracular, and other styles.

clause. The phrase type that corresponds to a sentence, whether it stands alone or is embedded in a larger sentence: _Ethan likes figs_; I wonder _whether Ethan likes figs_; The boy _who likes figs_ is here; The claim _that Ethan likes figs_ is false.

coherence connective. A word, phrase, or punctuation mark that signals the semantic relation between a clause or passage and one that preceded it: _Anna eats a lot of broccoli, because she likes the taste. Moreover, she thinks it's healthy. In contrast, Emile never touches the stuff. And neither does Anna's son._

complement. A phrase that is allowed or required to appear with a head, completing its meaning: _smell the glove_; scoot _into the cave_; I thought _you were dead_; a picture _of Mabel_; proud _of his daughter_.

conjunction. The traditional term for the grammatical category of words that link two phrases, including coordinating conjunctions (_and, or, nor, but, yet, so_) and subordinating conjunctions (_whether, if, to_). Following the _Cambridge Grammar_, I use the terms **coordinator** and **subordinator** instead.

coordinate. One of two or more phrases in a **coordination.**

coordination. A phrase consisting of two or more phrases with the same function, usually linked by a coordinator: _parsley, sage, rosemary, and thyme; She is poor but honest; To live and die in LA; Should I stay or should I go?; I came, I saw, I conquered._

coordinator. The **grammatical category** of words that link two or more phrases with the same function, such as _and, or, nor, but, yet,_ and _so._

definiteness. A semantic distinction marked by the **determiner** of a noun phrase, indicating whether the content of the head noun is sufficient to identify the referent in context. If I say _I bought the car_ (definite), I am assuming that you already know which car I'm talking about; if I say _I bought a car_ (indefinite), I'm introducing it to you for the first time.

denominal verb. A verb derived from a noun: _He elbowed his way in; She demonized him._

determinative. The name used in the *Cambridge Grammar* for the **grammatical category** of words that can function as **determiners,** including **articles** and **quantifiers.**

determiner. The part of a noun phrase that helps determine the referent of the head noun, answering the question "Which one?" or "How many?" The determiner function is carried out by **articles** (*a, an, the, this, that, these, those*), **quantifiers** (*some, any, many, few, one, two, three*), and **genitives** (*my mother; Sara's iPhone*). Note that **determiner** is a **grammatical function; determinative** a **grammatical category.**

diction. The choice of words. Not used here to refer to clarity of enunciation.

direct object. The object of the verb (or, if the verb has two objects, the second of the two), usually indicating the entity that is directly moved or affected by the action: *spank the monkey; If you give a muffin to a moose; If you give a moose a muffin; Cry me a river.*

discourse. A connected sequence of sentences, such as a conversation, a paragraph, a letter, a post, or an essay.

ellipsis. Omission of an obligatory phrase that can be recovered from the context: *Yes we can __! Abe flossed, and I did __ too; Where did you go? __To the lighthouse.*

factual remoteness. Whether a proposition refers to a remote possibility, namely a state of affairs that is untrue, highly hypothetical, or extremely improbable. The difference between *If my grandmother is free, she'll come over* (an open possibility) and *If my grandmother had wheels, she'd be a trolley* (a remote possibility).

foot. A sequence of syllables pronounced as a unit and with a specific rhythm: *The SUN / did not SHINE. / It was TOO / wet to PLAY.*

genitive. The technical term for what is loosely called "possessive" case, namely the case of a noun which functions as a determiner, such as *Ed's head* or *my theory.* Marked in English by the choice of certain pronouns (*my, your, his, her, their,* and so on) and, with all other noun phrases, the suffix *'s* or *s':* *John's guitar; The Troggs' drummer.*

gerund. The form of the verb with the suffix *–ing,* often functioning like a noun: *His drinking got out of hand.*

government. A traditional grammatical term covering the ways in which the head of a phrase may determine the grammatical properties of other words in the phrase, including agreement, case-marking, and the selection of complements.

grammatical category. A class of words that are interchangeable in their syntactic positions and in the way they are inflected: **noun**, **verb**, **adjective**, **adverb**, **preposition**, **determinative** (including **articles**), **coordinator**, **subordinator**, **interjection**. Also called a part of speech.

grammatical function. The role that a phrase plays inside a larger phrase, including subject, object, predicate, determiner, head, complement, modifier, and adjunct.

head. The word in a phrase that determines the meaning and properties of the whole phrase: *the _man_ who knew too much; _give_ a moose a muffin; _afraid_ of his own shadow; _under_ the boardwalk.*

hypercorrection. The overextension of a poorly grasped prescriptive rule to examples in which it does not apply, as in *I feel _terribly_; They planned a party for _she_ and her husband; one _fewer_ car; _Whomever_ did this should be punished.*

iambic. A weak-STRONG **meter:** *MICHELLE; AWAY; To BED!*

indicative. A term from traditional grammar for the **mood** of ordinary statements of fact, in contrast to subjunctive, imperative, interrogative, and other moods.

indirect object. The first of two consecutive objects of a verb, usually indicating a recipient or beneficiary: *If you give _a moose_ a muffin; Cry _me_ a river.*

infinitive. The plain, untensed form of the verb, sometimes (but not always) appearing with the **subordinator** *to: I want to _be_ alone; She helped him _pack_; You must _go_.*

inflection. The modification of the form of a word according to its role in the sentence, including the declension of nouns (*duck, ducks, duck's, ducks'*) and the conjugation of verbs (*quack, quacks, quacked, quacking*). Not to be confused with **intonation** or **prosody**.

intonation. The melody or pitch contour of speech.

intransitive. A verb that does not allow a direct object: *Martha fainted; The chipmunk darted under the car.*

irrealis. Literally "not real": a form of the verb that indicates **factual remoteness**. In English it is marked only on the verb *be: If I were a rich man,* as opposed to *If I was sick, I'd have a fever.* In traditional grammars, it tends to be conflated with the **subjunctive.**

main clause. The clause that expresses the principal assertion of a sentence, and in which subordinate clauses may be embedded: *She thinks [I'm crazy]; Peter repeated the gossip [that Melissa was pregnant] to Sherry.*

metadiscourse. Words that refer to the current discourse: *To sum up; In this essay I will make the following seventeen points; But I digress.*

meter. The rhythm of a word or set of words, consisting of a pattern of weak and strong syllables.

modal auxiliary. The auxiliaries *will, would, can, could, may, might, shall, should, must,* and *ought.* They convey necessity, possibility, obligation, future time, and other concepts related to modalities.

modality. Aspects of meaning relevant to the factual status of a proposition, including whether it is being asserted as fact, suggested as a possibility, posed as a question, or laid out as a command, a request, or an obligation. These are the meanings expressed by the grammatical system for **mood.**

modifier. An optional phrase that comments on or adds information to a head: *a nice boy; See you in the morning; The house that everyone tiptoes past.*

mood. Distinctions among the grammatical forms of a verb or clause that convey the semantic distinctions of **modality,** including the distinctions between an **indicative** statement (*He ate*), a question (*Did he eat?*), an imperative (*Eat!*), a **subjunctive** (*It's important that he eat*), and, for the verb *be,* an **irrealis** (*If I were you*).

morpheme. The smallest meaningful pieces into which words can be cut: *walk-s; in-divis-ibil-ity; crowd-sourc-ing.*

nominal. Something nouny: a noun, pronoun, proper name, or noun phrase.

nominalization. A noun formed out of a verb or an adjective: *a cancellation; a fail; an enactment; protectiveness; a fatality.*

noun. The grammatical category of words that refer to things, people, and other nameable or conceivable entities: *lily, joist, telephone, bargain, grace, prostitute, terror, Joshua, consciousness.*

noun phrase. A phrase headed by a noun: *Jeff; the muskrat; the man who would be king; anything you want.*

object. A complement that follows a verb or preposition, usually indicating an entity that is essential to defining the action, state, or situation: *spank the monkey; prove the theorem; into the cave; before the party.* Includes **direct, indirect,** and **oblique** objects.

oblique object. An object of a preposition: *under the door.*

open conditional. An *if-then* statement referring to an open possibility, one that the speaker does not know to be true or false: *If it rains, we'll cancel the game.*

participle. A form of the verb without a tense, which generally needs to appear with an auxiliary or other verb. English has two: the past participle, used in the passive voice (*It was eaten*) and perfect tense (*He has eaten*), and the gerund-participle, used in the progressive present tense (*He is running*) and in gerunds (*Getting there is half the fun*). Most verbs have regular past-participle forms, formed by the suffix *–ed* (*I have stopped; It was stopped*), but about 165 have irregular forms (*I have given it away; It was given to me; I have brought it; It was brought here*). All gerund-participles in English are formed with *–ing.*

part of speech. Traditional term for a **grammatical category**.

passive voice. One of the two major **voices** in English. A construction in which the usual object appears as the subject, and the usual subject is an object of *by* or absent altogether: *He was bitten by a rabbit* (compare the **active** *A rabbit bit him*); *We got screwed; Attacked by his own supporters, he had nowhere else to turn.*

past tense. A form of the verb used to indicate past time, **factual remoteness,** or **backshift:** *She left yesterday; If you left tomorrow, you'd save money; She said she left.* Most verbs have regular past-tense forms, formed by the suffix *–ed* (*I stopped*), but about 165 have irregular forms (*I gave it away; She brought it*). Also called the preterite.

person. The grammatical distinction between the speaker (first person), the addressee (second person), and those not participating in the conversation (third person). Marked only on pronouns: first person *I, me, we, us, my, our;* second person *you, your;* third person *he, him, she, her, they, their, it, its.*

phoneme. A minimal unit of sound, consisting of a spoken vowel or consonant: *p-e-n; g-r-oa-n.*

phrase. A group of words that behaves as a unit in a sentence and which typically has some coherent meaning: *in the dark; the man in the gray suit; dancing in the dark; afraid of the wolf.*

predicate. The **grammatical function** of a verb phrase, corresponding to a state, an event, or a relationship which is asserted to be true of the subject: *The boys <u>are back in town</u>; Tex <u>is tall</u>; The baby <u>ate a slug</u>.* The term is also sometimes used to refer to the verb that heads the predicate (e.g., *ate*), or, if the verb is *be*, the verb, noun, adjective, or preposition that heads its complement (e.g., *tall*).

preposition. The **grammatical category** of words that typically express spatial or temporal relationships: *in, on, at, near, by, for, under, before, after, up.*

pronoun. A small subcategory of nouns that includes personal pronouns (*I, me, my, mine, you, your, yours, he, him, his, she, her, hers, we, us, our, ours, they, them, their, theirs*) and interrogative and relative pronouns (*who, whom, whose, what, which, where, why, when*).

prosody. The melody, timing, and rhythm of speech.

quantifier. A word (usually a **determinative**) which specifies the amount or quantity of a head noun: *all, some, no, none, any, every, each, many, most, few.*

relative clause. A clause that modifies a noun, often containing a gap which indicates the role the noun plays inside that phrase: *five fat guys <u>who __ rock</u>; a clause <u>that __ modifies a noun</u>; women <u>we love __</u>; violet eyes <u>to die for __</u>; <u>fruit for the crows to pluck __</u>.*

remote conditional. An *if-then* statement referring to a remote possibility, one that the speaker believes to be false, purely hypothetical, or highly improbable: *If wishes were horses, beggars would ride; If pigs had wings, they could fly.*

semantics. The meaning of a word, phrase, or sentence. Does not refer to hairsplitting over exact definitions.

sequence of tenses. See **backshift.**

subject. The grammatical function of the phrase that the predicate is saying something about. In active sentences with action verbs it corresponds to the actor or cause of the action: *The boys are back in town; Tex is tall; The baby ate a slug; Debbie broke the violin.* In passive sentences it usually corresponds to the affected entity: *A slug was eaten.*

subjunctive. A **mood,** marked mainly in **subordinate clause**s, which uses the plain form of the verb, and indicates a hypothetical, demanded, or required situation: *It is essential that I be kept in the loop; He bought insurance lest someone sue him.*

subordinate clause. A clause embedded in a larger phrase, as opposed to the main clause of the sentence: *She thinks I'm crazy; Peter repeated the gossip that Melissa was pregnant to Sherry.*

subordinator. A grammatical category containing a small number of words that introduce a subordinate clause: *She said that it will work; I wonder whether he knows about the party; For her to stay home is unusual.* It corresponds roughly to the traditional category of subordinating conjunctions.

supplement. A loosely attached **adjunct** or **modifier,** set off from the rest of the sentence by pauses in speech and by punctuation in writing: *Fortunately, he got his job back; My point—and I do have one—is this; Let's eat, Grandma; The shoes, which cost $5,000, were hideous.*

syntax. The component of grammar that governs the arrangement of words into phrases and sentences.

tense. The marking of a verb to indicate the time of the state or event relative to the moment the sentence is uttered, including present tense (*He mows the lawn every week*) and past tense (*He mowed the lawn last week*). A tense may have several meanings in addition to its standard temporal one; see **past tense.**

topic. A sentence topic is the phrase that indicates what the sentence is about; in English it is usually the subject, though it can also be expressed in adjuncts such as *As for fish, I like scrod.* A **discourse** topic is what a conversation or text is about; it may be mentioned repeatedly throughout the discourse, sometimes in different words.

transitive. A verb that requires an **object:** *Biff fixed the lamp.*

verb. The **grammatical category** of words which are inflected for tense and which often refer to an action or a state: *He kicked the football; I thought I saw a pussycat; I am strong.*

verb phrase. A phrase headed by a verb which includes the verb together with its **complements** and **adjuncts:** *He tried to kick the football but missed; I thought I saw a pussycat; I am strong.*

voice. The difference between an **active** sentence (*Beavers build dams*) and a **passive** sentence (*Dams are built by beavers*).

word-formation. Also called morphology: the component of grammar that alters the forms of words (*rip* → *ripped*) or that creates new words from old ones (*a demagogue* → *to demagogue; priority* → *prioritize; crowd + source* → *crowd-source*).

zombie noun. Helen Sword's nickname for an unnecessary **nominalization** that hides the agent of the action. Her example: *The proliferation of nominal-izations in a discursive formation may be an indication of a tendency toward pomposity and abstraction* (instead of *Writers who overload their sentences with nouns derived from verbs and adjectives tend to sound pompous and abstract*).

Notes

PROLOGUE

1. From the introduction to *The Elements of Style* (Strunk & White, 1999), p. xv.
2. Pullum, 2009, 2010; J. Freeman, "Clever horses: Unhelpful advice from 'The Elements of Style,'" *Boston Globe*, April 12, 2009.
3. Williams, 1981; Pullum, 2013.
4. Eibach & Libby, 2009.
5. The examples are from Daniels, 1983.
6. Lloyd-Jones, 1976, cited in Daniels, 1983.
7. See Garvey, 2009, for a discussion of criticisms that have been leveled at Strunk & White for its insistence on plain style, and Lanham, 2007, for a critique of the one-dimensional approach to style which runs through what he calls The Books.
8. Herring, 2007; Connors & Lunsford, 1988; Lunsford & Lunsford, 2008; Lunsford, 2013; Thurlow, 2006.
9. Adams & Hunt, 2013; Cabinet Office Behavioural Insights Team, 2012; Sunstein, 2013.
10. Schriver, 2012. For more on plain language laws, see the Center for Plain Language (http://centerforplainlanguage.org) and the organizations called Plain (http://www.plainlanguage.gov) and Clarity (http://www.clarity-international.net).

11. K. Wiens, "I won't hire people who use poor grammar. Here's why," *Harvard Business Review Blog Network,* July 20, 2012, http://blogs.hbr.org/cs /2012/07/i_wont_hire_people_who_use_poo.html.

12. http:// blog.okcupid.com/index.php/online-dating-advice-exactly -what-to-say-in-a-first-message/. The quotation is from the writer Twist Phelan in "Apostrophe now: Bad grammar and the people who hate it," *BBC News Magazine,* May 13, 2013.

CHAPTER 1: GOOD WRITING

1. From "A few maxims for the instruction of the over-educated," first published anonymously in *Saturday Review,* Nov. 17, 1894.

2. Though commonly attributed to William Faulkner, the quotation comes from the English professor Sir Arthur Quiller-Couch in his 1916 lectures *On the art of writing.*

3. R. Dawkins, *Unweaving the rainbow: Science, delusion and the appetite for wonder* (Boston: Houghton Mifflin, 1998), p. 1.

4. According to the Google ngram viewer: http://ngrams.googlelabs.com.

5. R. N. Goldstein, *Betraying Spinoza: The renegade Jew who gave us modernity* (New York: Nextbook/Schocken, 2006), pp. 124–125.

6. Kosslyn, Thompson, & Ganis, 2006; H. Miller, 2004–2005; Sadoski, 1998; Shepard, 1978.

7. M. Fox, "Maurice Sendak, author of splendid nightmares, dies at 83," *New York Times,* May 8, 2012; "Pauline Phillips, flinty adviser to millions as Dear Abby, dies at 94," *New York Times,* Jan. 17, 2013; "Helen Gurley Brown, who gave 'Single Girl' a life in full, dies at 90," *New York Times,* Aug. 13, 2013. I have altered the punctuation to conform to the style of this book, and in the Phillips excerpt I have quoted two of the four "Dear Abby" letters in the original obituary and reordered them.

8. Poole et al., 2011.

9. McNamara, Crossley, & McCarthy, 2010; Poole et al., 2011.

10. Pinker, 2007, chap. 6.

11. M. Fox, "Mike McGrady, known for a literary hoax, dies at 78," *New York Times,* May 14, 2012.

12. I. Wilkerson, *The warmth of other suns: The epic story of America's great migration* (New York: Vintage, 2011), pp. 8–9, 14–15.

CHAPTER 2: A WINDOW ONTO THE WORLD

1. Versions of this saying have been expressed by the writing scholar James C. Raymond, the psychologist Philip Gough, the literary scholar Betsy Draine, and the poet Mary Ruefle.
2. For a discussion of the ubiquity of concrete metaphors in language, see Pinker, 2007, chap. 5.
3. Grice, 1975; Pinker, 2007, chap. 8.
4. Thomas & Turner, 1994, p. 81.
5. Thomas & Turner, 1994, p. 77.
6. Both quotations are from p. 79.
7. B. Greene, "Welcome to the multiverse," *Newseek/The Daily Beast*, May 21, 2012.
8. D. Dutton, "Language crimes: A lesson in how not to write, courtesy of the professoriate," *Wall Street Journal*, Feb. 5, 1999, http://denisdutton.com /bad_writing.htm.
9. Thomas & Turner, 1994, p. 60.
10. Thomas & Turner, 1994, p. 40.
11. Most likely said by the Kansas newspaper editor William Allen White, http://quoteinvestigator.com/2012/08/29/substitute-damn/.
12. "Avoid clichés like the plague" is one of the many self-undermining rules of writing popularized by William Safire in his 1990 book *Fumblerules*. The genre goes back at least to 1970s campus xeroxlore; see http://alt -usage-english.org/humorousrules.html.
13. Keysar et al., 2000; Pinker, 2007, chap. 5.
14. From the historian Niall Ferguson.
15. From the linguist Geoffrey Pullum.
16. From the politician, lawyer, executive, and immortal Montreal Canadiens goaltender Ken Dryden.
17. From the historian Anthony Pagden.
18. The Dickens simile is from *David Copperfield*.
19. Roger Brown, in an unpublished paper.
20. A. Bellow, "Skin in the game: A conservative chronicle," *World Affairs*, Summer 2008.
21. H. Sword, "Zombie nouns," *New York Times*, July 23, 2012.
22. G. Allport, "Epistle to thesis writers," photocopy handed down by generations of Harvard psychology graduate students, undated but presumably from the 1960s.

23. From the Pennsylvania Plain Language Consumer Contract Act, http://www.pacode.com/secure/data/037/chapter307/s307.10.html.

24. G. K. Pullum, "The BBC enlightens us on passives," *Language Log,* Feb. 22, 2011, http://languagelog.ldc.upenn.edu/nll/?p=2990.

CHAPTER 3: THE CURSE OF KNOWLEDGE

1. Sword, 2012.

2. Named after Robert J. Hanlon, who contributed it to Arthur Bloch's *Murphy's Law Book Two: More reasons why things go wrong!* (Los Angeles: Price/Stern/Sloan, 1980).

3. The term "curse of knowledge" was coined by Robin Hogarth and popularized by Camerer, Lowenstein, & Weber, 1989.

4. Piaget & Inhelder, 1956.

5. Fischhoff, 1975.

6. Ross, Greene, & House, 1977.

7. Keysar, 1994.

8. Wimmer & Perner, 1983.

9. Birch & Bloom, 2007.

10. Hayes & Bajzek, 2008; Nickerson, Baddeley, & Freeman, 1986.

11. Kelley & Jacoby, 1996.

12. Hinds, 1999.

13. Other researchers who have made this suggestion include John Hayes, Karen Schriver, and Pamela Hinds.

14. Cushing, 1994.

15. From the title of the 1943 style manual by Robert Graves and Alan Hodge, *The reader over your shoulder: A handbook for writers of prose* (New York: Random House; revised edition, 1979).

16. Epley, 2014.

17. Fischhoff, 1975; Hinds, 1999; Schriver, 2012.

18. Kelley & Jacoby, 1996.

19. Freedman, 2007, p. 22.

20. From p. 73 of the second edition (1972).

21. Attentive readers may notice that this definition of *syllepsis* is similar to the definition of *zeugma* I gave in connection with the Sendak obituary in chapter 1. The experts on rhetorical tropes don't have a consistent explanation of how they differ.

22. G. A. Miller, 1956.

23. Pinker, 2013.
24. Duncker, 1945.
25. Sadoski, 1998; Sadoski, Goetz, & Fritz, 1993; Kosslyn, Thompson, & Ganis, 2006.
26. Schriver, 2012.
27. Epley, 2014.

CHAPTER 4: THE WEB, THE TREE, AND THE STRING

1. Florey, 2006.
2. Pinker, 1997.
3. Pinker, 1994, chap. 4.
4. Pinker, 1994, chap. 8.
5. I use the analyses in *The Cambridge Grammar of the English Language* (Huddleston & Pullum, 2002) with a few simplifications, including those introduced in the companion *A Student's Introduction to English Grammar* (Huddleston & Pullum, 2005).
6. The incident is described in Liberman & Pullum, 2006.
7. Huddleston & Pullum, 2002; Huddleston & Pullum, 2005.
8. Bock & Miller, 1991.
9. Chomsky, 1965; see Pinker, 1994, chaps. 4 and 7.
10. Pinker, 1994, chap. 7. For more recent reviews of the experimental study of sentence processing, see Wolf & Gibson, 2003; Gibson, 1998; Levy, 2008; Pickering & van Gompel, 2006.
11. From Liberman & Pullum, 2006.
12. Mostly from the column of Aug. 6, 2013.
13. I have simplified the tree on page 100; the *Cambridge Grammar* would call for two additional levels of embedding in the clause *Did Henry kiss whom* to represent the inversion of the subject and the auxiliary.
14. The first example is from the *New York Times* "After Deadline" column; the second, from Bernstein, 1965.
15. Pinker, 1994; Wolf & Gibson, 2003.
16. Some of the examples come from Smith, 2001.
17. R. N. Goldstein, *36 Arguments for the existence of God: A work of fiction* (New York: Pantheon, 2010), pp. 18–19.
18. From "Types of sentence branching," *Report writing at the World Bank*, 2012, http://colelearning.net/rw_wb/module6/page7.html.

19. Here and elsewhere, I use the label Noun Phrase for the constituent the *Cambridge Grammar* calls "Nominal."

20. Zwicky et al., 1971/1992. See also http://itre.cis.upenn.edu/~myl/langua gelog/archives/001086.html.

21. Pinker, 1994, chap. 4; Gibson, 1998.

22. *Boston Globe*, May 23, 1999.

23. Fodor, 2002a, 2002b; Rayner & Pollatsek, 1989; Van Orden, Johnston, & Hale, 1988.

24. R. Rosenbaum, "Sex week at Yale," *Atlantic Monthly*, Jan./Feb. 2003; reprinted in Pinker, 2004.

25. The unattributed source for most of these emails is Lederer, 1987.

26. Spotted by *Language Log*, http://languagelog.ldc.upenn.edu/nll/?p=4401.

27. Bever, 1970.

28. Pinker, 1994, chap. 7; Fodor, 2002a; Gibson, 1998; Levy, 2008; Pickering & van Gompel, 2006; Wolf & Gibson, 2003.

29. Nunberg, 1990; Nunberg, Briscoe, & Huddleston, 2002.

30. Levy, 2008.

31. Pickering & Ferreira, 2008.

32. Cooper & Ross, 1975; Pinker & Birdsong, 1979.

33. The example is from Geoffrey Pullum.

34. Gordon & Lowder, 2012.

35. Huddleston & Pullum, 2002; Huddleston & Pullum, 2005.

CHAPTER 5: ARCS OF COHERENCE

1. Mostly from Lederer, 1987.

2. Wolf & Gibson, 2006.

3. Bransford & Johnson, 1972.

4. M. O'Connor, "Surviving winter: Heron," *The Cape Codder*, Feb. 28, 2003; reprinted in Pinker, 2004.

5. Huddleston & Pullum, 2002; Huddleston & Pullum, 2005.

6. Huddleston & Pullum, 2002; Huddleston & Pullum, 2005.

7. Gordon & Hendrick, 1998.

8. Mostly from Lederer, 1987.

9. Garrod & Sanford, 1977; Gordon & Hendrick, 1998.

10. Hume, 1748/1999.

11. Grosz, Joshi, & Weinstein, 1995; Hobbs, 1979; Kehler, 2002; Wolf & Gibson, 2006. Hume's connections between ideas, as he originally explained

them, are not identical to those distinguished by Kehler, but his trichotomy is a useful way to organize the coherence relations.

12. Clark & Clark, 1968; G. A. Miller & Johnson-Laird, 1976.
13. Grosz, Joshi, & Weinstein, 1995; Hobbs, 1979; Kehler, 2002; Wolf & Gibson, 2006.
14. Kamalski, Sanders, & Lentz, 2008.
15. P. Tyre, "The writing revolution," *The Atlantic,* Oct. 2012, http://www .theatlantic.com/magazine/archive/2012/10/the-writing-revolution /309090/.
16. Keegan, 1993, p. 3.
17. Clark & Chase, 1972; Gilbert, 1991; Horn, 2001; Huddleston & Pullum, 2002; Huddleston & Pullum, 2005; Miller & Johnson-Laird, 1976.
18. Gilbert, 1991; Goldstein, 2006; Spinoza, 1677/2000.
19. Gilbert, 1991; Wegner et al., 1987.
20. Clark & Chase, 1972; Gilbert, 1991; Miller & Johnson-Laird, 1976.
21. Huddleston & Pullum, 2002.
22. Liberman & Pullum, 2006; see also the many postings on "misnegation" in the blog *Language Log*, http://languagelog.ldc.upenn.edu/nll/.
23. Wason, 1965.
24. Huddleston & Pullum, 2002.
25. Huddleston & Pullum, 2002.
26. To be exact, he said, "We choose to go to the moon in this decade and do the other things, not because they are easy, but because they are hard . . . ," http://er.jsc.nasa.gov/seh/ricetalk.htm.
27. Keegan, 1993, pp. 3–4.
28. Keegan, 1993, p. 5.
29. Keegan, 1993, p. 12.
30. Williams, 1990.
31. Mueller, 2004, pp. 16–18.

CHAPTER 6: TELLING RIGHT FROM WRONG

1. Macdonald, 1962.
2. G. W. Bush, "Remarks by the President at the Radio-Television Correspondents Association 57th Annual Dinner," Washington Hilton Hotel, March 29, 2001.
3. Skinner, 2012.
4. Hitchings, 2011; *Merriam-Webster's Dictionary of English Usage,* 1994.

5. Lindgren, 1990.

6. *American Heritage Dictionary*, 2011; Copperud, 1980; Huddleston & Pullum, 2002; Huddleston & Pullum, 2005; Liberman & Pullum, 2006; *Merriam-Webster's Dictionary of English Usage*, 1994; Soukhanov, 1999. Online dictionaries: *The American Heritage Dictionary of the English Language* (http://www.ahdictionary.com/); *Dictionary.com* (http://dictionary.reference.com); *Merriam-Webster Unabridged* (http://unabridged.merriam-webster.com/); *Merriam-Webster Online* (http://www.merriam-webster.com/); *Oxford English Dictionary* (http://www.oed.com); *Oxford Dictionary Online* (http://www.oxforddictionaries.com). *Language Log*, http://languagelog.ldc.upenn.edu/nll. Other sources consulted in this discussion include Bernstein, 1965; Fowler, 1965; Haussaman, 1993; Lunsford, 2006; Lunsford & Lunsford, 2008; *Oxford English Dictionary*, 1991; Siegal & Connolly, 1999; Williams, 1990.

7. M. Liberman, "Prescribing terribly," *Language Log*, 2009, http://languagelog.ldc.upenn.edu/nll/?p=1360; M. Liberman, 2007, "Amid this vague uncertainty, who walks safe?" *Language Log*, http://itre.cis.upenn.edu/~myl/languagelog/archives/004231.html.

8. E. Bakovic, "Think this," *Language Log*, 2006, http://itre.cis.upenn.edu/~myl/languagelog/archives/003144.html.

9. The errors are taken from Lunsford, 2006, and Lunsford & Lunsford, 2008.

10. Haussaman, 1993; Huddleston & Pullum, 2002.

11. *Merriam-Webster's Dictionary of English Usage*, 1994, p. 218.

12. Nunnally, 1991.

13. This analysis is based on Huddleston & Pullum, 2002.

14. G. K. Pullum, "Menand's acumen deserts him," in Liberman & Pullum, 2006, and *Language Log*, 2003, http://itre.cis.upenn.edu/~myl/languagelog/archives/000027.html.

15. B. Zimmer, "A misattribution no longer to be put up with," *Language Log*, 2004, http://itre.cis.upenn.edu/~myl/languagelog/archives/001715.html.

16. M. Liberman, "Hot Dryden-on-Jonson action," *Language Log*, 2007, http://itre.cis.upenn.edu/~myl/languagelog/archives/004454.html.

17. These and other examples of errors in student papers are adapted from Lunsford, 2006, and Lunsford & Lunsford, 2008. For an explanation of tense and its relationship to time, see Pinker, 2007, chap. 4.

18. Called out as an error by the *New York Times*' "After Deadline" column, May 14, 2013.

19. Huddleston & Pullum, 2002.

20. Huddleston & Pullum, 2002, pp. 152–154.

21. Pinker, 2007, chap. 4.

22. G. K. Pullum, "Irrational terror over adverb placement at Harvard," *Language Log,* 2008, http://languagelog.ldc.upenn.edu/nll/?p=100.

23. Huddleston & Pullum, 2002, pp. 1185–1187.

24. M. Liberman, "Heaping of catmummies considered harmful," *Language Log,* 2008, http://languagelog.ldc.upenn.edu/nll/?p=514.

25. G. K. Pullum, "Obligatorily split infinitives in real life," *Language Log,* 2005, http://itre.cis.upenn.edu/~myl/languagelog/archives/002180.html.

26. A. M. Zwicky, "Not to or to not," *Language Log,* 2005, http://itre.cis.upenn.edu/~myl/languagelog/archives/002139.html.

27. A. M. Zwicky, "Obligatorily split infinitives," *Language Log,* 2004, http://itre.cis.upenn.edu/~myl/languagelog/archives/000901.html.

28. From Winston Churchill.

29. This analysis is based on Huddleston & Pullum, 2002, especially pp. 999–1000.

30. Huddleston & Pullum, 2002, p. 87.

31. Huddleston & Pullum, 2002; Huddleston & Pullum, 2005.

32. *Merriam-Webster's Dictionary of English Usage,* 1994, p. 343.

33. G. K. Pullum, "A rule which will live in infamy," *Chronicle of Higher Education,* Dec. 7, 2012; M. Liberman, "A decline in *which*-hunting?" *Language Log,* 2013, http://languagelog.ldc.upenn.edu/nll/?p=5479#more-5479.

34. G. K. Pullum, "More timewasting garbage, another copy-editing moron," *Language Log,* 2004, http://itre.cis.upenn.edu/~myl/languagelog/archives/000918.html; G. K. Pullum, "*Which* vs *that?* I have numbers!" *Language Log,* 2004, http://itre.cis.upenn.edu/~myl/languagelog/archives/001464.html.

35. *Merriam-Webster's Dictionary of English Usage,* 1994, p. 895.

36. Pinker, 1999/2011.

37. Flynn, 2007; see also Pinker, 2011, chap. 9.

38. M. Liberman, "*Whom* humor," *Language Log,* 2004, http://itre.cis.upenn.edu/~myl/languagelog/archives/000779.html.

39. *Merriam-Webster's Dictionary of English Usage,* 1994, p. 958; G. K. Pullum, "One rule to ring them all," *Chronicle of Higher Education,* Nov. 30, 2012, http://chronicle.com/blogs/linguafranca/2012/11/30/one-rule-to-ring-them-all/; Huddleston & Pullum, 2002.

40. According to the Google ngram viewer: http://ngrams.googlelabs.com.

41. A fifteenth-century curse discussed in my book *The stuff of thought*, chap. 7.

42. Quoted in *Merriam-Webster's Dictionary of English Usage,* 1994, p. 959.

43. *Merriam-Webster's Dictionary of English Usage,* 1994, pp. 689–690; Huddleston & Pullum, 2002, p. 506; *American Heritage Dictionary,* 2011, Usage Note for *one.*

44. For an analysis of the language of stuff and things, see Pinker, 2007, chap. 4.

45. J. Freeman, "One less thing to worry about," *Boston Globe,* May 24, 2009.

46. Originally published as "Ships in the night," *New York Times,* April 5, 1994.

47. White House Office of the Press Secretary, "Statement by the President on the Supreme Court's Ruling on Arizona v. the United States," June 25, 2012.

48. D. Gelernter, "Feminism and the English language," *Weekly Standard,* March 3, 2008; G. K. Pullum, "Lying feminist ideologues wreck English language, says Yale prof," *Language Log,* 2008, http://itre.cis.upenn.edu/~myl /languagelog/archives/005423.html.

49. Foertsch & Gernsbacher, 1997.

50. From G. K. Pullum, "Lying feminist ideologues wreck English language, says Yale prof," *Language Log,* 2008, http://itre.cis.upenn.edu/~myl /languagelog/archives/005423.html, and *Merriam-Webster's Dictionary of English Usage,* 1994.

51. Foertsch & Gernsbacher, 1997.

52. From G. J. Stigler, "The intellectual and the market place," Selected Papers No. 3, Graduate School of Business, University of Chicago, 1967.

53. H. Churchyard, "Everyone loves their Jane Austen," http://www.crossmyt .com/hc/linghebr/austheir.html.

54. G. K. Pullum, "Singular *they* with known sex," *Language Log,* 2006, http://itre.cis.upenn.edu/~myl/languagelog/archives/002742.html.

55. Pinker, 1994, chap. 12.

56. Foertsch & Gernsbacher, 1997; Sanforth & Filik, 2007; M. Liberman, "Prescriptivist science," *Language Log,* 2008, http://languagelog.ldc.upenn .edu/nll/?p=199.

57. Huddleston & Pullum, 2002, pp. 608–609.

58. Nunberg, 1990; Nunberg, Briscoe, & Huddleston, 2002.

59. Truss, 2003; L. Menand, "Bad comma," *New Yorker*, June 28, 2004; Crystal, 2006; J. Mullan, "The war of the commas," *The Guardian*, July 1, 2004, http://www.theguardian.com/books/2004/jul/02/referenceandlanguages .johnmullan.

60. Huddleston & Pullum, 2002; Huddleston & Pullum, 2005, p. 188.

61. Lunsford, 2006; Lunsford & Lunsford, 2008; B. Yagoda, "The most comma mistakes," *New York Times*, May 21, 2012; B. Yagoda, "Fanfare for the comma man," *New York Times*, April 9, 2012.

62. B. Yagoda, "Fanfare for the comma man," *New York Times*, April 9, 2012.

63. M. Norris, "In defense of 'nutty' commas," *New Yorker*, April 12, 2010.

64. Lunsford, 2006; Lunsford & Lunsford, 2008; B. Yagoda, "The most comma mistakes," *New York Times*, May 21, 2012.

65. The examples that follow are from Wikipedia, "Serial comma."

66. Siegal & Connolly, 1999.

67. At least according to the *New York Times Manual of Style and Usage* (Siegal & Connolly, 1999). Other manuals make an exception to this exception for classical names ending in *-as* or *-us*, and then make an exception to the exception to the exception for *Jesus*—but he would get by without the *'s* by virtue of the sound of his name anyway.

68. Pullum, 1984.

69. B. Yagoda, "The rise of 'logical punctuation,'" *Slate*, May 12, 2011.

70. D. F. Wallace, "Tense present: Democracy, English, and the wars over usage," *Harper's*, April 2001; D. Gelernter, "Feminism and the English language," *Weekly Standard*, March 3, 2008; J. Simon, *Paradigms lost* (New York: Clarkson Potter, 1980), p. 97; J. Simon, "First foreword," in Fiske, 2011, p. ix; Fiske, 2011, p. 213; Truss, 2003.

71. G. K. Pullum, "Lying feminist ideologues wreck English, says Yale prof," *Language Log*, 2008, http://itre.cis.upenn.edu/~myl/languagelog/archives /005423.html. See also M. Liberman, "At a loss for lexicons," *Language Log*, 2004, http://itre.cis.upenn.edu/~myl/languagelog/archives/000437.html.

72. Deck & Herson, 2010.

73. Kahneman, Slovic, & Tversky, 1982; Schacter, 2001.

74. K. A. McDonald, "Many of Mark Twain's famed humorous sayings are found to have been misattributed to him," *Chronicle of Higher Education*, Sept. 4, 1991, A8.

75. Haidt, 2012; Pinker, 2011, chap. 8.

References

Adams, P., & Hunt, S. 2013. *Encouraging consumers to claim redress: Evidence from a field trial.* London: Financial Conduct Authority.

American Heritage Dictionary of the English Language (5th ed.). 2011. Boston: Houghton Mifflin Harcourt.

Bernstein, T. M. 1965. *The careful writer: A modern guide to English usage.* New York: Atheneum.

Bever, T. G. 1970. The cognitive basis for linguistic structures. In J. R. Hayes (ed.), *Cognition and the development of language.* New York: Wiley.

Birch, S. A. J., & Bloom, P. 2007. The curse of knowledge in reasoning about false beliefs. *Psychological Science, 18*, 382–386.

Bock, K., & Miller, C. A. 1991. Broken agreement. *Cognitive Psychology, 23*, 45–93.

Bransford, J. D., & Johnson, M. K. 1972. Contextual prerequisites for understanding: Some investigations of comprehension and recall. *Journal of Verbal Learning and Verbal Behavior, 11*, 717–726.

Cabinet Office Behavioural Insights Team. 2012. *Applying behavioural insights to reduce fraud, error and debt.* London: Cabinet Office Behavioural Insights Team.

Camerer, C., Lowenstein, G., & Weber, M. 1989. The curse of knowledge in economic settings: An experimental analysis. *Journal of Political Economy, 97*, 1232–1254.

Chomsky, N. 1965. *Aspects of the theory of syntax*. Cambridge, Mass.: MIT Press.

Clark, H. H., & Chase, W. G. 1972. On the process of comparing sentences against pictures. *Cognitive Psychology, 3*, 472–517.

Clark, H. H., & Clark, E. V. 1968. Semantic distinctions and memory for complex sentences. *Quarterly Journal of Experimental Psychology, 20*, 129–138.

Connors, R. J., & Lunsford, A. A. 1988. Frequency of formal errors in current college writing, or Ma and Pa Kettle do research. *College Composition and Communication, 39*, 395–409.

Cooper, W. E., & Ross, J. R. 1975. World order. In R. E. Grossman, L. J. San, & T. J. Vance (eds.), *Papers from the parasession on functionalism of the Chicago Linguistics Society*. Chicago: University of Chicago Press.

Copperud, R. H. 1980. *American usage and style: The consensus*. New York: Van Nostrand Reinhold.

Crystal, D. 2006. *The fight for English: How language pundits ate, shot, and left*. New York: Oxford University Press.

Cushing, S. 1994. *Fatal words: Communication clashes and aircraft crashes*. Chicago: University of Chicago Press.

Daniels, H. A. 1983. *Famous last words: The American language crisis reconsidered*. Carbondale: Southern Illinois University Press.

Deck, J., & Herson, B. D. 2010. *The great typo hunt: Two friends changing the world, one correction at a time*. New York: Crown.

Duncker, K. 1945. On problem solving. *Psychological Monographs, 58*.

Eibach, R. P., & Libby, L. K. 2009. Ideology of the good old days: Exaggerated perceptions of moral decline and conservative politics. In J. T. Jost, A. Kay, & H. Thorisdottir (eds.), *Social and psychological bases of ideology and system justification*. Oxford: Oxford University Press.

Epley, N. 2014. *Mindwise: (Mis)understanding what others think, believe, feel, and want*. New York: Random House.

Fischhoff, B. 1975. Hindsight ≠ foresight: The effect of outcome knowledge on judgment under uncertainty. *Journal of Experimental Psychology: Human Perception and Performance, 1*, 288–299.

Fiske, R. H. 2011. *Robert Hartwell Fiske's Dictionary of Unendurable English*. New York: Scribner.

Florey, K. B. 2006. *Sister Bernadette's barking dog: The quirky history and lost art of diagramming sentences*. New York: Harcourt.

Flynn, J. R. 2007. *What is intelligence?* New York: Cambridge University Press.

Fodor, J. D. 2002a. Prosodic disambiguation in silent reading. Paper presented at the North East Linguistic Society.

Fodor, J. D. 2002b. Psycholinguistics cannot escape prosody. https://gc.cuny.edu/CUNY_GC/media/CUNY-Graduate-Center/PDF/Programs/Linguistics/Psycholinguistics-Cannot-Escape-Prosody.pdf.

Foertsch, J., & Gernsbacher, M. A. 1997. In search of gender neutrality: Is singular *they* a cognitively efficient substitute for generic *he*? *Psychological Science, 8*, 106–111.

Fowler, H. W. 1965. *Fowler's Modern English Usage* (2nd ed.; E. Gowers, ed.). New York: Oxford University Press.

Freedman, A. 2007. *The party of the first part: The curious world of legalese.* New York: Henry Holt.

Garrod, S., & Sanford, A. 1977. Interpreting anaphoric relations: The integration of semantic information while reading. *Journal of Verbal Learning and Verbal Behavior, 16*, 77–90.

Garvey, M. 2009. *Stylized: A slightly obsessive history of Strunk and White's "The Elements of Style."* New York: Simon & Schuster.

Gibson, E. 1998. Linguistic complexity: Locality of syntactic dependencies. *Cognition, 68*, 1–76.

Gilbert, D. T. 1991. How mental systems believe. *American Psychologist, 46*, 107–119.

Goldstein, R. N. 2006. *Betraying Spinoza: The renegade Jew who gave us modernity.* New York: Nextbook/Schocken.

Gordon, P. C., & Hendrick, R. 1998. The representation and processing of coreference in discourse. *Cognitive Science, 22*, 389–424.

Gordon, P. C., & Lowder, M. W. 2012. Complex sentence processing: A review of theoretical perspectives on the comprehension of relative clauses. *Language and Linguistics Compass, 6/7*, 403–415.

Grice, H. P. 1975. Logic and conversation. In P. Cole & J. L. Morgan (eds.), *Syntax & semantics* (Vol. 3, *Speech acts*). New York: Academic Press.

Grosz, B. J., Joshi, A. K., & Weinstein, S. 1995. Centering: A framework for modeling the local coherence of discourse. *Computational Linguistics, 21*, 203–225.

Haidt, J. 2012. *The righteous mind: Why good people are divided by politics and religion.* New York: Pantheon.

Haussaman, B. 1993. *Revising the rules: Traditional grammar and modern linguistics.* Dubuque, Iowa: Kendall/Hunt.

Hayes, J. R., & Bajzek, D. 2008. Understanding and reducing the knowledge effect: Implications for writers. *Written Communication, 25,* 104–118.

Herring, S. C. 2007. Questioning the generational divide: Technological exoticism and adult construction of online youth identity. In D. Buckingham (ed.), *Youth, identity, and digital media.* Cambridge, Mass.: MIT Press.

Hinds, P. J. 1999. The curse of expertise: The effects of expertise and debiasing methods on predictions of novel performance. *Journal of Experimental Psychology: Applied, 5,* 205–221.

Hitchings, H. 2011. *The language wars: A history of proper English.* London: John Murray.

Hobbs, J. R. 1979. Coherence and coreference. *Cognitive Science, 3,* 67–90.

Horn, L. R. 2001. *A natural history of negation.* Stanford, Calif.: Center for the Study of Language and Information.

Huddleston, R., & Pullum, G. K. 2002. *The Cambridge Grammar of the English Language.* New York: Cambridge University Press.

Huddleston, R., & Pullum, G. K. 2005. *A Student's Introduction to English Grammar.* New York: Cambridge University Press.

Hume, D. 1748/1999. *An enquiry concerning human understanding.* New York: Oxford University Press.

Kahneman, D., Slovic, P., & Tversky, A. 1982. *Judgment under uncertainty: Heuristics and biases.* New York: Cambridge University Press.

Kamalski, J., Sanders, T., & Lentz, L. 2008. Coherence marking, prior knowledge, and comprehension of informative and persuasive texts: Sorting things out. *Discourse Processes, 45,* 323–345.

Keegan, J. 1993. *A history of warfare.* New York: Vintage.

Kehler, A. 2002. *Coherence, reference, and the theory of grammar.* Stanford, Calif.: Center for the Study of Language and Information.

Kelley, C. M., & Jacoby, L. L. 1996. Adult egocentrism: Subjective experience versus analytic bases for judgment. *Journal of Memory and Language, 35,* 157–175.

Keysar, B. 1994. The illusory transparency of intention: Linguistic perspective taking in text. *Cognitive Psychology, 26,* 165–208.

Keysar, B., Shen, Y., Glucksberg, S., & Horton, W. S. 2000. Conventional language: How metaphorical is it? *Journal of Memory and Language, 43,* 576–593.

Kosslyn, S. M., Thompson, W. L., & Ganis, G. 2006. *The case for mental imagery.* New York: Oxford University Press.

Lanham, R. 2007. *Style: An anti-textbook*. Philadelphia: Paul Dry.

Lederer, R. 1987. *Anguished English*. Charleston, S.C.: Wyrick.

Levy, R. 2008. Expectation-based syntactic comprehension. *Cognition, 106,* 1126–1177.

Liberman, M., & Pullum, G. K. 2006. *Far from the madding gerund: And other dispatches from Language Log*. Wilsonville, Ore.: William, James & Co.

Lindgren, J. 1990. Fear of writing (review of *Texas Law Review Manual of Style*, 6th ed., and *Webster's Dictionary of English Usage*). *California Law Review, 78,* 1677–1702.

Lloyd-Jones, R. 1976. Is writing worse nowadays? *University of Iowa Spectator,* April.

Lunsford, A. A. 2006. Error examples. Unpublished document, Program in Writing and Rhetoric, Stanford University.

Lunsford, A. A. 2013. Our semi-literate youth? Not so fast. Unpublished manuscript, Dept. of English, Stanford University.

Lunsford, A. A., & Lunsford, K. J. 2008. "Mistakes are a fact of life": A national comparative study. *College Composition and Communication, 59,* 781–806.

Macdonald, D. 1962. The string untuned: A review of *Webster's New International Dictionary* (3rd ed.). *New Yorker,* March 10.

McNamara, D. S., Crossley, S. A., & McCarthy, P. M. 2010. Linguistic features of writing quality. *Written Communication, 27,* 57–86.

Merriam-Webster's Dictionary of English Usage. 1994. Springfield, Mass.: Merriam-Webster.

Miller, G. A. 1956. The magical number seven, plus or minus two: Some limits on our capacity for processing information. *Psychological Review, 63,* 81–96.

Miller, G. A., & Johnson-Laird, P. N. 1976. *Language and perception*. Cambridge, Mass.: Harvard University Press.

Miller, H. 2004–2005. Image into word: Glimpses of mental images in writers writing. *Journal of the Assembly for Expanded Perspectives on Learning, 10,* 62–72.

Mueller, J. 2004. *The remnants of war*. Ithaca, N.Y.: Cornell University Press.

Nickerson, R. S., Baddeley, A., & Freeman, B. 1986. Are people's estimates of what other people know influenced by what they themselves know? *Acta Psychologica, 64,* 245–259.

Nunberg, G. 1990. *The linguistics of punctuation*. Stanford, Calif.: Center for the Study of Language and Information.

Nunberg, G., Briscoe, T., & Huddleston, R. 2002. Punctuation. In R. Huddleston & G. K. Pullum, *The Cambridge Grammar of the English Language*. New York: Cambridge University Press.

Nunnally, T. 1991. The possessive with gerunds: What the handbooks say, and what they should say. *American Speech, 66,* 359–370.

Oxford English Dictionary. 1991. *The Compact Edition of the Oxford English Dictionary* (2nd ed.). New York: Oxford University Press.

Piaget, J., & Inhelder, B. 1956. *The child's conception of space.* London: Routledge.

Pickering, M. J., & Ferreira, V. S. 2008. Structural priming: A critical review. *Psychological Bulletin, 134,* 427–459.

Pickering, M. J., & van Gompel, R. P. G. 2006. Syntactic parsing. In M. Traxler & M. A. Gernsbacher (eds.), *Handbook of psycholinguistics* (2nd ed.). Amsterdam: Elsevier.

Pinker, S. 1994. *The language instinct.* New York: HarperCollins.

Pinker, S. 1997. *How the mind works.* New York: Norton.

Pinker, S. 1999. *Words and rules: The ingredients of language.* New York: HarperCollins.

Pinker, S. (ed.). 2004. *The best American science and nature writing 2004.* Boston: Houghton Mifflin.

Pinker, S. 2007. *The stuff of thought: Language as a window into human nature.* New York: Viking.

Pinker, S. 2011. *The better angels of our nature: Why violence has declined.* New York: Viking.

Pinker, S. 2013. George A. Miller (1920–2012). *American Psychologist, 68,* 467–468.

Pinker, S., & Birdsong, D. 1979. Speakers' sensitivity to rules of frozen word order. *Journal of Verbal Learning and Verbal Behavior, 18,* 497–508.

Poole, D. A., Nelson, L. D., McIntyre, M. M., VanBergen, N. T., Scharphorn, J. R., & Kastely, S. M. 2011. The writing styles of admired psychologists. Unpublished manuscript, Dept. of Psychology, Central Michigan University.

Pullum, G. K. 1984. Punctuation and human freedom. *Natural Language and Linguistic Theory, 2,* 419–425.

Pullum, G. K. 2009. 50 years of stupid grammar advice. *Chronicle of Higher Education,* Dec. 22.

Pullum, G. K. 2010. The land of the free and "The Elements of Style." *English Today, 26,* 34–44.

Pullum, G. K. 2013. Elimination of the fittest. *Chronicle of Higher Education,* April 11.

Rayner, K., & Pollatsek, A. 1989. *The psychology of reading.* Englewood Cliffs, N.J.: Prentice Hall.

Ross, L., Greene, D., & House, P. 1977. The "false consensus effect": An egocentric bias in social perception and attribution processes. *Journal of Experimental Social Psychology, 13,* 279–301.

Sadoski, M. 1998. Mental imagery in reading: A sampler of some significant studies. *Reading Online.* www.readingonline.org/researchSadoski.html.

Sadoski, M., Goetz, E. T., & Fritz, J. B. 1993. Impact of concreteness on comprehensibility, interest, and memory for text: Implications for dual coding theory and text design. *Journal of Educational Psychology, 85,* 291–304.

Sanforth, A. J., & Filik, R. 2007. "They" as a gender-unspecified singular pronoun: Eye tracking reveals a processing cost. *Quarterly Journal of Experimental Psychology, 60,* 171–178.

Schacter, D. L. 2001. *The seven sins of memory: How the mind forgets and remembers.* Boston: Houghton Mifflin.

Schriver, K. A. 2012. What we know about expertise in professional communication. In V. Berninger (ed.), *Past, present, and future contributions of cognitive writing research to cognitive psychology.* New York: Psychology Press.

Shepard, R. N. 1978. The mental image. *American Psychologist, 33,* 125–137.

Siegal, A. M., & Connolly, W. G. 1999. *The New York Times Manual of Style and Usage.* New York: Three Rivers Press.

Skinner, D. 2012. *The story of* ain't: *America, its language, and the most controversial dictionary ever published.* New York: HarperCollins.

Smith, K. 2001. *Junk English.* New York: Blast Books.

Soukhanov, A. 1999. *Encarta World English Dictionary.* New York: St. Martin's Press.

Spinoza, B. 1677/2000. *Ethics* (G. H. R. Parkinson, trans.). New York: Oxford University Press.

Strunk, W., & White, E. B. 1999. *The Elements of Style* (4th ed.). New York: Longman.

Sunstein, C. R. 2013. *Simpler: The future of government.* New York: Simon & Schuster.

Sword, H. 2012. *Stylish academic writing.* Cambridge, Mass.: Harvard University Press.

Thomas, F.-N., and Turner, M. 1994. *Clear and simple as the truth: Writing classic prose*. Princeton: Princeton University Press.

Thurlow, C. 2006. From statistical panic to moral panic: The metadiscursive construction and popular exaggeration of new media language in the print media. *Journal of Computer-Mediated Communication, 11.*

Truss, L. 2003. *Eats, shoots & leaves: The zero tolerance approach to punctuation*. London: Profile Books.

Van Orden, G. C., Johnston, J. C., & Hale, B. L. 1988. Word identification in reading proceeds from spelling to sound to meaning. *Journal of Experimental Psychology: Learning, Memory, and Cognition, 14,* 371–386.

Wason, P. C. 1965. The contexts of plausible denial. *Journal of Verbal Learning and Verbal Behavior, 4,* 7–11.

Wegner, D., Schneider, D. J., Carter, S. R. I., & White, T. L. 1987. Paradoxical effects of thought suppression. *Journal of Personality and Social Psychology, 53,* 5–13.

Williams, J. M. 1981. The phenomenology of error. *College Composition and Communication, 32,* 152–168.

Williams, J. M. 1990. *Style: Toward clarity and grace*. Chicago: University of Chicago Press.

Wimmer, H., & Perner, J. 1983. Beliefs about beliefs: Representation and constraining function of wrong beliefs in young children's understanding of deception. *Cognition, 13,* 103–128.

Wolf, F., & Gibson, E. 2003. Parsing: An overview. In L. Nadel (ed.), *Encyclopedia of Cognitive Science*. New York: Macmillan.

Wolf, F., & Gibson, E. 2006. *Coherence in natural language: Data structures and applications*. Cambridge, Mass.: MIT Press.

Zwicky, A. M., Salus, P. H., Binnick, R. I., & Vanek, A. L. (eds.). 1971/1992. *Studies out in left field: Defamatory essays presented to James D. McCawley on the occasion of his 33rd or 34th birthday*. Philadelphia: John Benjamins.

Index

Page numbers in **boldface** refer to glossary entries and main discussions; page numbers in *italics* refer to cartoons and other illustrations.

ALLEN LANE
an imprint of
PENGUIN BOOKS

Recently Published

Dominic Lieven, *Towards the Flame: Empire, War and the End of Tsarist Russia*

Noel Malcolm, *Agents of Empire: Knights, Corsairs, Jesuits and Spies in the Sixteenth-Century Mediterranean World*

James Rebanks, *The Shepherd's Life: A Tale of the Lake District*

David Brooks, *The Road to Character*

Joseph Stiglitz, *The Great Divide*

Ken Robinson and Lou Aronica, *Creative Schools: Revolutionizing Education from the Ground Up*

Clotaire Rapaille and Andrés Roemer, *Move UP: Why Some Cultures Advances While Others Don't*

Jonathan Keates, *William III and Mary II: Partners in Revolution*

David Womersley, *James II: The Last Catholic King*

Richard Barber, *Henry II: A Prince Among Princes*

Jane Ridley, *Victoria: Queen, Matriarch, Empress*

John Gray, *The Soul of the Marionette: A Short Enquiry into Human Freedom*

Emily Wilson, *Seneca: A Life*

Michael Barber, *How to Run a Government: So That Citizens Benefit and Taxpayers Don't Go Crazy*

Dana Thomas, *Gods and Kings: The Rise and Fall of Alexander McQueen and John Galliano*

Steven Weinberg, *To Explain the World: The Discovery of Modern Science*

Jennifer Jacquet, *Is Shame Necessary?: New Uses for an Old Tool*

Eugene Rogan, *The Fall of the Ottomans: The Great War in the Middle East, 1914-1920*